The Giant Book of Hollywood Trivia

3811 Questions About Hollywood's Movies and Celebrities

Copyright © 2019 by Meghan A. Faith

ALL RIGHTS RESERVED.

Let's Begin

1. Who was the composer for the 1989 film «The Fly II»?
Answer: Christopher Young

2. Who directed the 2019 film «The Highwaymen»?
Answer: John Lee Hancock

3. What's the birth name of Charlie Carver?
Answer: Charles Carver Martensen

4. For which film did Leonardo DiCaprio receive the «Silver Bear for Best Actor» award in 1997?
Answer: Romeo + Juliet

5. For his work in the movie «Million Dollar Baby», who won the «Academy Award for Best Supporting Actor» in 2004?
Answer: Morgan Freeman

6. What is the name of the character Viola Davis plays in the movie «Suicide Squad»?
Answer: Amanda Waller

7. What's the birth name of Ethan Embry?
Answer: Ethan Philan Randall

8. Whom did Deborah Raffin marry in the year 1974?
Answer: Michael Viner

9. Whom did Kaitlin Olson marry in the year 2008?
Answer: Rob McElhenney

10. Which film won the Academy Award for Best Original Score in the year 1982?
Answer: E.T. the Extra-Terrestrial

11. What is the full name of Zachary Gordon?
Answer: Zachary Adam Gordon

12. In which year did Fran Drescher marry Shiva Ayyadurai?
Answer: 2014

13. What is the name of the character Joe Pesci plays in the movie «Lethal Weapon 3»?
Answer: Leo Getz

14. In which year did Elaine Stritch marry John Bay?
Answer: 1973

15. Whom did Annette O'Toole marry in the year 1999?
Answer: Michael McKean

16. Who was the composer for the 2018 film «The Front Runner»?
Answer: Rob Simonsen

17. What's the birth name of Kid Cudi?
Answer: Scott Ramon Seguro Mescudi

18. Whom did Annabeth Gish marry in the year 2003?
Answer: Wade Allen

19. What is the full name of Jeremy Renner?
Answer: Jeremy Lee Renner

20. Where did Ron Perlman get his master's degree from?
Answer: University of Minnesota, in Minneapolis

21. Where was Lee Majors born?
Answer: Wyandotte

22. Who acted as Raymond III in the movie «Kingdom of Heaven»?
Answer: Jeremy Irons

23. Whom did Mel Harris marry in the year 1988?
Answer: Cotter Smith

24. For his work in the movie «Amadeus», who won the «Golden Globe Award for Best Director» in 1984?
Answer: Miloš Forman

25. What is the full name of Blake Anderson?
Answer: Blake Raymond Anderson

26. Who directed the 2015 film «Daddy's Home»?
Answer: Sean Anders

27. For his work in the movie «Reservoir Dogs», who won the «Independent Spirit Award for Best Supporting Male» in 1993?
Answer: Steve Buscemi

28. Whom did Christine Lahti marry in the year 1983?
Answer: Thomas Schlamme

29. In which year did Alexa Havins marry Justin Bruening?
Answer: 2005

30. Who directed the 2014 film «Fury»?
Answer: David Ayer

31. Which film won the Special Achievement Academy Award in the year 1976?
Answer: King Kong

32. Whom did Michelle Williams marry in the year 2018?
Answer: Phil Elverum

33. For which film did Halle Berry receive the «BET Award for Best Actor & Actress» in 2002?
Answer: Monster's Ball

34. Who directed the 1986 film «The Color of Money»?
Answer: Martin Scorsese

35. When did J. Smith-Cameron marry Kenneth Lonergan?

Answer: 2000

36. Who directed the 2017 film «Kong: Skull Island»?
Answer: Jordan Vogt-Roberts

37. Which film won the Academy Award for Best Picture in the year 1965?
Answer: My Fair Lady

38. Where did Mindy Kaling get her bachelor's degree from?
Answer: Dartmouth College, in Hanover

39. In which year did Glenne Headly marry John Malkovich?
Answer: 1982

40. What's the birth name of Denise Richards?
Answer: Denise Lee Richards

41. Who directed the 1996 film «The Rock»?
Answer: Michael Bay

42. Who acted as Patrick Verona in the movie «10 Things I Hate About You»?
Answer: Heath Ledger

43. What's the birth name of Corin Nemec?
Answer: Joseph Charles Nemec

44. What is the name of the character Nicolas Cage plays in the movie «Snowden»?
Answer: Hank Forrester

45. What is the name of the character Ben Kingsley plays in the movie «Exodus: Gods and Kings»?
Answer: Nun

46. What's the birth name of Simon Rex?
Answer: Simon Rex Cutright

47. What is the full name of Michael K. Williams?
Answer: Michael Kenneth Williams

48. Who directed the 2017 film «Wakefield»?
Answer: Robin Swicord

49. Where was Alan Ritchson born?
Answer: Grand Forks

50. What is the full name of Jelena Jensen?
Answer: Monique Reising

51. Whom did Alice Hirson marry in the year 1980?
Answer: Stephen Elliott

52. What is the full name of Shia LaBeouf?
Answer: Shia Saide LaBeouf

53. Who directed the 2018 film «Mandy»?
Answer: Panos Cosmatos

54. Whom did Jamie-Lynn Sigler marry in the year 2012?
Answer: Cutter Dykstra

55. For which film did Tom Cruise receive the «Golden Globe Award for Best Actor – Motion Picture Drama» in 1990?
Answer: Born on the Fourth of July

56. What is the full name of Tera Patrick?
Answer: Linda Ann Hopkins

57. For her work in the movie «A Patch of Blue», who won the «Academy Award for Best Supporting Actress» in 1965?
Answer: Shelley Winters

58. Which film won the Golden Globe Award for Best Screenplay in the year 1994?
Answer: Pulp Fiction

59. What is the name of the character Gene Hackman plays in the movie «Superman»?
Answer: Lex Luthor

60. Where did Mario Yedidia get his Bachelor of Arts degree from?
Answer: Columbia University, in Manhattan

61. Who directed the 1999 film «Blast from the Past»?
Answer: Hugh Wilson

62. Which film won the Academy Award for Best Picture in the year 1961?
Answer: The Apartment

63. What's the birth name of Josh Brolin?
Answer: Josh James Brolin

64. What is the full name of Eddie Murphy?
Answer: Edward Regan Murphy

65. For his work in the movie «Double Team», who won the «Golden Raspberry Award for Worst New Star» in 1997?
Answer: Dennis Rodman

66. What's the birth name of Jenna Elfman?
Answer: Jennifer Mary Butala

67. What is the name of the character Nicolas Cage plays in the movie «Left Behind»?
Answer: Rayford Steele

68. In which year did Marisa Miller marry Griffin Guess?
Answer: 2006

69. Where did Keith David get his Bachelor of Fine Arts degree from?
Answer: Juilliard School, in Manhattan

70. For her work in the movie «Ray», who won the «BET

Award for Best Actor & Actress» in 2005?
Answer: Regina King

71. Whom did Allyce Beasley marry in the year 1985?
Answer: Vincent Schiavelli

72. Whom did Jane Kaczmarek marry in the year 1992?
Answer: Bradley Whitford

73. For which film did Jack Lemmon receive the «Academy Award for Best Supporting Actor» in 1955?
Answer: Mister Roberts

74. Which film won the Academy Award for Best Picture in the year 1953?
Answer: The Greatest Show on Earth

75. What is the full name of Hank Azaria?
Answer: Henry Albert Azaria

76. Who acted as Valerie Veran in the movie «Little Nicky»?
Answer: Patricia Arquette

77. When did Marjorie Bransfield marry Jim Belushi?
Answer: 1990

78. Whom did Jennifer Lopez marry in the year 2001?
Answer: Cris Judd

79. Where did Katherine Dunham get her bachelor's degree from?
Answer: University of Chicago

80. Whom did Jennie Garth marry in the year 2001?
Answer: Peter Facinelli

81. Whom did Alfre Woodard marry in the year 1983?
Answer: Roderick Spencer

82. Where was Bryce Dallas Howard born?

Answer: Los Angeles

83. Where did Austin Stowell get his Bachelor of Fine Arts degree from?
Answer: University of Connecticut, in Storrs

84. Who was the composer for the 1995 film «Die Hard with a Vengeance»?
Answer: Michael Kamen

85. Who directed the 1995 film «Judge Dredd»?
Answer: Danny Cannon

86. Who was the composer for the 2014 film «Interstellar»?
Answer: Hans Zimmer

87. Who directed the 2014 film «November Man»?
Answer: Roger Donaldson

88. Who was the composer for the 2016 film «Collateral Beauty»?
Answer: Mychael Danna

89. Who was the composer for the 1997 film «Contact»?
Answer: Alan Silvestri

90. Who acted as Castor Troy in the movie «Face/Off»?
Answer: Nicolas Cage

91. Which film won the Academy Award for Best Sound Mixing in the year 2018?
Answer: Dunkirk

92. When did Karen Sillas marry Peter Stormare?
Answer: 1989

93. For which film did Steven Spielberg receive the «London Film Critics Circle Award for Director of the Year» in 1994?
Answer: Schindler's List

94. Who directed the 2015 film «The Throwaways»?
Answer: Tony Bui

95. Whom did Kiele Sanchez marry in the year 2001?
Answer: Zach Helm

96. Whom did Ami Dolenz marry in the year 2002?
Answer: Jerry Trimble

97. In which year did Shirley Mitchell marry Jay Livingston?
Answer: 1992

98. What is the name of the character William Hurt plays in the movie «Avengers: Infinity War»?
Answer: Thaddeus Ross

99. Who was the composer for the 1999 film «Notting Hill»?
Answer: Trevor Jones

100. Who directed the 1987 film «Good Morning, Vietnam»?
Answer: Barry Levinson

101. When did Kristanna Loken marry Noah Danby?
Answer: 2008

102. What is the full name of Jenny Lewis?
Answer: Jennifer Diane Lewis

103. What's the birth name of Jessica Biel?
Answer: Jessica Claire Biel

104. Who was the composer for the 2013 film «The Host»?
Answer: Antonio Pinto

105. Whom did Sarah Thompson marry in the year 2007?
Answer: Brad Caleb Kane

106. Whom did Angelina Jolie marry in the year 2000?

Answer: Billy Bob Thornton

107. In which year did Kassie DePaiva marry James DePaiva?
Answer: 1996

108. Whom did Irene Cara marry in the year 1986?
Answer: Conrad Palmisano

109. In which year did Ellen Barkin marry Ronald Perelman?
Answer: 2000

110. Whom did Emily Neves marry in the year 2011?
Answer: Andrew Love

111. When did Patti D'Arbanville marry Roger Miremont?
Answer: 1975

112. In which year did Susan Bernard marry Jason Miller?
Answer: 1974

113. What is the full name of Ty Burrell?
Answer: Tyler Gerald Burrell

114. Whom did Selena marry in the year 1992?
Answer: Chris Pérez

115. What is the name of the character Tom Cruise plays in the movie «Jack Reacher»?
Answer: Jack Reacher

117. For her work in the movie «The Pumpkin Eater», who won the «Cannes Film Festival Award for Best Actress» in 1964?
Answer: Anne Bancroft

118. Who was the composer for the 2018 film «Suspiria»?
Answer: Thom Yorke

119. Whom did Julie Condra marry in the year 1992?

Answer: Brandon Douglas

120. In which year did Anna Faris marry Chris Pratt?
Answer: 2009

121. For which film did William Hurt receive the «BAFTA Award for Best Actor in a Leading Role» in 1986?
Answer: Kiss of the Spider Woman

122. Who was the composer for the 2001 film «Enemy at the Gates»?
Answer: James Horner

123. Whom did Christina Applegate marry in the year 2001?
Answer: Johnathon Schaech

124. Whom did Jacinda Barrett marry in the year 2004?
Answer: Gabriel Macht

125. For his work in the movie «Saving Private Ryan», who won the «London Film Critics Circle Award for Film of the Year» in 1998?
Answer: Steven Spielberg

126. In which year did Bijou Phillips marry Danny Masterson?
Answer: 2011

127. Who was the composer for the 2017 film «Spider-Man: Homecoming»?
Answer: Michael Giacchino

128. Who directed the 2016 film «Synchronicity»?
Answer: Jacob Gentry

129. What is the full name of Madeline Carroll?
Answer: Marissa Madeline Carroll

130. Who was the composer for the 2005 film «King Kong»?
Answer: James Newton Howard

131. What is the full name of Kate Hudson?
Answer: Kate Garry Hudson

132. Who directed the 2019 film «Cold Pursuit»?
Answer: Hans Petter Moland

133. Who were the composers of the 2018 film «Solo: A Star Wars Story»?
Answer: John Williams and John Powell

134. What is the full name of Carmen Electra?
Answer: Tara Leigh Patrick

135. Who directed the 1991 film «Father of the Bride»?
Answer: Charles Shyer

136. What is the full name of Daniel Henney?
Answer: Daniel Phillip Henney

137. Where was Fred Thompson born?
Answer: Sheffield

138. Whom did Shera Danese marry in the year 1977?
Answer: Peter Falk

139. Who directed the 2015 film «Concussion»?
Answer: Peter Landesman

140. Who was the composer for the 1994 film «Street Fighter»?
Answer: Graeme Revell

141. For which film did Grace Kelly receive the «National Board of Review Award for Best Actress» in 1954?
Answer: Rear Window

142. For his work in the movie «City of Hope», who won the «Independent Spirit Award for Best Supporting Male» in 1992?
Answer: David Strathairn

143. Who was the composer for the 2019 film «The Prodigy»?
Answer: Joseph Bishara

144. Who directed the 2009 film «Post Grad»?
Answer: Vicky Jenson

145. What is the full name of Sam Jaeger?
Answer: Samuel Heath Jaeger

146. Who was the composer for the 2006 film «Flicka»?
Answer: Aaron Zigman

147. Who was the composer for the 1990 film «White Hunter Black Heart»?
Answer: Lennie Niehaus

148. Whom did Jennifer Lopez marry in the year 2004?
Answer: Marc Anthony

149. What is the full name of Blake Lively?
Answer: Blake Ellender Brown

150. For her work in the movie «The Wrestler», who won the «San Francisco Film Critics Circle Award for Best Supporting Actress» in 2008?
Answer: Marisa Tomei

151. In which year did Katherine LaNasa marry French Stewart?
Answer: 1998

152. Who directed the 1993 film «Demolition Man»?
Answer: Marco Brambilla

153. In which year did Deborah Rennard marry Paul Haggis?
Answer: 1997

154. What is the name of the character Nicolas Cage plays

in the movie «Trespass»?
Answer: Kyle Miller

155. Who directed the 2019 film «Booksmart»?
Answer: Olivia Wilde

156. Whom did Mireille Enos marry in the year 2008?
Answer: Alan Ruck

157. Who directed the 2018 film «Future World»?
Answer: James Franco

158. What is the full name of Tyler Posey?
Answer: Tyler Garcia Posey

159. For which film did Anne Hathaway receive the «Academy Award for Best Supporting Actress» in 2012?
Answer: Les Misérables

160. Who was the composer for the 1995 film «Fair Game»?
Answer: Mark Mancina

161. Where did Mark Harmon get his Bachelor of Arts degree from?
Answer: University of California, Los Angeles

162. Where did Bob Kirsh get his Bachelor of Arts degree from?
Answer: Temple University, in Philadelphia

163. What's the birth name of Ireland Baldwin?
Answer: Ireland Eliesse Basinger-Baldwin

164. What is the full name of Cynthia Nixon?
Answer: Cynthia Ellen Nixon

165. Who was the composer for the 1997 film «The Edge»?
Answer: Jerry Goldsmith

166. Where was Kelly Stables born?

Answer: St. Louis

167. Whom did Jenni Rivera marry in the year 2010?
Answer: Esteban Loaiza

168. Whom did Cindy Cheung marry in the year 2002?
Answer: Ed Lin

169. Who directed the 2011 film «Thor»?
Answer: Kenneth Branagh

170. What is the name of the character Angelina Jolie plays in the movie «Alexander»?
Answer: Olympias

171. For his work in the movie «Leaving Las Vegas», who won the «Screen Actors Guild Award for Outstanding Performance by a Male Actor in a Leading Role» in 1996?
Answer: Nicolas Cage

172. For which film did Mary Steenburgen receive the «Broadcast Film Critics Association Award for Best Cast» in 2011?
Answer: The Help

173. In which year did Sara Foster marry Tommy Haas?
Answer: 2010

174. Who directed the 2015 film «In the Heart of the Sea»?
Answer: Ron Howard

175. Who was the composer for the 2011 film «Mr. Popper's Penguins»?
Answer: Rolfe Kent

176. For her work in the movie «Xiu Xiu: The Sent Down Girl», who won the «Golden Horse Award for Best Director» in 1998?
Answer: Joan Chen

177. What's the birth name of Julia Roberts?
Answer: Julia Fiona Roberts

178. What is the full name of Manish Dayal?
Answer: Manish Sudhir Patel

179. For which film did Walter Brennan receive the «Academy Award for Best Supporting Actor» in 1938?
Answer: Kentucky

180. What is the name of the character Tilda Swinton plays in the movie «Doctor Strange»?
Answer: The Ancient One

181. Whom did Shannen Doherty marry in the year 1993?
Answer: Ashley Hamilton

182. Where was Seamus Dever born?
Answer: Flint

183. Who directed the 2009 film «The Proposal»?
Answer: Anne Fletcher

184. For her work in the movie «The Interpreter», who won the «Los Angeles Film Critics Association Award for Best Supporting Actress» in 2005?
Answer: Catherine Keener

185. For which film did Elizabeth Taylor receive the «David di Donatello for Best Foreign Actress» award in 1972?
Answer: Zee and Co.

186. Whom did Jennifer Grey marry in the year 2001?
Answer: Clark Gregg

187. When did KaDee Strickland marry Jason Behr?
Answer: 2006

188. For his work in the movie «Amistad», who won the «Broadcast Film Critics Association Award for Best Supporting Actor» in 1997?
Answer: Anthony Hopkins

189. What is the full name of Lisa Roberts Gillan?

Answer: Lisa Roberts

190. Whom did Alexandra Holden marry in the year 2010?
Answer: Johnny Strong

191. What's the birth name of Eion Bailey?
Answer: Eion Francis Hamilton Bailey

192. Which film won the Academy Award for Best Picture in the year 1951?
Answer: All About Eve

193. Who directed the 2011 film «Another Earth»?
Answer: Mike Cahill

194. Who directed the 1998 film «Pi»?
Answer: Darren Aronofsky

195. Which film won the Golden Globe Award for Best Motion Picture – Drama in the year 1960?
Answer: Spartacus

196. For which film did Lee Marvin receive the «Silver Bear» award in 1965?
Answer: Cat Ballou

197. Which film won the Golden Globe Award for Best Original Score in the year 2001?
Answer: Moulin Rouge!

198. Which film won the Golden Globe Award for Best Screenplay in the year 1970?
Answer: Love Story

199. When did Lin Shaye marry Clayton Landey?
Answer: 1988

200. Where did Shaquille O'Neal get his Bachelor of Arts degree from?
Answer: Louisiana State University, in Baton Rouge

201. What is the full name of Wesley John?
Answer: John Wesley Pantejo Managbanag

202. Which film won the Academy Award for Best Writing, Original Screenplay in the year 2015?
Answer: Birdman

203. Who acted as Lucius Fox in the movie «The Dark Knight»?
Answer: Morgan Freeman

204. For which film did Marisa Tomei receive the «Las Vegas Film Critics Society Award for Best Supporting Actress» in 2008?
Answer: The Wrestler

205. When did Jaime Ray Newman marry Guy Nattiv?
Answer: 2012

206. Which film won the Academy Award for Best Documentary Feature in the year 2009?
Answer: The Cove

207. Who acted as Brad's bud in the movie «Fast Times at Ridgemont High»?
Answer: Nicolas Cage

208. Whom did Laura Dern marry in the year 1993?
Answer: Jeff Goldblum

209. What is the full name of Katy Perry?
Answer: Katheryn Elizabeth Hudson

210. Who acted as John Jonah Jameson in the movie «Spider-Man»?
Answer: J. K. Simmons

211. What is the full name of Coby Bell?
Answer: Coby Scott Bell

212. Who directed the 2018 film «Lizzie»?

Answer: Craig Macneill

213. For which film did Joseph Schildkraut receive the «Academy Award for Best Supporting Actor» in 1937?
Answer: The Life of Emile Zola

214. Which film won the Academy Award for Best Writing, Original Screenplay in the year 1989?
Answer: Dead Poets Society

215. Which film won the Academy Award for Best Documentary Feature in the year 2008?
Answer: Man on Wire

216. Where did McLean Stevenson get his bachelor's degree from?
Answer: Northwestern University, in Illinois

217. For which film did Spencer Tracy receive the «Academy Award for Best Actor» in 1937?
Answer: Captains Courageous

218. For his work in the movie «The Paper Chase», who won the «Academy Award for Best Supporting Actor» in 1973?
Answer: John Houseman

219. For which film did Anne Bancroft receive the «National Board of Review Award for Best Actress» in 1977?
Answer: The Turning Point

220. Whom did Bianca Kajlich marry in the year 2006?
Answer: Landon Donovan

221. Whom did Lauren Bowles marry in the year 2004?
Answer: Patrick Fischler

222. When did Hilarie Burton marry Jeffrey Dean Morgan?
Answer: 2014

223. For which film did Sandra Bullock receive the «Academy Award for Best Actress» in 2010?
Answer: The Blind Side

224. Whom did Anne Hathaway marry in the year 2012?
Answer: Adam Shulman

225. Who was the composer for the 2004 film «Alien vs. Predator»?
Answer: Harald Kloser

226. For his work in the movie «My Own Private Idaho», who won the «Volpi Cup» award in 1991?
Answer: River Phoenix

227. Which film won the Golden Globe Award for Best Original Score in the year 1970?
Answer: Love Story

228. When did Arielle Dombasle marry Paul Albou?
Answer: 1976

229. Which film won the Academy Award for Best Visual Effects in the year 1996?
Answer: Independence Day

230. When did Calista Flockhart marry Harrison Ford?
Answer: 2010

231. When did Lisa Hartman marry Clint Black?
Answer: 1991

232. In which year did Lynn Whitfield marry Vantile Whitfield?
Answer: 1974

233. Whom did Julia Roberts marry in the year 1993?
Answer: Lyle Lovett

234. What's the birth name of Matt Bomer?
Answer: Matthew Staton Bomer

235. Whom did Alexa Vega marry in the year 2014?
Answer: Carlos Pena Jr

236. Whom did Veronica Cartwright marry in the year 1982?
Answer: Richard Compton

237. What's the birth name of Anton Yelchin?
Answer: Anton Viktorovich Yelchin

238. When did Mena Suvari marry Robert Brinkmann?
Answer: 2000

239. When did Gayle Hunnicutt marry Simon Jenkins?
Answer: 1978

240. For his work in the movie «Big», who won the «Golden Globe Award for Best Actor – Motion Picture Musical or Comedy» in 1989?
Answer: Tom Hanks

241. Which film won the Academy Award for Best Picture in the year 1997?
Answer: The English Patient

242. Which film won the Academy Award for Best Picture in the year 1985?
Answer: Amadeus

243. What's the birth name of Michael Zomick?
Answer: Michael Jared Zomick

244. For her work in the movie «State and Main», who won the «Florida Film Critics Circle Award for Best Cast» in 2000?
Answer: Patti LuPone

245. Whom did Vonetta McGee marry in the year 1987?
Answer: Carl Lumbly

246. Where was Ron Jeremy born?

Answer: Queens

247. Which film won the Academy Award for Best Picture in the year 1981?
Answer: Ordinary People

248. Who was the composer for the 2016 film «The Divergent Series: Allegiant»?
Answer: Joseph Trapanese

249. For which film did Gabourey Sidibe receive the «NAACP Image Award for Outstanding Actress in a Motion Picture» in 2010?
Answer: Precious

250. When did Gabrielle Union marry Chris Howard?
Answer: 2001

251. When did Christina Milian marry The-Dream?
Answer: 2009

252. Whom did Candice Bergen marry in the year 1980?
Answer: Louis Malle

253. Who was the composer for the 2012 film «Wanderlust»?
Answer: Craig Wedren

254. Who was the composer for the 1994 film «True Lies»?
Answer: Brad Fiedel

255. Who acted as Itzhak Stern in the movie «Schindler's List»?
Answer: Ben Kingsley

256. What is the full name of Anne Hathaway?
Answer: Anne Jacqueline Hathaway

257. For which film did Diane Keaton receive the «Satellite Award for Best Actress – Motion Picture Musical or

Comedy» in 2004?
Answer: Something's Gotta Give

258. For which film did Kristen Stewart receive the «MTV Movie Award for Best Female Performance» in 2009?
Answer: Twilight

259. Whom did Nancy Allen marry in the year 1992?
Answer: Craig Shoemaker

260. Whom did Vanessa Trump marry in the year 2005?
Answer: Donald Trump Jr.

261. Who acted as Robert Langdon in the movie «Inferno»?
Answer: Tom Hanks

262. Who acted as Aunt May in the movie «The Amazing Spider-Man»?
Answer: Sally Field

263. For his work in the movie «On the Waterfront», who won the «Academy Award for Best Actor» in 1954?
Answer: Marlon Brando

264. For his work in the movie «Adaptation», who won the «Academy Award for Best Supporting Actor» in 2002?
Answer: Chris Cooper

265. For which film did Winona Ryder receive the «Golden Globe Award for Best Supporting Actress – Motion Picture» in 1993?
Answer: The Age of Innocence

266. Who directed the 2014 film «The Good Dinosaur»?
Answer: Peter Sohn

267. Who directed the 2002 film «25th Hour»?
Answer: Spike Lee

268. For which film did Cuba Gooding Jr. receive the

«Academy Award for Best Supporting Actor» in 1996?
Answer: Jerry Maguire

269. For her work in the movie «Sophie's Choice», who won the «Academy Award for Best Actress» in 1983?
Answer: Meryl Streep

270. Where did Lee Majors get his bachelor's degree from?
Answer: Eastern Kentucky University, in Richmond

271. For which film did Jason Lee receive the «Online Film Critics Society Award for Best Cast» in 2000?
Answer: Almost Famous

272. For her work in the movie «Closer», who won the «Golden Globe Award for Best Supporting Actress – Motion Picture» in 2005?
Answer: Natalie Portman

273. Whom did Marian Nixon marry in the year 1974?
Answer: Ben Lyon

274. Who was the composer for the 2017 film «Everything, Everything»?
Answer: Ludwig Göransson

275. Who directed the 1989 film «Blaze»?
Answer: Ron Shelton

276. What's the birth name of Tia Carrere?
Answer: Althea Rae Janairo

277. For which film did Adam Sandler receive the «Golden Raspberry Award for Worst Actor» in 2012?
Answer: Big Daddy

278. Whom did Idina Menzel marry in the year 2003?
Answer: Taye Diggs

279. What's the birth name of Alexander Chaplin?

Answer: Alexander Gaberman

280. Who directed the 2011 film «War Horse»?
Answer: Steven Spielberg

281. For which film did Gary Cooper receive the «Academy Award for Best Actor» in 1941?
Answer: Sergeant York

282. For which film did Robert De Niro receive the «Academy Award for Best Supporting Actor» in 1974?
Answer: The Godfather Part II

283. Whom did Stephanie March marry in the year 2005?
Answer: Bobby Flay

284. Whom did Margot Kidder marry in the year 1975?
Answer: Thomas McGuane

285. What's the birth name of Jennifer Lawrence?
Answer: Jennifer Shrader Lawrence

286. For which film did Dianne Wiest receive the «Academy Award for Best Supporting Actress» in 1986?
Answer: Hannah and Her Sisters

287. Whom did Faune A. Chambers marry in the year 2010?
Answer: Fonzworth Bentley

288. Whom did Blake Lively marry in the year 2012?
Answer: Ryan Reynolds

289. Whom did Maggie Gyllenhaal marry in the year 2009?
Answer: Peter Sarsgaard

290. What is the full name of John Cena?
Answer: Richard Hammerbush

291. Who was the composer for the 2018 film «Bad Times at the El Royale»?

Answer: Michael Giacchino

292. In which year did Alley Mills marry Orson Bean?
Answer: 1993

293. What is the full name of Ross Bagley?
Answer: Ross Elliot Bagley

294. In which year did Amanda Righetti marry Jordan Alan?
Answer: 2006

295. Which film won the Golden Globe Award for Best Screenplay in the year 1973?
Answer: The Exorcist

296. Who was the composer for the 2008 film «The Incredible Hulk»?
Answer: Craig Armstrong

297. For her work in the movie «Ray», who won the «NAACP Image Award for Outstanding Supporting Actress in a Motion Picture» in 2005?
Answer: Regina King

298. Whom did Grace Byers marry in the year 2016?
Answer: Trai Byers

299. In which year did Connie Sellecca marry Gil Gerard?
Answer: 1979

300. Which film won the Academy Award for Best Visual Effects in the year 1968?
Answer: 2001: A Space Odyssey

301. For her work in the movie «Erin Brockovich», who won the «Golden Globe Award for Best Actress – Motion Picture Drama» in 2000?
Answer: Julia Roberts

302. Who was the composer for the 1987 film «Lethal

Weapon»?
Answer: Michael Kamen

303. Which film won the Academy Award for Best Picture in the year 1957?
Answer: Around the World in 80 Days

304. Which film won the Academy Award for Best Documentary Feature in the year 1988?
Answer: Hôtel Terminus: The Life and Times of Klaus Barbie

305. In which year did Holly Marie Combs marry Bryan Smith?
Answer: 1993

306. For his work in the movie «Superman Returns», who won the «Empire Award for Best Male Newcomer» in 2006?
Answer: Brandon Routh

307. Who was the composer for the 2018 film «Entebbe»?
Answer: Rodrigo Amarante

308. Who was the composer for the 2011 film «Beastly»?
Answer: Marcelo Zarvos

309. For his work in the movie «Sayonara», who won the «Golden Globe Award for New Star of the Year – Actor» in 1957?
Answer: James Garner

310. What is the name of the character Anna Paquin plays in the movie «X-Men: The Last Stand»?
Answer: Rogue

311. When did Sarah Wayne Callies marry Josh Winterhalt?
Answer: 2002

312. Who directed the 2016 film «Gods of Egypt»?
Answer: Alex Proyas

313. Who was the composer for the 2003 film «Peter Pan»?
Answer: James Newton Howard

314. Which film won the Academy Award for Best Picture in the year 1979?
Answer: The Deer Hunter

315. Whom did Ione Skye marry in the year 2008?
Answer: Ben Lee

316. For her work in the movie «Capote», who won the «Chlotrudis Award for Best Supporting Actress» in 2006?
Answer: Catherine Keener

317. Who was the composer for the 2001 film «The Royal Tenenbaums»?
Answer: Mark Mothersbaugh

318. Who directed the 1990 film «Die Hard 2»?
Answer: Renny Harlin

319. Whom did Karen Black marry in the year 1987?
Answer: Stephen Eckelberry

320. What is the full name of Amy Acker?
Answer: Amy Louise Acker
321. For his work in the movie «Moneyball», who won the «New York Film Critics Circle Award for Best Actor» in 2011?
Answer: Brad Pitt

322. Whom did Rachel Ticotin marry in the year 1984?
Answer: David Caruso

323. Where was Ron Perlman born?
Answer: Washington Heights

324. Which film won the Academy Award for Best Documentary Feature in the year 1989?
Answer: Common Threads: Stories from the Quilt

325. In which year did Jaime King marry Kyle Newman?
Answer: 2007

326. When did Carrie Coon marry Tracy Letts?
Answer: 2013

327. Whom did Rhonda Fleming marry in the year 1978?
Answer: Hall Bartlett

328. For his work in the movie «Big Night», who won the «National Society of Film Critics Award for Best Supporting Actor» in 1996?
Answer: Tony Shalhoub

329. Who directed the 2006 film «Kinky Boots»?
Answer: Julian Jarrold

330. Whom did Candy Clark marry in the year 1978?
Answer: Marjoe Gortner

331. Which film won the Academy Award for Best Film Editing in the year 1968?
Answer: Bullitt

332. Whom did Vera Farmiga marry in the year 2008?
Answer: Renn Hawkey

333. Who was the composer for the 1993 film «Addams Family Values»?
Answer: Marc Shaiman

334. For which film did Robert De Niro receive the «Academy Award for Best Actor» in 1980?
Answer: Raging Bull

335. For which film did Jack Nicholson receive the «Academy Award for Best Actor» in 1998?
Answer: As Good as It Gets

336. Whom did Monet Mazur marry in the year 2005?

Answer: Alex De Rakoff

337. Who acted as Russell Billiu Long in the movie «JFK»?
Answer: Walter Matthau

338. When did Linda Purl marry Desi Arnaz, Jr.?
Answer: 1980

339. For her work in the movie «Kings Row», who won the «National Board of Review Award for Best Actress» in 1942?
Answer: Ann Sheridan

340. For her work in the movie «Suddenly, Last Summer», who won the «Golden Globe Award for Best Actress – Motion Picture Drama» in 1959?
Answer: Elizabeth Taylor

341. What's the birth name of Mara Wilson?
Answer: Mara Elizabeth Wilson

342. Which film won the Academy Award for Best Writing, Original Screenplay in the year 1968?
Answer: The Producers

343. Who was the composer for the 2005 film «Son of the Mask»?
Answer: Randy Edelman

344. What is the full name of Bridget Moynahan?
Answer: Kathryn Bridget Moynahan

345. Where was Patton Oswalt born?
Answer: Portsmouth

346. Who directed the 2008 film «Defiance»?
Answer: Edward Zwick

347. Whom did Loretta Young marry in the year 1993?
Answer: Jean Louis

348. For which film did Bryan Singer receive the «Saturn Award for Best Director» in 2001?
Answer: X-Men

349. Which film won the Academy Award for Best Documentary Feature in the year 1979?
Answer: Best Boy

350. Whom did Claire Danes marry in the year 2009?
Answer: Hugh Dancy

351. Whom did Elizabeth Bogush marry in the year 2005?
Answer: Lukas Reiter

352. What's the birth name of Lauren Ambrose?
Answer: Lauren Anne D'Ambruoso

353. For his work in the movie «Shadowlands», who won the «National Board of Review Award for Best Actor» in 1993?
Answer: Anthony Hopkins

354. Who was the composer for the 2014 film «Earth to Echo»?
Answer: Joseph Trapanese

355. In which year did Stacey Dash marry Emmanuel Xuereb?
Answer: 2007

356. For which film did Leonardo DiCaprio receive the «BAFTA Award for Best Actor in a Leading Role» in 2016?
Answer: The Revenant

357. For her work in the movie «Bonnie and Clyde», who won the «Academy Award for Best Supporting Actress» in 1968?
Answer: Estelle Parsons

358. Whom did Gail O'Grady marry in the year 1991?
Answer: Severin Wunderman

359. Who acted as James Gordon in the movie «The Dark Knight»?
Answer: Gary Oldman

360. For his work in the movie «The Rock», who won the «MTV Movie Award for Best On-Screen Duo» in 1997?
Answer: Nicolas Cage

361. Who directed the 1995 film «Apollo 13»?
Answer: Ron Howard

362. Who directed the 1997 film «Picture Perfect»?
Answer: Glenn Gordon Caron

363. Who directed the 2016 film «Suicide Squad»?
Answer: David Ayer

364. Which film won the Academy Award for Best Makeup and Hairstyling in the year 2001?
Answer: Dr. Seuss' How the Grinch Stole Christmas

365. Whom did Molly Sims marry in the year 2011?
Answer: Scott Stuber

366. What is the full name of Vanessa Williams?
Answer: Vanessa Lynn Williams

367. Where did Jon Hamm get his Bachelor of Arts degree from?
Answer: University of Missouri

368. What is the full name of Rebecca Hall?
Answer: Rebecca Maria Hall

369. For which film did Anthony Hopkins receive the «National Board of Review Award for Best Supporting Actor» in 1991?
Answer: The Silence of the Lambs

370. Who directed the 1998 film «Lethal Weapon 4»?

Answer: Richard Donner

371. Who directed the 2016 film «Fantastic Beasts and Where to Find Them»?
Answer: David Yates

372. Who was the composer for the 1995 film «Bad Boys»?
Answer: Mark Mancina

373. Who was the composer for the 2016 film «A Heavenly Christmas»?
Answer: Michael Richard Plowman

374. In which year did Michelle Branch marry Teddy Landau?
Answer: 2004

375. Who were the directors of the 2000 film «Men of Honor»?
Answer: Alex Lam and George Tillman, Jr.

376. What is the full name of Demetrius Shipp, Jr.?
Answer: Demetrius Antionne Shipp

377. Who were the directors of the 2014 film «Sin City: A Dame to Kill For»?
Answer: Robert Rodriguez and Frank Miller

378. Who directed the 2019 film «Cliffs of Freedom»?
Answer: Van Ling

379. Who directed the 2011 film «Unknown»?
Answer: Jaume Collet-Serra

380. For her work in the movie «Black Swan», who won the «BAFTA Award for Best Actress in a Leading Role» in 2010?
Answer: Natalie Portman

381. When did Alison Lohman marry Mark Neveldine?
Answer: 2009

382. Who were the composers of the 1987 film «Spaceballs»?
Answer: Jon Bon Jovi, John Morris, and Mel Brooks

383. Who acted as Odin in the movie «Thor»?
Answer: Anthony Hopkins

384. For which film did Robin Williams receive the «Academy Award for Best Supporting Actor» in 1997?
Answer: Good Will Hunting

385. In which year did Linda Kozlowski marry Paul Hogan?
Answer: 1990

386. Who was the composer for the 2018 film «Looking Glass»?
Answer: Mark Adler

387. Which film won the Golden Globe Award for Best Original Score in the year 1968?
Answer: The Shoes of the Fisherman

388. For her work in the movie «The Country Girl», who won the «Academy Award for Best Actress» in 1954?
Answer: Grace Kelly

389. In which year did Faith Ford marry Campion Murphy?
Answer: 1998

390. For which film did Matt Damon receive the «Satellite Award for Best Cast – Motion Picture» in 2006?
Answer: The Departed

391. In which year did Kate del Castillo marry Luis García Postigo?
Answer: 2001

392. Who were the composers of the 2017 film «Blade Runner 2049»?

Answer: Hans Zimmer and Benjamin Wallfisch

393. For her work in the movie «Black Swan», who won the «Golden Globe Award for Best Actress – Motion Picture Drama» in 2011?
Answer: Natalie Portman

394. Where did Katherine Dunham get her bachelor's degree from?
Answer: University of Chicago

395. What is the full name of Jimmy Fallon?
Answer: James Thomas Fallon

396. When did Jennifer Beals marry Alexandre Rockwell?
Answer: 1986

397. Who was the composer for the 2017 film «Dragonheart: Battle for the Heartfire»?
Answer: Mark McKenzie

398. Which film won the Academy Award for Best Writing, Original Screenplay in the year 1995?
Answer: Pulp Fiction

399. Which film won the Academy Award for Best Production Design in the year 1931?
Answer: Cimarron

400. For his work in the movie «Dog Day Afternoon», who won the «BAFTA Award for Best Actor in a Leading Role» in 1976?
Answer: Al Pacino

401. In which year did Lea Thompson marry Howard Deutch?
Answer: 1989

402. Which film won the Academy Award for Best Documentary Feature in the year 2000?
Answer: Into the Arms of Strangers: Stories of the

403. Which film won the Academy Award for Best Picture in the year 2002?
Answer: A Beautiful Mind

404. When did Pamela Des Barres marry Michael Des Barres?
Answer: 1977

406. Who directed the 2015 film «Chappie»?
Answer: Neill Blomkamp

407. In which year did Eva Longoria marry Tyler Christopher?
Answer: 2002

408. Which film won the Golden Globe Award for Best Screenplay in the year 1996?
Answer: The People vs. Larry Flynt

409. Who was the composer for the 2006 film «The Guardian»?
Answer: Trevor Rabin

410. Which film won the Academy Award for Best Picture in the year 2010?
Answer: The Hurt Locker

411. In which year did Sherry Boucher marry George Peppard?
Answer: 1975

412. For his work in the movie «Mulholland Drive», who won the «Cannes Best Director Award» in 2001?
Answer: David Lynch

413. Who was the composer for the 1991 film «Barton Fink»?
Answer: Carter Burwell

414. When did Sally Struthers marry William C. Rader?
Answer: 1977

415. Which film won the Academy Award for Best Writing, Adapted Screenplay in the year 1965?
Answer: Doctor Zhivago

416. Whom did Debra Winger marry in the year 1996?
Answer: Arliss Howard

417. Who was the composer for the 2016 film «Snowden»?
Answer: Craig Armstrong

418. For which film did Yul Brynner receive the «Academy Award for Best Actor» in 1956?
Answer: The King and I

419. Who were the directors of the 1991 film «Barton Fink»?
Answer: Ethan Coen and Joel Coen

420. Whom did Mary Elizabeth McGlynn marry in the year 1988?
Answer: Daran Norris

421. What is the full name of Téa Leoni?
Answer: Elizabeth Téa Pantaleoni

422. For which film did Brad Pitt receive the «National Society of Film Critics Award for Best Actor» in 2011?
Answer: The Tree of Life

423. For which film did Kristen Stewart receive the «MTV Movie Award for Best Kiss» in 2012?
Answer: The Twilight Saga: Breaking Dawn – Part 1

424. For which film did Joanne Woodward receive the «BAFTA Award for Best Actress in a Leading Role» in 1974?
Answer: Summer Wishes, Winter Dreams

425. Where was Amy Poehler born?
Answer: Newton

426. Who directed the 2016 film «Rogue One»?
Answer: Gareth Edwards

427. For her work in the movie «Silver Linings Playbook», who won the «Independent Spirit Award for Best Female Lead» in 2013?
Answer: Jennifer Lawrence

428. Who was the composer for the 2019 film «The Highwaymen»?
Answer: Thomas Newman

429. Whom did Elizabeth Banks marry in the year 2003?
Answer: Max Handelman

430. For his work in the movie «The Silence of the Lambs», who won the «Boston Society of Film Critics Award for Best Supporting Actor» in 1991?
Answer: Anthony Hopkins

431. Whom did Christine Taylor marry in the year 2000?
Answer: Ben Stiller

432. For which film did Ed Harris receive the «Southeastern Film Critics Association Award for Best Supporting Actor» in 1999?
Answer: The Truman Show

433. For her work in the movie «Silver Linings Playbook», who won the «MTV Movie Award for Best Female Performance» in 2013?
Answer: Jennifer Lawrence

434. What is the full name of Adam Brody?
Answer: Adam Jared Brody

435. Who directed the 2018 film «Mortal Engines»?

Answer: Christian Rivers

436. For his work in the movie «Mississippi Burning», who won the «Silver Bear for Best Actor» award in 1989?
Answer: Gene Hackman

437. Where did Bill Wallace get his master's degree from?
Answer: University of Memphis

438. What is the name of the character Morgan Freeman plays in the movie «The Dark Knight Rises»?
Answer: Lucius Fox

439. In which year did Adrienne Barbeau marry John Carpenter?
Answer: 1979

440. Who was the composer for the 1995 film «Four Rooms»?
Answer: Combustible Edison

441. What is the full name of Ali Hillis?
Answer: Alecia Deann Hillis

442. Whom did LisaRaye McCoy-Misick marry in the year 2006?
Answer: Michael Misick

443. Whom did Sigrid Valdis marry in the year 1970?
Answer: Bob Crane

444. Who directed the 2013 film «The Wolverine»?
Answer: James Mangold

445. When did Kate Levering marry Reza Jahangiri?
Answer: 2013

446. What is the name of the character Jennifer Connelly plays in the movie «Noah»?
Answer: Naamah
447. What is the full name of Nick Jonas?

Answer: Nicholas Jerry Jonas

448. Who directed the 2013 film «Big Ass Spider!»?
Answer: Mike Mendez

449. Who was the composer for the 2015 film «Chappie»?
Answer: Hans Zimmer

450. Where was Jaclyn Hales born?
Answer: Syracuse

451. Who was the composer for the 2000 film «Autumn in New York»?
Answer: Gabriel Yared

452. When did Thalía marry Tommy Mottola?
Answer: 2000

453. Where was Paul Simon born?
Answer: Newark

454. For his work in the movie «Whiplash», who won the «Academy Award for Best Supporting Actor» in 2015?
Answer: J. K. Simmons

455. Which film won the Academy Award for Best Documentary Feature in the year 1990?
Answer: American Dream

456. Which film won the Academy Award for Best Sound Mixing in the year 1995?
Answer: Apollo 13

457. Who directed the 2009 film «My Life in Ruins»?
Answer: Donald Petrie

458. In which year did Susan Anton marry Jeff Lester?
Answer: 1992

459. Who was the composer for the 1998 film «Titanic»?
Answer: James Horner

460. For which film did Fred Astaire receive the «Golden Globe Award for Best Actor – Motion Picture Musical or Comedy» in 1950?
Answer: Three Little Words

461. Whom did Torrey DeVitto marry in the year 2011?
Answer: Paul Wesley

462. For her work in the movie «Something's Gotta Give», who won the «National Board of Review Award for Best Actress» in 2003?
Answer: Diane Keaton

463. What is the full name of Kieran Culkin?
Answer: Kieran Kyle Culkin

464. Where was Erik Jensen born?
Answer: Minnesota

465. Who directed the 1990 film «RoboCop 2»?
Answer: Irvin Kershner

466. For her work in the movie «The Accused», who won the «David di Donatello for Best Foreign Actress» award in 1989?
Answer: Jodie Foster

467. When did Diane Lane marry Christopher Lambert?
Answer: 1988

468. When did Jennifer Rubin marry Elias Koteas?
Answer: 1987

469. Who was the composer for the 2015 film «The Hunger Games: Mockingjay – Part 2»?
Answer: James Newton Howard

470. For which film did Martin Scorsese receive the «Golden Globe Award for Best Director» in 2006?
Answer: The Departed

471. Whom did Robin Tunney marry in the year 1997?
Answer: Bob Gosse

472. Who directed the 2016 film «Bridget Jones's Baby»?
Answer: Sharon Maguire

473. What is the full name of Lucas Black?
Answer: Lucas York Black

474. For which film did Denzel Washington receive the «MTV Movie Award for Best Villain» in 2002?
Answer: Training Day

475. For which film did Jason Robards receive the «Academy Award for Best Supporting Actor» in 1977?
Answer: Julia

476. Who directed the 2004 film «Troy»?
Answer: Wolfgang Petersen

477. Which film won the Academy Award for Best Picture in the year 2005?
Answer: Million Dollar Baby

478. Whom did Sheila Kelley marry in the year 1996?
Answer: Richard Schiff

479. When did Catherine Oxenberg marry Casper Van Dien?
Answer: 1999

480. For her work in the movie «The Wrestler», who won the «San Diego Film Critics Society Award for Best Supporting Actress» in 2008?
Answer: Marisa Tomei

481. In which year did Nikki Reed marry Ian Somerhalder?
Answer: 2015

482. For his work in the movie «Looking for Richard», who won the «Directors Guild of America Award for

Outstanding Directing – Documentaries» in 1997?
Answer: Al Pacino

483. Whom did Allison Miller marry in the year 2012?
Answer: Nee Brothers

484. In which year did Nicole Kidman marry Keith Urban?
Answer: 2006

485. Who directed the 2018 film «Annihilation»?
Answer: Alex Garland

486. For which film did Anne Bancroft receive the «Academy Award for Best Actress» in 1962?
Answer: The Miracle Worker

487. For which film did Edward Norton receive the «Boston Society of Film Critics Award for Best Supporting Actor» in 1996?
Answer: The People vs. Larry Flynt

488. When did Joan Chen marry Jim Lau?
Answer: 1985

489. Who directed the 1994 film «Bad Girls»?
Answer: Jonathan Kaplan

490. What's the birth name of Kristin Davis?
Answer: Kristin Landen Davis

491. For her work in the movie «Dreamgirls», who won the «Broadcast Film Critics Association Award for Best Supporting Actress» in 2006?
Answer: Jennifer Hudson

492. For which film did Nicolas Cage receive the «Golden Globe Award for Best Actor – Motion Picture Drama» in 1996?
Answer: Leaving Las Vegas

493. In which year did Kim Kardashian marry Kris

Humphries?
Answer: 2011

494. Whom did Zsa Zsa Gabor marry in the year 1983?
Answer: Felipe de Alba

495. Which film won the Academy Award for Best Original Song in the year 1993?
Answer: Philadelphia

496. For her work in the movie «A Beautiful Mind», who won the «Broadcast Film Critics Association Award for Best Supporting Actress» in 2001?
Answer: Jennifer Connelly

497. Who was the composer for the 2017 film «Thor: Ragnarok»?
Answer: Mark Mothersbaugh

498. Who directed the 2018 film «Pacific Rim Uprising»?
Answer: Steven S. DeKnight

499. For his work in the movie «Waterworld», who won the «Golden Raspberry Award for Worst Supporting Actor» in 1995?
Answer: Dennis Hopper

500. Who was the composer for the 2005 film «The Land Before Time XI: Invasion of the Tinysauruses»?
Answer: Michael Tavera

501. Which film won the Academy Award for Best Production Design in the year 1996?
Answer: The English Patient

502. Who acted as Lee Harvey Oswald in the movie «JFK»?
Answer: Gary Oldman

503. Whom did Catherine Keener marry in the year 1990?
Answer: Dermot Mulroney

504. When did Ione Skye marry Adam Horowitz?
Answer: 1992

505. Which film won the Golden Globe Award for Best Original Score in the year 1988?
Answer: Gorillas in the Mist

506. Who acted as Padmé Amidala in the movie «Star Wars Episode II: Attack of the Clones»?
Answer: Natalie Portman

507. Who was the composer for the 2002 film «The Emperor's Club»?
Answer: James Newton Howard

508. In which year did Aviva Baumann marry Ken Baumann?
Answer: 2012

509. In which year did Kate del Castillo marry Aarón Díaz?
Answer: 2009

510. Who were the composers of the 1998 film «Armageddon»?
Answer: Harry Gregson-Williams and Trevor Rabin

511. Who was the composer for the 2006 film «The Texas Chainsaw Massacre: The Beginning»?
Answer: Steve Jablonsky

512. When did Sharon Stone marry Phil Bronstein?
Answer: 1998

513. What is the full name of Mira Sorvino?
Answer: Mira Katherine Sorvino

514. Who were the directors of the 1990 film «Rocky V»?
Answer: John G. Avildsen and Sylvester Stallone

515. Whom did Jennifer Garner marry in the year 2005?

Answer: Ben Affleck

516. What is the full name of James Franco?
Answer: James Edward Franco

517. Who directed the 2018 film «Woman Walks Ahead»?
Answer: Susanna White

518. What is the full name of Reese Witherspoon?
Answer: Laura Jeanne Reese Witherspoon

519. In which year did Gloria Swanson marry William Dufty?
Answer: 1976

520. When did Mia Farrow marry André Previn?
Answer: 1970

521. Who directed the 2013 film «Ender's Game»?
Answer: Gavin Hood

522. When did Milla Jovovich marry Luc Besson?
Answer: 1997

523. Whom did Julianna Margulies marry in the year 2007?
Answer: Keith Lieberthal

524. In which year did Marilyn Flores marry Yonel Cohen?
Answer: 2018

525. Whom did Audra Lindley marry in the year 1972?
Answer: James Whitmore

526. Who was the composer for the 1995 film «Father of the Bride Part II»?
Answer: Alan Silvestri

527. Where was Bob Kirsh born?
Answer: Bristol

528. When did Jennifer Jones marry Norton Simon?

Answer: 1971

529. What's the birth name of Shawn Levy?
Answer: Shawn Adam Levy

530. Whom did Debbie Allen marry in the year 1984?
Answer: Norm Nixon

531. Whom did Kelly Preston marry in the year 1991?
Answer: John Travolta

532. Who directed the 2004 film «Alien vs. Predator»?
Answer: Paul W. S. Anderson

533. Who was the composer for the 1995 film «Mortal Kombat»?
Answer: George S. Clinton

534. For which film did Holly Hunter receive the «Las Vegas Film Critics Society Award for Best Supporting Actress» in 2004?
Answer: Thirteen

535. When did Candice King marry Joe King?
Answer: 2014

536. Who directed the 1993 film «Jurassic Park»?
Answer: Steven Spielberg

537. Who was the composer for the 1994 film «The Next Karate Kid»?
Answer: Bill Conti

538. Which film won the Academy Award for Best Live Action Short Film in the year 2018?
Answer: Skin

539. Which film won the Academy Award for Best Writing, Original Screenplay in the year 1958?
Answer: The Defiant Ones

540. What is the full name of Bobby Lashley?
Answer: Franklin Roberto Lashley

541. Where did Meryl Streep get her Master of Fine Arts degree from?
Answer: Yale University, in New Haven

542. Who was the composer for the 2017 film «Diary of a Wimpy Kid: The Long Haul»?
Answer: Edward Shearmur

543. Which film won the Academy Award for Best Picture in the year 2014?
Answer: 12 Years a Slave

544. Whom did Sutton Foster marry in the year 2006?
Answer: Christian Borle

545. Whom did Kate Burton marry in the year 1984?
Answer: Michael Ritchie

546. For which film did Ed Harris receive the «National Society of Film Critics Award for Best Supporting Actor» in 2005?
Answer: A History of Violence

547. What's the birth name of Eliza Dushku?
Answer: Eliza Patricia Dushku

548. When did Christina Aguilera marry Jordan Bratman?
Answer: 2005

549. For which film did Barkhad Abdi receive the «BAFTA Award for Best Actor in a Supporting Role» in 2014?
Answer: Captain Phillips

550. Whom did Anna Wood marry in the year 2012?
Answer: Dane DeHaan

551. Who directed the 2018 film «Welcome to Marwen»?
Answer: Robert Zemeckis

552. For which film did Mel Brooks receive the «Writers Guild of America Award for Best Original Screenplay» in 1969?
Answer: The Producers

553. Who directed the 2012 film «Wanderlust»?
Answer: David Wain

554. Who was the composer for the 1989 film «Star Trek V: The Final Frontier»?
Answer: Jerry Goldsmith

555. Who was the composer for the 2016 film «Solace»?
Answer: BT

556. Which film won the Academy Award for Best Film Editing in the year 2007?
Answer: The Bourne Ultimatum

557. For which film did Brandon Routh receive the «Saturn Award for Best Actor» in 2006?
Answer: Superman Returns

558. For his work in the movie «The Hurt Locker», who won the «Washington D.C. Area Film Critics Association Award for Best Ensemble» in 2009?
Answer: Jeremy Renner

559. Who was the composer for the 2007 film «Pathfinder»?
Answer: Jonathan Elias

560. Where did Erik Jensen get his Bachelor of Fine Arts degree from?
Answer: Carnegie Mellon University, in Pittsburgh

561. For her work in the movie «The Little Girl Who Lives Down the Lane», who won the «Saturn Award» in 1978?
Answer: Jodie Foster

562. Whom did Talia Shire marry in the year 1970?

Answer: David Shire

563. What is the full name of David Arquette?
Answer: David James Arquette

564. What is the name of the character Kate Winslet plays in the movie «Titanic»?
Answer: Rose DeWitt Bukater

565. Who directed the 2018 film «A Simple Favor»?
Answer: Paul Feig

566. For her work in the movie «Desperately Seeking Susan», who won the «BAFTA Award for Best Actress in a Supporting Role» in 1986?
Answer: Rosanna Arquette

567. For which film did Burgess Meredith receive the «Saturn Award for Best Supporting Actor» in 1981?
Answer: Clash of the Titans

568. Where was Keith David born?
Answer: New York City

569. Who was the composer for the 2018 film «Shock and Awe»?
Answer: Jeff Beal

570. In which year did Zandy Hartig marry David Wain?
Answer: 2009

571. What is the name of the character George Clooney plays in the movie «From Dusk till Dawn»?
Answer: Seth Gecko

572. When did Sissy Spacek marry Jack Fisk?
Answer: 1974

573. For which film did Sharon Stone receive the «Golden Raspberry Award for Worst Actress» in 1994?
Answer: The Specialist

574. In which year did Kate Walsh marry Alex Young?
Answer: 2007

575. Who directed the 2004 film «13 Going on 30»?
Answer: Gary Winick

576. For which film did Kim Basinger receive the «Academy Award for Best Supporting Actress» in 1998?
Answer: L.A. Confidential

577. Which film won the Academy Award for Best Documentary Feature in the year 2013?
Answer: 20 Feet from Stardom

578. Whom did Paula Abdul marry in the year 1992?
Answer: Emilio Estevez

579. Whom did Carrie Underwood marry in the year 2010?
Answer: Mike Fisher

580. Who directed the 1994 film «Wyatt Earp»?
Answer: Lawrence Kasdan

581. Whom did Jerry Hall marry in the year 2016?
Answer: Rupert Murdoch

582. Who directed the 2017 film «Patriots Day»?
Answer: Peter Berg

583. What is the full name of Scoot McNairy?
Answer: John Marcus McNairy

584. Whom did Rachel Nichols marry in the year 2014?
Answer: Michael Kershaw

585. Whom did Gillian Anderson marry in the year 2004?
Answer: Julian Ozanne

586. Whom did Rebecca Romijn marry in the year 1998?
Answer: John Stamos

587. Who directed the 2003 film «Terminator 3: Rise of the Machines»?
Answer: Jonathan Mostow

588. Who was the composer for the 2018 film «Skyscraper»?
Answer: Steve Jablonsky

589. In which year did Tawny Kitaen marry David Coverdale?
Answer: 1989

590. Who was the composer for the 2017 film «Alien: Covenant»?
Answer: Jed Kurzel

591. Whom did America Olivo marry in the year 2009?
Answer: Christian Campbell

592. For which film did Anne Bancroft receive the «BAFTA Award for Best Actress in a Leading Role» in 1988?
Answer: 84 Charing Cross Road

593. Who was the composer for the 2000 film «The Beach»?
Answer: Angelo Badalamenti

594. Whom did Elisabeth Moss marry in the year 2009?
Answer: Fred Armisen

595. For which film did Sigourney Weaver receive the «BAFTA Award for Best Actress in a Supporting Role» in 1998?
Answer: The Ice Storm

596. Whom did Lauren Ambrose marry in the year 2001?
Answer: Sam Handel

597. Which film won the Academy Award for Best Sound Mixing in the year 1973?

Answer: The Exorcist

598. Who directed the 1987 film «Lethal Weapon»?
Answer: Richard Donner

599. In which year did Jill Clayburgh marry David Rabe?
Answer: 1979

600. In which year did Aaliyah marry R. Kelly?
Answer: 1994

601. In which year did Diora Baird marry Jonathan Togo?
Answer: 2013

602. In which year did Coral Browne marry Vincent Price?
Answer: 1974

603. Whom did Aimee Mann marry in the year 1997?
Answer: Michael Penn

604. For which film did Jennifer Hudson receive the «BET Award for Best Actor & Actress» in 2007?
Answer: Dreamgirls

605. For which film did Ron Howard receive the «Academy Award for Best Director» in 2001?
Answer: A Beautiful Mind

606. Who was the composer for the 2005 film «7 Seconds»?
Answer: Neal Acree

607. For which film did Jennifer Connelly receive the «Academy Award for Best Supporting Actress» in 2002?
Answer: A Beautiful Mind

608. Who directed the 2003 film «Thirteen»?
Answer: Catherine Hardwicke

609. Whom did Daisy Donovan marry in the year 2005?
Answer: Dan Mazer

610. What is the name of the character Michael Douglas plays in the movie «Ant-Man»?
Answer: Hank Pym

611. Who directed the 2018 film «First Man»?
Answer: Damien Chazelle

612. Which film won the Academy Award for Best Sound Editing in the year 1964?
Answer: Goldfinger

613. What is the full name of Alexis Amore?
Answer: Fabiola Melgar García

614. Who directed the 1991 film «JFK»?
Answer: Oliver Stone

615. Who directed the 2008 film «Choke»?
Answer: Clark Gregg

616. Who acted as Newt Scamander in the movie «Fantastic Beasts: The Crimes of Grindelwald»?
Answer: Eddie Redmayne

617. Who was the composer for the 2009 film «My Sister's Keeper»?
Answer: Aaron Zigman

618. Whom did Majandra Delfino marry in the year 2011?
Answer: David Walton

619. Whom did Daphne Maxwell Reid marry in the year 1982?
Answer: Tim Reid
620. What is the full name of Oscar Isaac?
Answer: Óscar Isaac Hernández Estrada

621. Who was the composer for the 1998 film «The Thin Red Line»?
Answer: Hans Zimmer

622. Who were the directors of the 1999 film «The Matrix»?
Answer: Lilly Wachowski and Lana Wachowski

623. Who directed the 2016 film «Ghostbusters»?
Answer: Paul Feig

624. What is the full name of Paula Abdul?
Answer: Paula Julie Abdul

625. Who acted as Obi-Wan Kenobi in the movie «Star Wars Episode VI: Return of the Jedi»?
Answer: Alec Guinness

626. For which film did Ernest Borgnine receive the «Academy Award for Best Actor» in 1955?
Answer: Marty

627. Who was the composer for the 1991 film «Hot Shots!»?
Answer: Sylvester Levay

628. What is the full name of Joshua Jackson?
Answer: Joshua Carter Jackson

629. Who acted as Mia Dolan in the movie «La La Land»?
Answer: Emma Stone

630. Who was the composer for the 1990 film «Arachnophobia»?
Answer: Trevor Jones

631. When did Jackie Sandler marry Adam Sandler?
Answer: 2003

632. Which film won the Academy Award for Best Documentary Feature in the year 1992?
Answer: The Panama Deception

633. For his work in the movie «Chicago», who won the

«Golden Globe Award for Best Actor – Motion Picture Musical or Comedy» in 2002?
Answer: Richard Gere

634. Whom did Holly Marie Combs marry in the year 2004?
Answer: David W. Donoho

635. Whom did Bryce Dallas Howard marry in the year 2006?
Answer: Seth Gabel

636. Who directed the 2018 film «Damsel»?
Answer: David Zellner

637. Who acted as Hela in the movie «Thor: Ragnarok»?
Answer: Cate Blanchett

638. In which year did Moira Harris marry Gary Sinise?
Answer: 1981

639. Who directed the 2013 film «Scary Movie 5»?
Answer: Malcolm D. Lee

640. Whom did Leeza Gibbons marry in the year 1991?
Answer: Stephen Meadows

641. What's the birth name of Alexandra Daddario?
Answer: Alexandra Anna Daddario

642. What's the birth name of Joaquin Phoenix?
Answer: Joaquín Rafael Bottom

643. Which film won the Academy Award for Best Picture in the year 1941?
Answer: Rebecca

644. When did Liza Minnelli marry Jack Haley, Jr.?
Answer: 1974

645. Who was the composer for the 2019 film «Happy

Death Day 2U»?
Answer: Bear McCreary

646. For which film did Katharine Hepburn receive the «Academy Award for Best Actress» in 1968?
Answer: The Lion in Winter

647. Who directed the 1987 film «Adventures in Babysitting»?
Answer: Chris Columbus

648. Who was the composer for the 2015 film «Concussion»?
Answer: James Newton Howard

649. Whom did Jenny McCarthy marry in the year 2014?
Answer: Donnie Wahlberg

650. Who directed the 1986 film «Top Gun»?
Answer: Tony Scott

651. What is the name of the character Tom Cruise plays in the movie «Mission: Impossible – Fallout»?
Answer: Ethan Hunt

652. What is the full name of Matthew Perry?
Answer: Matthew Langford Perry

653. Whom did Zsa Zsa Gabor marry in the year 1986?
Answer: Frédéric Prinz von Anhalt

654. Which film won the Academy Award for Best Documentary Feature in the year 1986?
Answer: Down and Out in America

655. Who acted as Jack Dawson in the movie «Titanic»?
Answer: Leonardo DiCaprio

656. When did Jaclyn Smith marry Dennis Cole?
Answer: 1978

657. For which film did Leonardo DiCaprio receive the «MTV Movie Award for Best Jaw Dropping Moment» in 2014?
Answer: The Wolf of Wall Street

658. What is the full name of Nicolas Cage?
Answer: Nicolas Kim Coppola

659. Where was Richard Riehle born?
Answer: Menomonee Falls

660. What's the birth name of Joe Jonas?
Answer: Joseph Adam Jonas

661. Who directed the 1997 film «Starship Troopers»?
Answer: Paul Verhoeven

662. Whom did Cindy Crawford marry in the year 1998?
Answer: Rande Gerber

663. Who directed the 2013 film «Iron Man 3»?
Answer: Shane Black

664. Which film won the Academy Award for Best Documentary Feature in the year 1955?
Answer: Helen Keller in Her Story

665. Whom did Melanie Griffith marry in the year 1989?
Answer: Don Johnson

666. Which film won the Academy Award for Best Documentary Feature in the year 1944?
Answer: The Fighting Lady

667. Who was the composer for the 2000 film «The Next Best Thing»?
Answer: Gabriel Yared

668. What is the full name of Dakota Johnson?
Answer: Dakota Mayi Johnson

669. Which film won the Academy Award for Best Documentary Feature in the year 1957?
Answer: Albert Schweitzer

670. What's the birth name of Craig Bierko?
Answer: Craig Philip Bierko

671. For which film did Christopher Lloyd receive the «Independent Spirit Award for Best Supporting Male» in 1994?
Answer: Twenty Bucks

672. What's the birth name of Michael Fishman?
Answer: Michael Aaron Fishman

673. Who was the composer for the 1994 film «Double Dragon»?
Answer: Jay Ferguson

674. Who acted as Moses in the movie «Exodus: Gods and Kings»?
Answer: Christian Bale

675. When did Kim Basinger marry Ron Snyder?
Answer: 1980

676. Who directed the 2016 film «Southside with You»?
Answer: Richard Tanne

677. Who directed the 2005 film «Good Night, and Good Luck.»?
Answer: George Clooney

678. Who were the composers of the 2016 film «A Hologram for the King»?
Answer: Johnny Klimek and Tom Tykwer

679. Who directed the 2016 film «A Hologram for the King»?
Answer: Tom Tykwer

680. For her work in the movie «The Accused», who won the «Academy Award for Best Actress» in 1988?
Answer: Jodie Foster

681. For her work in the movie «L.A. Confidential», who won the «Screen Actors Guild Award for Outstanding Performance by a Female Actor in a Supporting Role» in 1997?
Answer: Kim Basinger

682. When did Amber Heard marry Johnny Depp?
Answer: 2015

683. For which film did Steven Spielberg receive the «National Society of Film Critics Award for Best Director» in 1993?
Answer: Schindler's List

684. Who was the composer for the 2007 film «300»?
Answer: Tyler Bates

685. Whom did Alaina Reed Hall marry in the year 1988?
Answer: Kevin Peter Hall

686. Who acted as Kay Adams-Corleone in the movie «The Godfather»?
Answer: Diane Keaton

687. Whom did Danneel Harris marry in the year 2010?
Answer: Jensen Ackles
688. What's the birth name of James Deen?
Answer: Bryan Matthew Sevilla

689. Who directed the 1996 film «From Dusk till Dawn»?
Answer: Robert Rodriguez

690. Who directed the 1990 film «The Hunt for Red October»?
Answer: John McTiernan

691. Who directed the 2017 film «The Belco Experiment»?

Answer: Greg McLean

692. Which film won the Academy Award for Best Sound Editing in the year 1992?
Answer: Terminator 2: Judgment Day

693. What's the birth name of Charles Esten?
Answer: Charles Esten Puskar III

694. What is the full name of Demi Lovato?
Answer: Demetria Devonne Lovato

695. In which year did Katrina Bowden marry Ben Jorgensen?
Answer: 2013

696. Who was the composer for the 2000 film «Without Evidence»?
Answer: Franco Piersanti

697. For his work in the movie «Cocoon», who won the «Saturn Award for Best Director» in 1986?
Answer: Ron Howard

698. What is the full name of Misha Collins?
Answer: Misha Dmitri Tippens Krushnic

699. What's the birth name of Gwen Stefani?
Answer: Gwen Renée Stefani

700. What is the full name of 50 Cent?
Answer: Curtis James Jackson III

701. Whom did Tara Strong marry in the year 2000?
Answer: Craig Strong

702. Who directed the 2015 film «The Martian»?
Answer: Ridley Scott

703. What's the birth name of Kirsten Dunst?
Answer: Kirsten Caroline Dunst

704. Who was the composer for the 1998 film «Deep Impact»?
Answer: James Horner

705. For which film did Elia Kazan receive the «Academy Award for Best Director» in 1954?
Answer: On the Waterfront

706. For her work in the movie «The Hunger Games: Catching Fire», who won the «MTV Movie Award for Best Female Performance» in 2014?
Answer: Jennifer Lawrence

708. Which film won the Academy Award for Best Picture in the year 1952?
Answer: An American in Paris

709. For which film did William Hurt receive the «Los Angeles Film Critics Association Award for Best Actor» in 1985?
Answer: Kiss of the Spider Woman

710. Where was McLean Stevenson born?
Answer: Normal

711. Who was the composer for the 2015 film «Watchers of the Sky»?
Answer: Dougie Bowne

712. Who was the composer for the 2017 film «Kingsman: The Golden Circle»?
Answer: Henry Jackman

713. For which film did Jared Leto receive the «Academy Award for Best Supporting Actor» in 2013?
Answer: Dallas Buyers Club

714. Whom did Nikki Cox marry in the year 2006?
Answer: Jay Mohr

715. What is the name of the character Kevin Spacey plays in the movie «Superman Returns»?
Answer: Lex Luthor

716. Who directed the 2011 film «The Big Year»?
Answer: David Frankel

717. For which film did Derek Luke receive the «BET Award for Best Actor & Actress» in 2003?
Answer: Antwone Fisher

718. For which film did Allison Janney receive the «Screen Actors Guild Award for Outstanding Performance by a Cast in a Motion Picture» in 2000?
Answer: American Beauty

719. Who directed the 1997 film «Event Horizon»?
Answer: Paul W. S. Anderson

720. Who directed the 1993 film «Mrs. Doubtfire»?
Answer: Chris Columbus

721. When did Emily Deschanel marry David Hornsby?
Answer: 2010

722. Who directed the 2018 film «The Spy Who Dumped Me»?
Answer: Susanna Fogel

723. For his work in the movie «Cat Ballou», who won the «Golden Globe Award for Best Actor – Motion Picture Musical or Comedy» in 1965?
Answer: Lee Marvin

724. Where did Jon Hamm get his Bachelor of Arts degree from?
Answer: University of Missouri, in Boone County

725. Who directed the 2014 film «Teenage Mutant Ninja Turtles»?
Answer: Jonathan Liebesman

726. For his work in the movie «Apollo 13», who won the «Broadcast Film Critics Association Award for Best Supporting Actor» in 1995?
Answer: Ed Harris

727. Who was the composer for the 2019 film «John Wick: Chapter 3 – Parabellum»?
Answer: Tyler Bates

728. What is the full name of Jennifer Stone?
Answer: Jennifer Lindsay Stone

729. What is the name of the character Julianne Moore plays in the movie «The Hunger Games: Mockingjay – Part 2»?
Answer: Alma Coin

730. For which film did Richard Gere receive the «David di Donatello for Best Foreign Actor» award in 1979?
Answer: Days of Heaven

731. What is the full name of Cedric the Entertainer?
Answer: Cedric Antonio Kyles

732. When did Tera Patrick marry Evan Seinfeld?
Answer: 2004

733. In which year did Helen Hunt marry Hank Azaria?
Answer: 1999

734. Whom did Caroline McWilliams marry in the year 1982?
Answer: Michael Keaton

735. When did Shanna Moakler marry Travis Barker?
Answer: 2004

736. Whom did Holly Hunter marry in the year 1995?
Answer: Janusz Kamiński

737. In which year did Faye Dunaway marry Peter Wolf?

Answer: 1974

738. When did Mamie Gummer marry Justin Hartley?
Answer: 2011

739. For which film did Martin Scorsese receive the «Golden Globe Award» in 2003?
Answer: Gangs of New York

740. Who was the composer for the 1994 film «Forrest Gump»?
Answer: Alan Silvestri

741. What is the full name of Anne Dudek?
Answer: Anne Louise Dudek

742. Who directed the 2015 film «The Big Short»?
Answer: Adam McKay

743. Whom did Olivia Brown marry in the year 1983?
Answer: Mykelti Williamson

744. Who was the composer for the 2014 film «Dawn of the Planet of the Apes»?
Answer: Michael Giacchino

745. Whom did Marley Shelton marry in the year 2001?
Answer: Beau Flynn

746. Whom did Janet Jackson marry in the year 1991?
Answer: René Elizondo, Jr.

747. For which film did Steven Spielberg receive the «Broadcast Film Critics Association Award for Best Director» in 2002?
Answer: Minority Report

748. For which film did Ida Lupino receive the «Saturn Award for Best Supporting Actress» in 1976?
Answer: The Devil's Rain

749. What's the birth name of Mahershala Ali?
Answer: Mahershalalhashbaz Gilmore

750. Who was the composer for the 2015 film «The Woman in Gold»?
Answer: Hans Zimmer

751. Whom did Milla Jovovich marry in the year 1992?
Answer: Shawn Andrews

752. For which film did Ed Harris receive the «Toronto Film Critics Association Award for Best Actor» in 2001?
Answer: Pollock

753. Where did Arnold Schwarzenegger get his Bachelor of Arts degree from?
Answer: University of Wisconsin–Superior

754. Who was the composer for the 1990 film «Pretty Woman»?
Answer: James Newton Howard

755. For which film did Brad Pitt receive the «San Diego Film Critics Society Award for Best Performance by an Ensemble» in 2009?
Answer: Inglourious Basterds

756. For his work in the movie «Hud», who won the «Academy Award for Best Supporting Actor» in 1963?
Answer: Melvyn Douglas

757. Who directed the 2018 film «Tomb Raider»?
Answer: Roar Uthaug

758. For her work in the movie «The Three Faces of Eve», who won the «Golden Globe Award for Best Actress – Motion Picture Drama» in 1957?
Answer: Joanne Woodward

759. Who were the directors of the 1995 film «Smoke»?
Answer: Wayne Wang and Paul Auster

760. Who directed the 2010 film «Let Me In»?
Answer: Matt Reeves

761. What's the birth name of Solange Knowles?
Answer: Solange Piaget Knowles

762. Who was the composer for the 1997 film «Picture Perfect»?
Answer: Carter Burwell

763. Who were the directors of the 2014 film «22 Jump Street»?
Answer: Chris Miller and Phil Lord

764. Whom did Darcy LaPier marry in the year 1994?
Answer: Jean-Claude Van Damme

765. What is the name of the character Kate Winslet plays in the movie «Titanic»?
Answer: Rose DeWitt Bukater

766. What's the birth name of Vin Diesel?
Answer: Mark Sinclair

767. For which film did Eli Wallach receive the «BAFTA Award for Most Promising Newcomer to Leading Film Roles» in 1957?
Answer: Baby Doll

768. For which film did Joan Allen receive the «Broadcast Film Critics Association Award for Best Supporting Actress» in 1996?
Answer: The Crucible

769. Who was the composer for the 2006 film «Superman Returns»?
Answer: John Ottman

770. Who directed the 2017 film «Monster Trucks»?
Answer: Chris Wedge

771. When did Valerie Bertinelli marry Eddie Van Halen?
Answer: 1981

772. What is the name of the character Charlton Heston plays in the movie «Tombstone»?
Answer: Henry Hooker

773. Who was the composer for the 2012 film «Seeking a Friend for the End of the World»?
Answer: Rob Simonsen

774. Who was the composer for the 2011 film «Water for Elephants»?
Answer: James Newton Howard

775. For which film did Oscar Isaac receive the «AACTA Award for Best Actor in a Supporting Role» in 2009?
Answer: Balibo

776. What is the name of the character Forest Whitaker plays in the movie «Black Panther»?
Answer: Zuri

777. For her work in the movie «Mogambo», who won the «Golden Globe Award for Best Supporting Actress – Motion Picture» in 1953?
Answer: Grace Kelly

778. When did Jessica Lange marry Paco Grande?
Answer: 1971

779. What is the full name of Marilyn Manson?
Answer: Brian Hugh Warner

780. What's the birth name of Danny Masterson?
Answer: Daniel Peter Masterson

781. What's the birth name of Huckleberry Fox?
Answer: George Miller Fox

782. In which year did Eileen Davidson marry Christopher Mayer?

Answer: 1985

783. What is the full name of Matt Schulze?
Answer: Matthew Steven Schulze

784. Who was the composer for the 1993 film «Gettysburg»?
Answer: Randy Edelman

785. In which year did Kristen Cloke marry Glen Morgan?
Answer: 1998

786. What's the birth name of Chris Brown?
Answer: Christopher Maurice Brown

787. Who was the composer for the 2003 film «The Matrix Reloaded»?
Answer: Don Davis

788. When did Jessica Walter marry Ron Leibman?
Answer: 1983

789. Which film won the Academy Award for Best Documentary (Short Subject) in the year 2019?
Answer: Period. End of Sentence.

790. For which film did Alan Arkin receive the «Independent Spirit Award for Best Supporting Male» in 2007?
Answer: Little Miss Sunshine

791. What's the birth name of Renée Estevez?
Answer: Renée Pilar Estevez

792. Whom did Mackenzie Phillips marry in the year 1996?
Answer: Shane Fontayne

793. Who was the composer for the 2018 film «White Boy Rick»?
Answer: Max Richter

794. For his work in the movie «Ordinary People», who

won the «Academy Award for Best Supporting Actor» in 1980?
Answer: Timothy Hutton

795. What is the full name of America Ferrera?
Answer: America Georgine Ferrera

796. For his work in the movie «From Here to Eternity», who won the «Academy Award for Best Supporting Actor» in 1953?
Answer: Frank Sinatra

797. What is the name of the character Nicolas Cage plays in the movie «Joe»?
Answer: Joe Ransom

798. Whom did Debbi Morgan marry in the year 1989?
Answer: Charles S. Dutton

799. Who directed the 2014 film «Jack Ryan: Shadow Recruit»?
Answer: Kenneth Branagh

800. In which year did Lily Tomlin marry Jane Wagner?
Answer: 2013

801. What's the birth name of Angelina Jolie?
Answer: Angelina Jolie Voight

802. When did Susan Anspach marry Mark Goddard?
Answer: 1970

803. What is the full name of Macaulay Culkin?
Answer: Macaulay Carson Culkin

804. Whom did Eliza Dushku marry in the year 2018?
Answer: Peter Palandjian
805. For his work in the movie «Kiss of the Spider Woman», who won the «David di Donatello for Best Foreign Actor» award in 1986?
Answer: William Hurt

806. Who acted as Edward Garlick in the movie «Good Morning, Vietnam»?
Answer: Forest Whitaker

807. Whom did Shannon Elizabeth marry in the year 2002?
Answer: Joseph D. Reitman

808. Who were the directors of the 2000 film «O Brother, Where Art Thou?»?
Answer: Ethan Coen and Joel Coen

809. Who was the composer for the 2010 film «The Karate Kid»?
Answer: James Horner

810. Where did Amy Poehler get her British Columbia Certificate of Graduation degree from?
Answer: Burlington High School, in Massachusetts

811. Whom did Donna Dixon marry in the year 1983?
Answer: Dan Aykroyd

812. Whom did Leilani Sarelle marry in the year 1991?
Answer: Miguel Ferrer

813. Whom did Alicia Silverstone marry in the year 2005?
Answer: Christopher Jarecki

814. Who was the composer for the 2018 film «I Feel Pretty»?
Answer: Michael Andrews

815. Whom did Gabrielle Union marry in the year 2014?
Answer: Dwyane Wade

816. For which film did Steven Spielberg receive the «Academy Award for Best Director» in 1993?
Answer: Schindler's List

817. For her work in the movie «Capote», who won the

«Boston Society of Film Critics Award for Best Supporting Actress» in 2005?
Answer: Catherine Keener

818. Who directed the 2005 film «Proof»?
Answer: John Madden

819. Which film won the Academy Award for Best Documentary Feature in the year 1998?
Answer: The Last Days

820. Who was the composer for the 1996 film «From Dusk till Dawn»?
Answer: Graeme Revell

821. Who directed the 2014 film «Monuments Men»?
Answer: George Clooney

822. Which film won the Academy Award for Best Cinematography in the year 2002?
Answer: Road to Perdition

823. In which year did Sônia Braga marry Antonio Guerreiro?
Answer: 1976

824. Who was the composer for the 2018 film «Uncle Drew»?
Answer: Christopher Lennertz

825. What's the birth name of Todd Sible?
Answer: Todd Steven Sible

826. When did Meryl Streep marry Don Gummer?
Answer: 1978

827. For his work in the movie «Gentleman's Agreement», who won the «Academy Award for Best Director» in 1947?
Answer: Elia Kazan

828. Who was the composer for the 2009 film «Space Buddies»?

Answer: Brahm Wenger

829. When did Jayne Atkinson marry Michel Gill?
Answer: 1998

830. When did Kirsten Price marry Barrett Blade?
Answer: 2004

831. Where did Danielle Panabaker get her Bachelor of Arts degree from?
Answer: University of California, Los Angeles

832. Where did Wendell Pierce get his Bachelor of Fine Arts degree from?
Answer: Juilliard School, in Manhattan

833. Who directed the 1999 film «The Thirteenth Floor»?
Answer: Josef Rusnak

834. For which film did Halle Berry receive the «Golden Raspberry Award for Worst Actress» in 2004?
Answer: Catwoman

835. What's the birth name of Tisha Campbell-Martin?
Answer: Tisha Michelle Campbell

836. When did Jenna Stern marry Brennan Brown?
Answer: 1998

837. Whom did Lili Taylor marry in the year 2009?
Answer: Nick Flynn

838. What is the full name of Jaden Smith?
Answer: Jaden Christopher Syre Smith

839. Who was the composer for the 1992 film «Society»?
Answer: Mark Ryder

840. In which year did Carmen Electra marry Dave Navarro?
Answer: 2003

841. In which year did Amy Ryan marry Eric Slovin?
Answer: 2011

842. Whom did Jenny McCarthy marry in the year 1999?
Answer: John Mallory Asher

843. Who were the composers of the 2015 film «The Throwaways»?
Answer: Alex Kovacs and Jérôme Leroy

844. Which film won the Academy Award for Best Sound Mixing in the year 1996?
Answer: The English Patient

845. What's the birth name of Andy Dick?
Answer: Andrew Roane Dick

846. What's the birth name of Oliver Hudson?
Answer: Oliver Rutledge Hudson

847. What's the birth name of Tom Cruise?
Answer: Thomas Cruise Mapother IV

848. Which film won the Academy Award for Best Documentary Feature in the year 1985?
Answer: Broken Rainbow

849. Whom did Julie Brown marry in the year 1983?
Answer: Terrence E. McNally

850. In which year did Carroll Baker marry Donald Burton?
Answer: 1978

851. For his work in the movie «My Own Private Idaho», who won the «National Society of Film Critics Award for Best Actor» in 1991?
Answer: River Phoenix

852. Whom did Maggie Siff marry in the year 2012?

Answer: Paul Ratliff

853. Whom did Heather Paige Kent marry in the year 1999?
Answer: Terry Dubrow

854. What is the full name of Judy Greer?
Answer: Judith Therese Evans

855. Who was the composer for the 1990 film «Teenage Mutant Ninja Turtles»?
Answer: John Du Prez

856. Whom did Carey Lowell marry in the year 2002?
Answer: Richard Gere

857. When did Lynn Collins marry Steven Strait?
Answer: 2007

858. Who directed the 2009 film «Fame»?
Answer: Kevin Tancharoen

859. Who was the composer for the 2001 film «Donnie Darko»?
Answer: Michael Andrews

860. Who acted as William Marshal, 1st Earl of Pembroke in the movie «Robin Hood»?
Answer: William Hurt

861. Whom did Kobe Tai marry in the year 1997?
Answer: Mark Davis

862. What's the birth name of Gregory Smith?
Answer: Gregory Edward Smith

863. For which film did Kevin Kline receive the «Academy Award for Best Supporting Actor» in 1988?
Answer: A Fish Called Wanda

864. Whom did Leslie Parrish marry in the year 1977?
Answer: Richard David Bach

865. For his work in the movie «Friday Night Lights», who won the «Best Sports Movie ESPY Award» in 2005?
Answer: Peter Berg

866. Who acted as Mandarin in the movie «Iron Man 3»?
Answer: Ben Kingsley

867. Whom did Halle Berry marry in the year 2013?
Answer: Olivier Martinez

868. Who were the composers of the 2018 film «Widows»?
Answer: Hans Zimmer and Thomas Newman

869. When did Michelle Forbes marry Ross Kettle?
Answer: 1990

870. Who was the composer for the 1990 film «Joe Versus the Volcano»?
Answer: Georges Delerue

871. For which film did Robin Williams receive the «National Board of Review Award for Best Actor» in 1990?
Answer: Awakenings

872. Which film won the Academy Award for Best Documentary Feature in the year 1973?
Answer: The Great American Cowboy

873. For which film did Shang Guan Lingfeng receive the «Golden Horse Award for Best Leading Actress» in 1973?
Answer: Back Alley Princess

874. Who were the directors of the 1991 film «Star Trek VI: The Undiscovered Country»?
Answer: Steven-Charles Jaffe, Ralph Winter, and Nicholas Meyer

875. Whom did Vanessa Marcil marry in the year 2010?
Answer: Carmine Giovinazzo

876. For her work in the movie «My Cousin Vinny», who won the «Academy Award for Best Supporting Actress» in 1992?
Answer: Marisa Tomei

877. In which year did Francesca Le marry Mark Wood?
Answer: 2001

878. Whom did Vanessa Williams marry in the year 1987?
Answer: Ramon Hervey II

879. What is the full name of Ezra Miller?
Answer: Ezra Matthew Miller

880. For which film did Paul Dano receive the «Chlotrudis Award for Best Supporting Actor» in 2008?
Answer: There Will Be Blood

881. For his work in the movie «The Thin Red Line», who won the «Satellite Award for Best Cast – Motion Picture» in 1999?
Answer: John Cusack

882. Which film won the Academy Award for Best Documentary Feature in the year 1963?
Answer: Robert Frost: A Lover's Quarrel with the World

883. For her work in the movie «Leaving Las Vegas», who won the «Independent Spirit Award for Best Female Lead» in 1995?
Answer: Elisabeth Shue

884. For his work in the movie «Cast Away», who won the «Golden Globe Award for Best Actor – Motion Picture Drama» in 2001?
Answer: Tom Hanks

885. When did Anjelica Huston marry Robert Graham?
Answer: 1992

886. Whom did Emmy Rossum marry in the year 2008?

Answer: Justin Siegel

887. Who directed the 2016 film «Collateral Beauty»?
Answer: David Frankel

888. When did Jenna Fischer marry James Gunn?
Answer: 2000

889. Who was the composer for the 2009 film «Everybody's Fine»?
Answer: Dario Marianelli

890. Who directed the 1989 film «See You in the Morning»?
Answer: Alan J. Pakula

891. For his work in the movie «Magic», who won the «Saturn Award for Best Supporting Actor» in 1978?
Answer: Burgess Meredith

892. For which film did Walter Brennan receive the «Academy Award for Best Supporting Actor» in 1936?
Answer: Come and Get It

893. Who directed the 1994 film «Richie Rich»?
Answer: Donald Petrie

894. In which year did Jennifer Connelly marry Paul Bettany?
Answer: 2003

895. In which year did Christine Baranski marry Matthew Cowles?
Answer: 1983

896. For her work in the movie «Million Dollar Baby», who won the «Academy Award for Best Actress» in 2004?
Answer: Hilary Swank

897. For his work in the movie «The Truman Show», who won the «National Board of Review Award for Best

Supporting Actor» in 1998?
Answer: Ed Harris

898. In which year did Julia Duffy marry Jerry Lacy?
Answer: 1984

899. When did Lyndsy Fonseca marry Matthew Smiley?
Answer: 2009

900. Which film won the Academy Award for Best Picture in the year 2019?
Answer: Green Book

901. In which year did Sarah Michelle Gellar marry Freddie Prinze?
Answer: 2002

902. Whom did Susan May Pratt marry in the year 2006?
Answer: Kenneth Mitchell

903. Whom did Rosie Perez marry in the year 2013?
Answer: Eric Haze

904. Whom did La La Anthony marry in the year 2010?
Answer: Carmelo Anthony

905. What is the full name of Zac Efron?
Answer: Zachary David Alexander Efron

906. What's the birth name of Jacob Pitts?
Answer: Jacob Rives Pitts

907. Where was Ron Perlman born?
Answer: Washington Heights

908. What's the birth name of Zoe Saldana?
Answer: Zoë Yadira Saldaña Nazario

909. When did Rachel Weisz marry Daniel Craig?
Answer: 2011

910. Where was Jesse Williams born?
Answer: Chicago

911. For which film did Sally Field receive the «Academy Award for Best Actress» in 1979?
Answer: Norma Rae

912. For her work in the movie «The Upside of Anger», who won the «San Diego Film Critics Society Award for Best Actress» in 2005?
Answer: Joan Allen

913. For which film did Karl Malden receive the «Academy Award for Best Supporting Actor» in 1951?
Answer: A Streetcar Named Desire

914. Who was the composer for the 2010 film «Predators»?
Answer: John Debney

915. Who was the composer for the 1993 film «Sister Act 2: Back in the Habit»?
Answer: Miles Goodman

916. Where did S. Epatha Merkerson get her Bachelor of Fine Arts degree from?
Answer: Wayne State University, in Detroit

917. What is the full name of Haley Paige?
Answer: Maryam Irene Haley

918. For his work in the movie «Raiders of the Lost Ark», who won the «Saturn Award for Best Director» in 1982?
Answer: Steven Spielberg

919. What is the full name of Josh Gad?
Answer: Joshua Ilan Gad

920. Who was the composer for the 2016 film «Bridget Jones's Baby»?
Answer: Craig Armstrong

921. What's the birth name of Kyle Kinane?
Answer: Kyle Christian Kinane

922. Who was the composer for the 2018 film «Dog Days»?
Answer: Craig Wedren

923. For which film did Mary Steenburgen receive the «National Society of Film Critics Award for Best Supporting Actress» in 1980?
Answer: Melvin and Howard

924. What's the birth name of Paul Butcher?
Answer: Paul Matthew Hawke Butcher

925. For which film did Joan Allen receive the «Chicago Film Critics Association Award for Best Actress» in 2006?
Answer: The Upside of Anger

926. What's the birth name of Daryl Sabara?
Answer: Daryl Christofer Sabara

927. Who directed the 2011 film «Rise of the Planet of the Apes»?
Answer: Rupert Wyatt

928. Who was the composer for the 2015 film «Ant-Man»?
Answer: Christophe Beck

929. When did Bette Midler marry Martin von Haselberg?
Answer: 1984

930. For which film did Clark Gregg receive the «Florida Film Critics Circle Award for Best Cast» in 2000?
Answer: State and Main

931. Who directed the 1997 film «Anaconda»?
Answer: Luis Llosa

932. What is the name of the character Gene Hackman

plays in the movie «Enemy of the State»?
Answer: Brill

933. What's the birth name of Robert Rodriguez?
Answer: Robert Anthony Rodríguez

934. For which film did Halle Berry receive the «NAACP Image Award for Outstanding Actress in a Motion Picture» in 2002?
Answer: Swordfish

935. Who was the composer for the 1996 film «The Rock»?
Answer: Nick Glennie-Smith

936. When did Karen Black marry L. M. Kit Carson?
Answer: 1975

937. Which film won the Golden Globe Award for Best Original Score in the year 1949?
Answer: The Inspector General

938. Whom did Jewel marry in the year 2008?
Answer: Ty Murray

939. Where did Stacy Keach get his Master of Fine Arts degree from?
Answer: Yale University, in New Haven

940. Who was the composer for the 1995 film «Waterworld»?
Answer: James Newton Howard

941. For his work in the movie «The Birdcage», who won the «Screen Actors Guild Award for Outstanding Performance by a Cast in a Motion Picture» in 1997?
Answer: Robin Williams

942. For his work in the movie «Inside Llewyn Davis», who won the «National Society of Film Critics Award for Best Actor» in 2013?

Answer: Oscar Isaac

943. Which film won the Academy Award for Best Film Editing in the year 1989?
Answer: Born on the Fourth of July

944. For which film did Helen Hunt receive the «Golden Globe Award for Best Actress – Motion Picture Musical or Comedy» in 1997?
Answer: As Good as It Gets

945. Who directed the 2002 film «Spy Kids 2: The Island of Lost Dreams»?
Answer: Robert Rodriguez

946. Who acted as Donna Sheridan-Carmichael in the movie «Mamma Mia! Here We Go Again»?
Answer: Meryl Streep

947. Whom did Pamela Anderson marry in the year 1995?
Answer: Tommy Lee

948. Who directed the 2016 film «10 Cloverfield Lane»?
Answer: Dan Trachtenberg

949. For which film did Anton Yelchin receive the «Boston Society of Film Critics Award for Best Cast» in 2009?
Answer: Star Trek

950. When did Kelly Lynch marry Mitch Glazer?
Answer: 1992

951. For which film did Julie Harris receive the «Primetime Emmy Award for Outstanding Voice-Over Performance» in 2000?
Answer: Not for Ourselves Alone

952. When did Katy Perry marry Russell Brand?
Answer: 2010

953. In which year did Pamela Anderson marry Kid Rock?
Answer: 2006

954. For her work in the movie «Five Corners», who won the «Independent Spirit Award for Best Female Lead» in 1989?
Answer: Jodie Foster

955. What is the full name of Ben Gibbard?
Answer: Benjamin Gibbard

956. In which year did Cynthia Ettinger marry Wally Kurth?
Answer: 1990

957. In which year did Colleen Camp marry John Goldwyn?
Answer: 1986

958. What's the birth name of Tawny Peaks?
Answer: Michele Ann Laird

959. For which film did Jack Albertson receive the «Academy Award for Best Supporting Actor» in 1968?
Answer: The Subject Was Roses

960. Where was Joan Allen born?
Answer: Rochelle

961. Where did Jessica Hecht get her Bachelor of Fine Arts degree from?
Answer: New York University Tisch School of the Arts, in New York City

962. For her work in the movie «The Picture of Dorian Gray», who won the «Golden Globe Award for Best Supporting Actress – Motion Picture» in 1945?
Answer: Angela Lansbury

963. For her work in the movie «Doubt», who won the «Screen Actors Guild Award for Outstanding Performance by a Female Actor in a Leading Role» in 2009?
Answer: Meryl Streep

964. When did Asia Carrera marry Bud Lee?
Answer: 1995

965. What's the birth name of Lea Thompson?
Answer: Lea Katherine Thompson

966. For which film did Brad Pitt receive the «National Society of Film Critics Award for Best Actor» in 2011?
Answer: Moneyball

967. For which film did James Coburn receive the «Academy Award for Best Supporting Actor» in 1999?
Answer: Affliction

968. What is the full name of Mindy Kaling?
Answer: Vera Mindy Chokalingam

969. Whom did Jessica Alba marry in the year 2008?
Answer: Cash Garner Warren

970. Where did Fred Thompson get his Bachelor of Arts degree from?
Answer: University of Memphis

971. What is the full name of Paul Schneider?
Answer: Paul Andrew Schneider

972. What is the name of the character Michael Douglas plays in the movie «Ant-Man»?
Answer: Hank Pym

973. In which year did A. J. Langer marry Charles Courtenay, Lord Courtenay?
Answer: 2005

974. Who directed the 2019 film «Hellboy»?
Answer: Neil Marshall

975. Whom did Eva LaRue marry in the year 1992?
Answer: John O'Hurley

976. In which year did Rebecca Herbst marry Michael Saucedo?
Answer: 2001

977. Who directed the 2018 film «Second Act»?
Answer: Peter Segal

978. For his work in the movie «The Hurt Locker», who won the «Las Vegas Film Critics Society Award for Best Actor» in 2009?
Answer: Jeremy Renner

979. When did Paget Brewster marry Steve Damstra?
Answer: 2014

980. Who directed the 2018 film «Halloween»?
Answer: David Gordon Green

981. For which film did Jodie Foster receive the «Academy Award for Best Actress» in 1991?
Answer: The Silence of the Lambs

982. What is the full name of Cassie Ventura?
Answer: Casandra Elizabeth Ventura

983. For which film did Gene Hackman receive the «BAFTA Award for Best Actor in a Supporting Role» in 1993?
Answer: Unforgiven

984. In which year did Nikki Tyler marry Bobby Vitale?
Answer: 1996

985. What's the birth name of Nora Zehetner?
Answer: Nora Angela Zehetner

986. When did Casey Wilson marry David Caspe?
Answer: 2014

987. When did Elizabeth Montgomery marry Robert Foxworth?

Answer: 1993

988. In which year did Priscilla Pointer marry Robert Symonds?
Answer: 1981

989. In which year did Judith Hoag marry Vince Grant?
Answer: 1988

990. Whom did Patricia Wettig marry in the year 1982?
Answer: Ken Olin

991. Whom did Sophia Bush marry in the year 2005?
Answer: Chad Michael Murray

992. Who directed the 1997 film «Con Air»?
Answer: Simon West

993. In which year did Rachel Ticotin marry Peter Strauss?
Answer: 1998

994. Who was the composer for the 2006 film «The Nativity Story»?
Answer: Mychael Danna

995. When did Mia Sara marry Jason Connery?
Answer: 1996

996. What's the birth name of Kevin Hart?
Answer: Kevin Darnell Hart

997. For his work in the movie «Schindler's List», who won the «London Film Critics Circle Award for Film of the Year» in 1994?
Answer: Steven Spielberg

998. Where was S. Epatha Merkerson born?
Answer: Saginaw

999. For his work in the movie «The French Connection»,

who won the «BAFTA Award for Best Actor in a Leading Role» in 1973?
Answer: Gene Hackman

1000. For which film did Alan Arkin receive the «Genie Award for Best Supporting Actor» in 1986?
Answer: Joshua Then and Now

1001. Who acted as Alfred Pennyworth in the movie «The Dark Knight»?
Answer: Michael Caine

1002. Where did Steve Harris get his Master of Fine Arts degree from?
Answer: University of Delaware, in Newark

1003. Whom did Anna Gunn marry in the year 1990?
Answer: Alastair Duncan

1004. For his work in the movie «The Revenant», who won the «Screen Actors Guild Award» in 2016?
Answer: Leonardo DiCaprio

1005. Whom did Rae Dawn Chong marry in the year 1989?
Answer: Christopher Thomas Howell

1006. For which film did Kristen Stewart receive the «Golden Raspberry Award for Worst Actress» in 2012?
Answer: Snow White and the Huntsman

1007. For which film did Rachel Weisz receive the «Screen Actors Guild Award for Outstanding Performance by a Female Actor in a Supporting Role» in 2006?
Answer: The Constant Gardener

1008. Who directed the 2006 film «Casino Royale»?
Answer: Martin Campbell

1009. What's the birth name of Jimmy Pop?
Answer: James Moyer Franks

1010. What's the birth name of Jennifer Hudson?

Answer: Jennifer Kate Hudson

1011. Who directed the 2000 film «Autumn in New York»?
Answer: Joan Chen

1012. Which film won the Golden Globe Award for Best Screenplay in the year 1978?
Answer: Midnight Express

1013. Whom did Asa Akira marry in the year 2012?
Answer: Toni Ribas

1014. For which film did Nate Parker receive the «U.S. Grand Jury Prize: Dramatic» award in 2016?
Answer: The Birth of a Nation

1015. Which film won the Academy Award for Best Sound Mixing in the year 1992?
Answer: Terminator 2: Judgment Day

1016. Who were the composers of the 2005 film «Sin City»?
Answer: Graeme Revell and John Debney

1017. Who was the composer for the 2005 film «Good Night, and Good Luck.»?
Answer: Dianne Reeves

1018. Who was the composer for the 1997 film «Wag the Dog»?
Answer: Mark Knopfler

1019. Who was the composer for the 2008 film «Defiance»?
Answer: James Newton Howard

1020. Who were the directors of the 1989 film «New York Stories»?
Answer: Francis Ford Coppola, Woody Allen, and Martin Scorsese

1021. What is the name of the character Robert Duvall plays in the movie «The Godfather»?
Answer: Tom Hagen

1022. Who directed the 1994 film «3 Ninjas Kick Back»?
Answer: Charles T. Kanganis

1023. Who acted as John Jonah Jameson in the movie «Spider-Man 3»?
Answer: J. K. Simmons

1024. Who was the composer for the 2014 film «22 Jump Street»?
Answer: Mark Mothersbaugh

1025. Who was the composer for the 2005 film «The Skeleton Key»?
Answer: Edward Shearmur

1026. Who was the composer for the 2004 film «Scooby-Doo 2: Monsters Unleashed»?
Answer: David Newman

1027. Who was the composer for the 1999 film «South Park: Bigger, Longer & Uncut»?
Answer: Trey Parker

1028. Who acted as Harry Hart in the movie «Kingsman: The Secret Service»?
Answer: Colin Firth

1029. Who was the composer for the 1992 film «Sarafina!»?
Answer: Stanley Myers

1030. For which film did Ron Howard receive the «Academy Award for Best Director» in 2002?
Answer: A Beautiful Mind

1031. Which film won the Academy Award for Best Sound Editing in the year 2012?

Answer: Skyfall

1032. For which film did Frances McDormand receive the «BAFTA Award for Best Actress in a Leading Role» in 2018?
Answer: Three Billboards Outside Ebbing, Missouri

1033. Who was the composer for the 2015 film «The Martian»?
Answer: Harry Gregson-Williams

1034. Who acted as Aunt May in the movie «The Amazing Spider-Man 2»?
Answer: Sally Field

1035. Which film won the Academy Award for Best Picture in the year 1959?
Answer: Gigi

1036. For which film did Denzel Washington receive the «Academy Award for Best Supporting Actor» in 1989?
Answer: Glory

1037. Whom did Kiersten Warren marry in the year 2005?
Answer: Kirk Acevedo

1038. For which film did Edward Burns receive the «U.S. Grand Jury Prize: Dramatic» award in 1995?
Answer: The Brothers McMullen

1039. Who acted as Chester Phillips in the movie «Captain America: The First Avenger»?
Answer: Tommy Lee Jones

1040. For which film did Jennifer Aniston receive the «MTV Movie Award for Best Villain» in 2012?
Answer: Horrible Bosses

1041. For his work in the movie «The Hurt Locker», who won the «Satellite Award for Best Actor – Motion Picture» in 2009?
Answer: Jeremy Renner

1042. What is the full name of Jake T. Austin?
Answer: Jake Austin Szymanski

1043. For his work in the movie «The Town», who won the «Washington D.C. Area Film Critics Association Award for Best Ensemble» in 2010?
Answer: Owen Burke

1044. Who was the composer for the 1995 film «Judge Dredd»?
Answer: Alan Silvestri

1045. What is the name of the character Christopher Walken plays in the movie «Batman Returns»?
Answer: Max Shreck

1046. What's the birth name of Demi Moore?
Answer: Demetria Gene Guynes

1047. For his work in the movie «The Usual Suspects», who won the «Academy Award for Best Supporting Actor» in 1995?
Answer: Kevin Spacey

1048. Who directed the 2018 film «Eighth Grade»?
Answer: Bo Burnham

1049. What is the name of the character Benicio del Toro plays in the movie «Guardians of the Galaxy»?
Answer: Collector (comics)

1050. What is the full name of Charlie Sheen?
Answer: Carlos Irwin Estévez

1051. For which film did Brad Pitt receive the «New York Film Critics Circle Award for Best Actor» in 2011?
Answer: The Tree of Life

1052. Whom did Demi Moore marry in the year 1980?
Answer: Freddy Moore

1053. In which year did Tori Spelling marry Dean McDermott?
Answer: 2006

1054. Whom did Terri Conn marry in the year 2011?
Answer: Austin Peck

1055. For which film did Mary Tyler Moore receive the «Golden Globe Award for Best Actress – Motion Picture Drama» in 1980?
Answer: Ordinary People

1056. Where did Jaclyn Hales get her Bachelor of Science degree from?
Answer: Utah Valley University, in Orem

1057. Who was the composer for the 2003 film «The Life of David Gale»?
Answer: Alex Parker

1058. For his work in the movie «My Girl», who won the «MTV Movie Award for Best Kiss» in 1992?
Answer: Macaulay Culkin

1059. For his work in the movie «Hugo», who won the «Golden Globe Award for Best Director» in 2011?
Answer: Martin Scorsese

1060. What is the full name of Mopreme Shakur?
Answer: Maurice Williams

1061. For which film did Van Heflin receive the «Academy Award for Best Supporting Actor» in 1942?
Answer: Johnny Eager

1062. What's the birth name of Johnny Knoxville?
Answer: Philip John Clapp

1063. Who was the composer for the 2015 film «Sicario»?
Answer: Jóhann Jóhannsson

1064. What is the full name of Wanda D'Isidoro?
Answer: Wanda Catherine D'Isidoro Arcolín

1065. For which film did Sean Penn receive the «Academy Award for Best Actor» in 2003?
Answer: Mystic River

1066. Who was the composer for the 2018 film «Peppermint»?
Answer: Simon Franglen

1067. What is the name of the character Natalie Portman plays in the movie «Thor»?
Answer: Jane Foster

1068. For which film did Mark Ruffalo receive the «New York Film Critics Circle Award for Best Saupporting Actor» in 2010?
Answer: The Kids Are All Right

1069. For his work in the movie «The Godfather», who won the «Academy Award for Best Actor» in 1972?
Answer: Marlon Brando

1070. Whom did Mary Beth Hurt marry in the year 1982?
Answer: Paul Schrader

1071. In which year did Robin Wright marry Dane Witherspoon?
Answer: 1986

1072. Whom did Becki Newton marry in the year 2005?
Answer: Chris Diamantopoulos

1073. Whom did Arthel Neville marry in the year 2001?
Answer: Taku Hirano

1074. Whom did Gigi Rice marry in the year 1991?
Answer: Ted McGinley

1075. Whom did Lacey Chabert marry in the year 2013?

Answer: David Nehdar

1076. Whom did Annie Potts marry in the year 1990?
Answer: James Hayman

1077. For which film did Thomas Haden Church receive the «Los Angeles Film Critics Association Award for Best Supporting Actor» in 2004?
Answer: Sideways

1078. Who directed the 1997 film «The Man Who Knew Too Little»?
Answer: Jon Amiel

1079. For his work in the movie «Double Team», who won the «Golden Raspberry Award for Worst Screen Couple/Ensemble» in 1997?
Answer: Dennis Rodman

1080. In which year did Zooey Deschanel marry Ben Gibbard?
Answer: 2009

1081. Who was the composer for the 1993 film «Demolition Man»?
Answer: Elliot Goldenthal

1082. What's the birth name of Paul McCrane?
Answer: Paul David McCrane

1083. Which film won the Academy Award for Best Writing, Adapted Screenplay in the year 1931?
Answer: Cimarron

1084. For which film did Ed Harris receive the «Screen Actors Guild Award for Outstanding Performance by a Cast in a Motion Picture» in 1996?
Answer: Apollo 13

1085. For which film did Al Pacino receive the «BAFTA Award for Best Actor in a Leading Role» in 1976?
Answer: The Godfather Part II

1086. What is the full name of Kirsten Vangsness?
Answer: Kirsten Simone Vangsness

1087. For her work in the movie «Boyhood», who won the «Academy Award for Best Supporting Actress» in 2015?
Answer: Patricia Arquette

1088. Whom did Julie McCullough marry in the year 2001?
Answer: David Sutcliffe

1089. In which year did America Ferrera marry Ryan Piers Williams?
Answer: 2011

1090. Who was the composer for the 1991 film «One Good Cop»?
Answer: David Foster

1091. Where did Anders Holm get his high school diploma from?
Answer: Evanston Township High School, in Illinois

1092. Who was the composer for the 1997 film «Volcano»?
Answer: Alan Silvestri

1093. Who directed the 2000 film «Gun Shy»?
Answer: Eric Blakeney

1094. When did Lindsay Price marry Shawn Piller?
Answer: 2004

1095. For which film did Jennifer Lawrence receive the «Academy Award for Best Actress» in 2012?
Answer: Silver Linings Playbook

1096. What's the birth name of Douglas Smith?
Answer: Douglas Alexander Smith

1097. For which film did Joe Pesci receive the «Academy Award for Best Supporting Actor» in 1990?

Answer: Goodfellas

1098. Who acted as Zuri in the movie «Black Panther»?
Answer: Forest Whitaker

1099. For her work in the movie «Lost in Translation», who won the «BAFTA Award for Best Actress in a Leading Role» in 2004?
Answer: Scarlett Johansson

1100. For which film did Chris Messina receive the «Screen Actors Guild Award for Outstanding Performance by a Cast in a Motion Picture» in 2013?
Answer: Argo

1101. In which year did Emily Blunt marry John Krasinski?
Answer: 2010

1102. Whom did Jennifer Hale marry in the year 2009?
Answer: Barry Oswick

1103. When did Jo Ann Pflug marry Chuck Woolery?
Answer: 1972

1104. Who was the composer for the 1993 film «Mrs. Doubtfire»?
Answer: Howard Shore

1105. Who directed the 1994 film «Street Fighter»?
Answer: Steven E. de Souza

1106. What's the birth name of Julia Stiles?
Answer: Julia O'Hara Stiles

1107. What is the full name of Loreto Peralta?
Answer: Loreto Peralta Jacobson

1108. For his work in the movie «Sideways», who won the «Screen Actors Guild Award for Outstanding Performance by a Cast in a Motion Picture» in 2005?

Answer: Thomas Haden Church

1109. Whom did Kristen Wiig marry in the year 2005?
Answer: Hayes Hargrove

1110. Who acted as God in the movie «Bruce Almighty»?
Answer: Morgan Freeman

1111. For which film did Steven Spielberg receive the «Golden Globe Award for Best Director» in 1998?
Answer: Saving Private Ryan

1112. Which film won the Academy Award for Best Picture in the year 1932?
Answer: Grand Hotel

1113. For his work in the movie «Goodfellas», who won the «Silver Lion» award in 1990?
Answer: Martin Scorsese

1114. What's the birth name of Shane Dawson?
Answer: Shane Mouthpop Yaw

1115. Whom did Christie Brinkley marry in the year 1994?
Answer: Richard Taubman

1116. For which film did Diane Keaton receive the «BAFTA Award for Best Actress in a Leading Role» in 1978?
Answer: Annie Hall

1117. What is the name of the character Morgan Freeman plays in the movie «Batman Begins»?
Answer: Lucius Fox

1118. Who directed the 2017 film «The Blackcoat's Daughter»?
Answer: Oz Perkins

1119. In which year did Kelli Williams marry Ajay Sahgal?
Answer: 1996

1120. Who acted as Forrest Gump in the movie «Forrest Gump»?
Answer: Tom Hanks

1121. When did Debrah Farentino marry Tony Adams?
Answer: 1992

1122. What's the birth name of Brie Larson?
Answer: Brianne Sidonie Desaulniers

1123. For his work in the movie «The Remains of the Day», who won the «Southeastern Film Critics Association Award for Best Actor» in 1993?
Answer: Anthony Hopkins

1124. Where was Billy Crystal born?
Answer: New York City

1125. Who directed the 2016 film «The Divergent Series: Allegiant»?
Answer: Robert Schwentke

1126. In which year did Kristine Sutherland marry John Pankow?
Answer: 1986

1127. Who directed the 2017 film «Inconceivable»?
Answer: Jonathan Baker

1128. When did Stockard Channing marry David Debin?
Answer: 1976

1129. Whom did Missi Pyle marry in the year 2000?
Answer: Antonio Sacre

1130. Who was the composer for the 2005 film «Blast»?
Answer: Danny Saber

1131. For which film did Lee Daniels receive the «U.S. Grand Jury Prize: Dramatic» award in 2009?
Answer: Precious

1132. When did Elizabeth Marvel marry Bill Camp?
Answer: 2004

1133. What is the name of the character Sigourney Weaver plays in the movie «Alien: Resurrection»?
Answer: Ellen Ripley

1134. In which year did Patricia Kalember marry Daniel Gerroll?
Answer: 1986

1135. Who directed the 2012 film «The Dark Knight Rises»?
Answer: Christopher Nolan

1136. Where was Beulah Bondi born?
Answer: Valparaiso

1137. Who acted as Hank Pym in the movie «Ant-Man and the Wasp»?
Answer: Michael Douglas

1138. When did Amy Van Nostrand marry Tim Daly?
Answer: 1982

1139. Who directed the 1991 film «The Marrying Man»?
Answer: Jerry Rees

1140. Which film won the Academy Award for Best Film Editing in the year 1987?
Answer: Platoon

1141. For which film did Mel Brooks receive the «Nebula Award for Best Script» in 1975?
Answer: Young Frankenstein

1142. Who acted as Richard Phillips in the movie «Captain Phillips»?
Answer: Tom Hanks

1143. For which film did Burl Ives receive the «Academy

Award for Best Supporting Actor» in 1958?
Answer: The Big Country

1144. For his work in the movie «Tender Mercies», who won the «Academy Award for Best Actor» in 1984?
Answer: Robert Duvall

1145. For his work in the movie «Good Will Hunting», who won the «Screen Actors Guild Award for Outstanding Performance by a Male Actor in a Supporting Role» in 1998?
Answer: Robin Williams

1146. What is the full name of Stephen Colbert?
Answer: Stephen Tyrone Colbert

1147. Who was the composer for the 2018 film «Aquaman»?
Answer: Rupert Gregson-Williams

1148. Who was the composer for the 2013 film «Broken City»?
Answer: Atticus Ross

1149. For his work in the movie «The Unbearable Lightness of Being», who won the «BAFTA Award for Best Adapted Screenplay» in 1989?
Answer: Philip Kaufman

1150. Which film won the Academy Award for Best Film Editing in the year 1999?
Answer: The Matrix

1151. For which film did Mark Ruffalo receive the «MTV Movie Award for Best Fight» in 2013?
Answer: The Avengers

1152. When did Michelle Pfeiffer marry David E. Kelley?
Answer: 1993

1153. What is the name of the character Jeremy Irons

plays in the movie «Batman v Superman: Dawn of Justice»?
Answer: Alfred Pennyworth

1154. Who was the composer for the 2003 film «The Matrix Revolutions»?
Answer: Don Davis

1155. Whom did Beyoncé marry in the year 2008?
Answer: Jay-Z

1156. Whom did Marian Seldes marry in the year 1990?
Answer: Garson Kanin

1157. Who directed the 1992 film «The Hand That Rocks the Cradle»?
Answer: Curtis Hanson

1158. Who was the composer for the 2018 film «Jurassic World: Fallen Kingdom»?
Answer: Michael Giacchino

1159. What is the full name of Bobbi Starr?
Answer: Elizabeth Evans

1160. When did Alicia Keys marry Swizz Beatz?
Answer: 2010

1161. Who was the composer for the 1991 film «The Naked Gun 2½: The Smell of Fear»?
Answer: Ira Newborn

1162. Who was the composer for the 2018 film «Golden Exits»?
Answer: Keegan DeWitt

1163. For which film did Miloš Forman receive the «BAFTA Award for Best Film» in 1977?
Answer: One Flew Over the Cuckoo's Nest

1164. For his work in the movie «The Birdcage», who won

the «Screen Actors Guild Award for Outstanding Performance by a Cast in a Motion Picture» in 1997?
Answer: Dan Futterman

1165. What is the full name of Anson Mount?
Answer: Anson Adams Mount IV

1166. Which film won the Academy Award for Best Writing, Adapted Screenplay in the year 2013?
Answer: 12 Years a Slave

1167. Who was the composer for the 2016 film «Bad Moms»?
Answer: Christopher Lennertz

1168. In which year did JoBeth Williams marry John Pasquin?
Answer: 1982

1169. What is the full name of La La Anthony?
Answer: Alani Vazquez

1170. Who directed the 2019 film «Gemini Man»?
Answer: Ang Lee

1171. When did Scarlett Johansson marry Romain Dauriac?
Answer: 2014

1172. Who were the directors of the 2010 film «The Book of Eli»?
Answer: Allen Hughes and Albert Hughes

1173. For her work in the movie «My Cousin Vinny», who won the «MTV Movie Award for Best Breakthrough Performance» in 1993?
Answer: Marisa Tomei

1174. Who was the composer for the 1997 film «Home Alone 3»?
Answer: Nick Glennie-Smith

1175. In which year did Kathy Najimy marry Dan Finnerty?
Answer: 1995

1176. When did Carey Lowell marry Griffin Dunne?
Answer: 1989

1177. Which film won the Academy Award for Best Writing, Adapted Screenplay in the year 1940?
Answer: Gone with the Wind

1178. Who was the composer for the 1995 film «Sudden Death»?
Answer: John Debney

1179. In which year did Roseanne Barr marry Thomas Duane Arnold?
Answer: 1990

1180. Whom did Eve Gordon marry in the year 1987?
Answer: Todd Waring

1181. When did Lala Sloatman marry Chris Robinson?
Answer: 1996

1182. What is the full name of Jordin Sparks?
Answer: Jordin Brianna Sparks

1183. Where did Patti LuPone get her Bachelor of Fine Arts degree from?
Answer: Juilliard School, in Manhattan

1184. In which year did Kathleen Kinmont marry Jere Burns?
Answer: 1997

1185. Who directed the 2008 film «Punisher: War Zone»?
Answer: Lexi Alexander

1186. Who directed the 2016 film «Allied»?
Answer: Robert Zemeckis

1187. When did Leven Rambin marry Jim Parrack?
Answer: 2015

1188. When did Whoopi Goldberg marry David Claessen?
Answer: 1986

1189. Which film won the Academy Award for Best Sound Editing in the year 1982?
Answer: E.T. the Extra-Terrestrial

1190. For which film did Anthony Hopkins receive the «Dallas-Fort Worth Film Critics Association Award for Best Actor» in 1991?
Answer: The Silence of the Lambs

1191. Who directed the 1996 film «Curdled»?
Answer: Reb Braddock

1192. For her work in the movie «Obsessed», who won the «MTV Movie Award for Best Fight» in 2010?
Answer: Beyoncé

1193. Who directed the 2011 film «Super 8»?
Answer: J. J. Abrams

1194. What is the name of the character Sigourney Weaver plays in the movie «Alien»?
Answer: Ellen Ripley

1195. For which film did Steven Spielberg receive the «New York Film Critics Circle Award for Best Film» in 1993?
Answer: Schindler's List

1196. Whom did Patty Duke marry in the year 1972?
Answer: John Astin

1197. Whom did Stacey Dash marry in the year 2005?
Answer: James Maby

1198. Whom did Portia de Rossi marry in the year 2008?

Answer: Ellen DeGeneres

1199. Who directed the 2017 film «Murder on the Orient Express»?
Answer: Kenneth Branagh

1200. What's the birth name of Jesse Metcalfe?
Answer: Jesse Eden Metcalfe

1201. For her work in the movie «Annie Hall», who won the «Golden Globe Award for Best Actress – Motion Picture Musical or Comedy» in 1977?
Answer: Diane Keaton

1202. Whom did Suzy Amis Cameron marry in the year 2000?
Answer: James Cameron

1203. Where was Shaquille O'Neal born?
Answer: Newark

1204. Who was the composer for the 2018 film «The Girl in the Spider's Web»?
Answer: Roque Baños

1205. For his work in the movie «Capote», who won the «Independent Spirit Award for Best Screenplay» in 2006?
Answer: Dan Futterman

1206. For her work in the movie «Summer Wishes, Winter Dreams», who won the «New York Film Critics Circle Award for Best Actress» in 1973?
Answer: Joanne Woodward

1207. When did Heidi Lenhart marry Robin Dunne?
Answer: 2002

1208. Where did Ron Jeremy get his Bachelor of Arts degree from?
Answer: Queens College

1209. Whom did Jennifer Blanc marry in the year 2009?
Answer: Michael Biehn

1210. What's the birth name of Belladonna?
Answer: Michelle Anne Sinclair

1211. For which film did Miloš Forman receive the «Los Angeles Film Critics Association Award for Best Director» in 1984?
Answer: Amadeus

1212. Who directed the 2018 film «Solo: A Star Wars Story»?
Answer: Ron Howard

1213. Who directed the 2019 film «Madeline's Madeline»?
Answer: Josephine Decker

1214. When did Jennifer Love Hewitt marry Brian Hallisay?
Answer: 2013

1215. Who directed the 2018 film «Shock and Awe»?
Answer: Rob Reiner

1217. For which film did Aaron Sorkin receive the «New York Film Critics Circle Award for Best Screenplay» in 2011?
Answer: Moneyball

1218. In which year did Janet Margolin marry Ted Wass?
Answer: 1979

1219. In which year did Kelli McCarty marry Matt Dearborn?
Answer: 2000

1220. Whom did Melissa Gilbert marry in the year 1995?
Answer: Bruce Boxleitner

1221. Who acted as Romeo in the movie «Romeo + Juliet»?
Answer: Leonardo DiCaprio

1222. In which year did Chelsea Noble marry Kirk Cameron?
Answer: 1991

1223. What is the full name of Michael Kelly?
Answer: Michael Joseph Kelly

1224. For which film did Catherine Keener receive the «Los Angeles Film Critics Association Award for Best Supporting Actress» in 2005?
Answer: Capote

1225. What's the birth name of Amy Adams?
Answer: Amy Lou Adams

1226. Whom did Paige Turco marry in the year 2003?
Answer: Jason O'Mara

1227. What's the birth name of Winona Ryder?
Answer: Winona Laura Horowitz

1228. When did Mary Ellen Trainor marry Robert Zemeckis?
Answer: 1980

1229. What is the full name of Megan Nicole?
Answer: Megan Nicole Flores

1230. Whom did Kate Jackson marry in the year 1991?
Answer: Tom Hart

1231. For her work in the movie «Cruel Intentions», who won the «MTV Movie Award for Best Kiss» in 2000?
Answer: Sarah Michelle Gellar

1232. In which year did Jaime Bergman marry David Boreanaz?

Answer: 2001

1233. Who acted as Batman in the movie «Batman Begins»?
Answer: Christian Bale

1234. In which year did Phylicia Rashād marry Ahmad Rashad?
Answer: 1985

1235. Which film won the Academy Award for Best Picture in the year 1968?
Answer: In the Heat of the Night

1236. Whom did Sofia Coppola marry in the year 1999?
Answer: Spike Jonze

1237. For which film did Wallace Beery receive the «Academy Award for Best Actor» in 1932?
Answer: The Champ

1238. Who was the composer for the 1995 film «Apollo 13»?
Answer: James Horner

1239. When did Genevieve Padalecki marry Jared Padalecki?
Answer: 2010

1240. What's the birth name of Rob Corddry?
Answer: Robert William Corddry

1241. Who acted as Thomas Bryan Reynolds in the movie «Enemy of the State»?
Answer: Jon Voight

1242. Who directed the 2006 film «Copying Beethoven»?
Answer: Agnieszka Holland

1243. For which film did Martin Scorsese receive the «BAFTA Award for Best Adapted Screenplay» in 1991?

Answer: Goodfellas

1244. Which film won the Academy Award for Best Picture in the year 1975?
Answer: The Godfather Part II

1245. For which film did Jodie Foster receive the «Golden Globe Award for Best Actress – Motion Picture Drama» in 1988?
Answer: The Accused

1246. For his work in the movie «The Thin Red Line», who won the «Satellite Award for Best Cast – Motion Picture» in 1999?
Answer: Dash Mihok

1247. In which year did Julianne Moore marry John Gould Rubin?
Answer: 1986

1248. What's the birth name of Aimee Teegarden?
Answer: Aimee Richelle Teegarden

1249. When did Pamela Anderson marry Rick Salomon?
Answer: 2007

1250. Who directed the 2018 film «Blindspotting»?
Answer: Carlos López Estrada

1251. In which year did Patti Hansen marry Keith Richards?
Answer: 1983

1252. Who acted as Chester Phillips in the movie «Captain America: The First Avenger»?
Answer: Tommy Lee Jones

1253. For which film did Tom Hanks receive the «Screen Actors Guild Award for Outstanding Performance by a Male Actor in a Leading Role» in 1995?
Answer: Forrest Gump

1254. Which film won the Academy Award for Best Sound Mixing in the year 1987?
Answer: Platoon

1255. For her work in the movie «Walk the Line», who won the «British Academy of Film and Television Arts» award in 2006?
Answer: Reese Witherspoon

1256. Who acted as Uncle Ben in the movie «Spider-Man 3»?
Answer: Cliff Robertson

1257. For her work in the movie «Annie Hall», who won the «National Society of Film Critics Award for Best Actress» in 1977?
Answer: Diane Keaton

1258. In which year did Cindy Pickett marry Lyman Ward?
Answer: 1986

1259. Whom did Sharon Stone marry in the year 1984?
Answer: Michael Greenburg

1260. Where was Andrea Anders born?
Answer: Madison

1261. Whom did Keyshia Cole marry in the year 2011?
Answer: Daniel Gibson

1262. Whom did Jenny O'Hara marry in the year 1986?
Answer: Nick Ullett

1263. When did Maria Canals-Barrera marry David Barrera?
Answer: 1999

1264. For which film did Tim Robbins receive the «Academy Award for Best Supporting Actor» in 2004?
Answer: Mystic River

1265. Who was the composer for the 1988 film «Die Hard»?
Answer: Michael Kamen

1266. Who was the composer for the 2002 film «Maid in Manhattan»?
Answer: Alan Silvestri

1267. Who directed the 2016 film «La La Land»?
Answer: Damien Chazelle

1268. Who was the composer for the 2014 film «Sin City: A Dame to Kill For»?
Answer: Robert Rodriguez

1269. Who directed the 1995 film «Sudden Death»?
Answer: Peter Hyams

1270. What's the birth name of Seamus Davey-Fitzpatrick?
Answer: Seamus Liam Davey-Fitzpatrick

1271. What's the birth name of Chyna?
Answer: Joan Marie Laurer

1272. When did Johanna Braddy marry Josh Blaylock?
Answer: 2012

1273. What is the full name of Sofia Coppola?
Answer: Sofia Carmina Coppola

1274. For which film did Casey Affleck receive the «Academy Award for Best Actor» in 2017?
Answer: Manchester by the Sea

1275. For her work in the movie «Dreamgirls», who won the «BAFTA Award for Best Actress in a Supporting Role» in 2007?
Answer: Jennifer Hudson

1276. Who acted as Zuri in the movie «Black Panther»?
Answer: Forest Whitaker

1277. Who was the composer for the 2006 film «Jesus Camp»?
Answer: Force Theory

1278. For which film did Stephen Boyd receive the «Golden Globe Award for Best Supporting Actor – Motion Picture» in 1959?
Answer: Ben-Hur

1279. What's the birth name of Fergie?
Answer: Stacy Ann Ferguson

1280. For his work in the movie «Kiss of the Spider Woman», who won the «Cannes Film Festival Award for Best Actor» in 1985?
Answer: William Hurt

1281. Where did Julianne Moore get her Bachelor of Fine Arts degree from?
Answer: Boston University, in Massachusetts

1282. In which year did Marg Helgenberger marry Alan Rosenberg?
Answer: 1989

1283. Whom did Kathryn Morris marry in the year 2010?
Answer: Johnny Messner

1284. What's the birth name of Scott Eastwood?
Answer: Scott Clinton Reeves

1285. Who was the composer for the 2011 film «Season of the Witch»?
Answer: Atli Örvarsson

1286. What is the name of the character Christopher Walken plays in the movie «A View to a Kill»?
Answer: Max Zorin

1287. Whom did Dedee Pfeiffer marry in the year 2009?
Answer: Kevin Ryan

1288. Whom did Summer Phoenix marry in the year 2006?
Answer: Casey Affleck

1289. What is the full name of Riley Keough?
Answer: Danielle Riley Keough

1290. What is the full name of Audrina Patridge?
Answer: Audrina Cathleen Patridge

1291. Who acted as Maria Altmann in the movie «The Woman in Gold»?
Answer: Helen Mirren

1292. Who was the composer for the 1987 film «Superman IV: The Quest for Peace»?
Answer: Alexander Courage

1293. In which year did Faith Evans marry The Notorious B.I.G.?
Answer: 1994

1294. In which year did Amy Acker marry James Carpinello?
Answer: 2003

1295. For his work in the movie «Kinsey», who won the «Los Angeles Film Critics Association Award for Best Actor» in 2004?
Answer: Liam Neeson

1296. When did Sigourney Weaver marry Jim Simpson?
Answer: 1984

1297. For his work in the movie «Stagecoach», who won the «Academy Award for Best Supporting Actor» in 1939?
Answer: Thomas Mitchell

1298. For her work in the movie «Butterfield 8», who won the «Academy Award for Best Actress» in 1960?
Answer: Elizabeth Taylor

1299. In which year did Lois Chiles marry Richard Gilder?
Answer: 2005

1300. Who directed the 1996 film «Primal Fear»?
Answer: Gregory Hoblit

1301. Where did Ron Perlman get his master's degree from?
Answer: University of Minnesota, in Saint Paul

1302. What's the birth name of Sarah Paulson?
Answer: Sarah Catharine Paulson

1303. Who was the composer for the 2007 film «The Pixar Story»?
Answer: Jeff Beal

1304. Whom did Edie Adams marry in the year 1972?
Answer: Pete Candoli

1305. For her work in the movie «Hustle & Flow», who won the «BET Award for Best Actor & Actress» in 2006?
Answer: Taraji P. Henson

1306. Where was Andrea Anders born?
Answer: Madison

1307. Where did Beulah Bondi get her bachelor's degree from?
Answer: Valparaiso University

1308. For his work in the movie «Schindler's List», who won the «Academy Award for Best Picture» in 1993?
Answer: Steven Spielberg

1309. What is the full name of Samantha Droke?
Answer: Samantha Raye Droke

1310. Who was the composer for the 1988 film «A Fish Called Wanda»?
Answer: John Du Prez

1311. Who was the composer for the 1999 film «Universal Soldier: The Return»?
Answer: Don Davis

1312. Who acted as Batman in the movie «The Dark Knight»?
Answer: Christian Bale

1313. When did Shiva Rose marry Dylan McDermott?
Answer: 1995

1314. Who was the composer for the 1994 film «The House of the Spirits»?
Answer: Hans Zimmer

1315. What's the birth name of Taylor Parks?
Answer: Taylor Monet Parks

1316. What is the full name of Brendan Fraser?
Answer: Brendan James Fraser

1317. When did Debrah Farentino marry Gregory Hoblit?
Answer: 1994

1318. Whom did Tuesday Weld marry in the year 1985?
Answer: Pinchas Zukerman

1319. Whom did Sheryl Lee Ralph marry in the year 2005?
Answer: Vincent Hughes

1320. Who acted as Zaphod Beeblebrox in the movie «The Hitchhiker's Guide to the Galaxy»?
Answer: Sam Rockwell

1321. Who directed the 2019 film «The Rhythm Section»?
Answer: Reed Morano

1322. What's the birth name of Christian Slater?
Answer: Christian Michael Leonard Slater

1323. For her work in the movie «Three Billboards Outside

Ebbing, Missouri», who won the «Academy Award for Best Actress» in 2018?
Answer: Frances McDormand

1324. Who directed the 1999 film «The World Is Not Enough»?
Answer: Michael Apted

1325. For his work in the movie «Schindler's List», who won the «Golden Globe Award» in 1994?
Answer: Steven Spielberg

1326. What's the birth name of Steve Zahn?
Answer: Steven James Zahn

1327. Whom did Kim Delaney marry in the year 1984?
Answer: Charles Grant

1328. What is the name of the character Tommy Lee Jones plays in the movie «JFK»?
Answer: Clay Bertrand

1329. What's the birth name of Anna Nicole Smith?
Answer: Vickie Lynn Hogan

1330. Who directed the 1989 film «National Lampoon's Christmas Vacation»?
Answer: Jeremiah S. Chechik

1331. Who acted as Jack Dawson in the movie «Titanic»?
Answer: Leonardo DiCaprio

1332. For which film did Jennifer Carpenter receive the «MTV Movie Award for Best Scared-As-St Performance» in 2006?**
Answer: The Exorcism of Emily Rose

1333. What's the birth name of Katie Morgan?
Answer: Sarah Carradine

1334. Who was the composer for the 2016 film

«Passengers»?
Answer: Thomas Newman

1335. Where did Kelly Stables get her bachelor's degree from?
Answer: University of Missouri, in Boone County

1336. In which year did Rebecca Romijn marry Jerry O'Connell?
Answer: 2007

1337. Who acted as The Joker in the movie «Suicide Squad»?
Answer: Jared Leto

1338. Who was the composer for the 1999 film «Cradle Will Rock»?
Answer: Dave Robbins

1339. What is the full name of David Gallagher?
Answer: David Lee Gallagher

1340. What is the full name of Sam Robards?
Answer: Sam Prideaux Robards

1341. Where did Al Franken get his Bachelor of Arts degree from?
Answer: Harvard College, in Cambridge

1342. In which year did Paula Marshall marry Danny Nucci?
Answer: 2003

1343. What is the name of the character Marlon Brando plays in the movie «Superman Returns»?
Answer: Jor-El

1344. In which year did Gail O'Grady marry Jeffrey Byron?
Answer: 1990

1345. When did Laura Johnson marry Harry Hamlin?
Answer: 1985

1346. Who was the composer for the 2001 film «A.I. Artificial Intelligence»?
Answer: John Williams

1347. Who acted as Irina Spalko in the movie «Indiana Jones and the Kingdom of the Crystal Skull»?
Answer: Cate Blanchett

1348. Who was the composer for the 2018 film «Damsel»?
Answer: The Octopus Project

1349. Who acted as Odin in the movie «Thor: The Dark World»?
Answer: Anthony Hopkins

1350. In which year did Tina Fey marry Jeff Richmond?
Answer: 2001

1351. What is the full name of Tom Goss?
Answer: Thomas Patrick Goss

1352. Who was the composer for the 1993 film «Hot Shots! Part Deux»?
Answer: Basil Poledouris

1353. What's the birth name of Luke Wilson?
Answer: Luke Cunningham Wilson

1354. For her work in the movie «Romeo + Juliet», who won the «MTV Movie Award for Best Female Performance» in 1997?
Answer: Claire Danes

1355. What's the birth name of Alexander Zemeckis?
Answer: Alexander Francis Zemeckis

1356. What's the birth name of Shannon Elizabeth?
Answer: Shannon Elizabeth Fadal

1357. Who was the composer for the 1997 film

«Anaconda»?
Answer: Randy Edelman

1358. Who was the composer for the 2014 film «300: Rise of an Empire»?
Answer: Junkie XL

1359. What is the name of the character Nicole Kidman plays in the movie «Aquaman»?
Answer: Atlanna

1360. In which year did Mariska Hargitay marry Peter Hermann?
Answer: 2004

1361. For which film did Edward Norton receive the «Satellite Award for Best Actor – Motion Picture» in 1999?
Answer: American History X

1362. For which film did Jennifer Lawrence receive the «Broadcast Film Critics Association Award for Best Cast» in 2012?
Answer: Silver Linings Playbook

1363. What's the birth name of Robert Sean Leonard?
Answer: Robert Lawrence Leonard

1364. For which film did Sydney Pollack receive the «Academy Award for Best Picture» in 1986?
Answer: Out of Africa

1365. What is the name of the character Alec Guinness plays in the movie «Star Wars Episode V: The Empire Strikes Back»?
Answer: Obi-Wan Kenobi

1366. What's the birth name of Vanessa Blue?
Answer: Tanya M. Faulkner

1367. Who directed the 2001 film «The Musketeer»?
Answer: Peter Hyams

1368. Who were the composers of the 2017 film «Patriots Day»?
Answer: Atticus Ross, Trent Reznor, and Steve Jablonsky

1369. Who was the composer for the 2015 film «Daddy's Home»?
Answer: Michael Andrews

1370. Whom did Cheryl Ladd marry in the year 1973?
Answer: David Ladd

1371. What's the birth name of Tara Strong?
Answer: Tara Lyn Charendoff-Strong

1372. Who directed the 2018 film «Show Dogs»?
Answer: Raja Gosnell

1373. For his work in the movie «Training Day», who won the «MTV Movie Award for Best Cameo» in 2002?
Answer: Snoop Dogg

1374. When did Jennifer Grant marry Randall Zisk?
Answer: 1993

1375. Whom did Joely Fisher marry in the year 1996?
Answer: Christopher Duddy

1376. What's the birth name of Danielle Harris?
Answer: Danielle Andrea Harris

1377. What's the birth name of Calista Flockhart?
Answer: Calista Kay Flockhart

1378. Who was the composer for the 1989 film «Dead Poets Society»?
Answer: Maurice Jarre

1379. For which film did Mervyn LeRoy receive the «Golden Globe for Best Film Promoting International Understanding» award in 1961?
Answer: A Majority of One

1380. Which film won the Academy Award for Best Film Editing in the year 1995?
Answer: Apollo 13

1381. For which film did Clark Gregg receive the «Online Film Critics Society Award for Best Cast» in 2000?
Answer: State and Main

1382. What is the full name of Bam Margera?
Answer: Brandon Cole Margera

1383. Who was the composer for the 2016 film «Captain America: Civil War»?
Answer: Henry Jackman

1384. What's the birth name of Ricki Lake?
Answer: Ricki Pamela Lake

1385. For his work in the movie «High Noon», who won the «Academy Award for Best Actor» in 1952?
Answer: Gary Cooper

1386. When did Christina Ricci marry James Heerdegen?
Answer: 2013

1387. When did Pia Zadora marry Jonathan Kaufer?
Answer: 1995

1388. Who was the composer for the 1990 film «The Godfather Part III»?
Answer: Carmine Coppola

1389. When did Kathryn Erbe marry Terry Kinney?
Answer: 1993

1390. Where did Eli Wallach get his Master of Education degree from?
Answer: City College of New York, in Manhattan

1391. Who was the composer for the 2019 film «Miss Bala»?

Answer: Alex Heffes

1392. For which film did Lauren Bacall receive the «Golden Globe Award for Best Supporting Actress – Motion Picture» in 1996?
Answer: The Mirror Has Two Faces

1393. Who directed the 2003 film «Spy Kids 3-D: Game Over»?
Answer: Robert Rodriguez

1394. Where did Shaquille O'Neal get his Master of Business Administration degree from?
Answer: University of Phoenix

1395. Who directed the 2007 film «Live Free or Die Hard»?
Answer: Len Wiseman

1396. When did Cecilia Hart marry Bruce Weitz?
Answer: 1971

1397. In which year did Eva Amurri marry Kyle Martino?
Answer: 2011

1398. When did Janet Jackson marry Wissam Al Mana?
Answer: 2012

1399. What is the full name of Ryan Merriman?
Answer: Ryan Earl Merriman

1400. For his work in the movie «Ghost World», who won the «National Society of Film Critics Award for Best Supporting Actor» in 2001?
Answer: Steve Buscemi

1401. Who directed the 2015 film «Creed»?
Answer: Ryan Coogler

1402. When did Angelina Jolie marry Billy Bob Thornton?
Answer: 2000

1403. Which film won the Academy Award for Best Documentary Feature in the year 1952?
Answer: The Sea Around Us

1404. What's the birth name of Robert Downey Jr.?
Answer: Robert John Downey

1405. Who directed the 2011 film «Water for Elephants»?
Answer: Francis Lawrence

1406. For his work in the movie «Cadillac Records», who won the «Black Reel Award for Best Ensemble» in 2008?
Answer: Adrien Brody

1407. For which film did Wendi McLendon-Covey receive the «MTV Movie Award for Best Jaw Dropping Moment» in 2012?
Answer: Bridesmaids

1409. For which film did Leonardo DiCaprio receive the «AACTA Award for Best Actor in a Leading Role» in 2013?
Answer: The Great Gatsby

1410. When did Heidi Mark marry Vince Neil?
Answer: 2000

1411. What's the birth name of Britney Spears?
Answer: Britney Jean Spears

1412. For which film did Halle Berry receive the «Academy Award for Best Actress» in 2001?
Answer: Monster's Ball

1413. Whom did Doris Day marry in the year 1976?
Answer: Barry Comden

1414. Who was the composer for the 2017 film «The Florida Project»?
Answer: Lorne Balfe

1415. In which year did Kyra Sedgwick marry Kevin

Bacon?
Answer: 1988

1416. Whom did Kate Jackson marry in the year 1978?
Answer: Andrew Stevens

1417. Whom did Frances Conroy marry in the year 1992?
Answer: Jan Munroe

1418. Which film won the Academy Award for Best Picture in the year 1946?
Answer: The Lost Weekend

1419. What is the name of the character Russell Crowe plays in the movie «Robin Hood»?
Answer: Robin Hood

1420. Whom did Cass Elliot marry in the year 1971?
Answer: Donald von Wiedenman

1421. Who was the composer for the 2018 film «The Cloverfield Paradox»?
Answer: Bear McCreary

1422. What is the full name of Makenzie Vega?
Answer: Makenzie Jade Vega

1423. For which film did Catherine Keener receive the «Los Angeles Film Critics Association Award for Best Supporting Actress» in 2005?
Answer: The Ballad of Jack and Rose

1424. Who acted as John Jonah Jameson in the movie «Spider-Man 2»?
Answer: J. K. Simmons

1425. What is the full name of Eve Torres?
Answer: Eve Marie Torres

1426. Who acted as James Gordon in the movie «Justice League»?

Answer: J. K. Simmons

1427. When did Leigh Taylor-Young marry Craig Sheffer?
Answer: 2003

1428. Which film won the Academy Award for Best Picture in the year 1978?
Answer: Annie Hall

1429. Who directed the 1999 film «Instinct»?
Answer: Jon Turteltaub

1430. For his work in the movie «They Shoot Horses, Don't They?», who won the «Academy Award for Best Supporting Actor» in 1969?
Answer: Gig Young

1431. What's the birth name of Ben Affleck?
Answer: Benjamin Geza Affleck

1432. Which film won the Academy Award for Best Picture in the year 2015?
Answer: Birdman

1433. In which year did Irene Bedard marry Denny Wilson?
Answer: 1993

1434. When did Lauren Holly marry Jim Carrey?
Answer: 1996

1435. In which year did Debbie Reynolds marry Richard Hamlett?
Answer: 1984

1436. Which film won the Academy Award for Best Picture in the year 1992?
Answer: The Silence of the Lambs

1437. In which year did Jessica Drake marry Evan Stone?
Answer: 2002

1438. For his work in the movie «Apollo 13», who won the «Screen Actors Guild Award for Outstanding Performance by a Male Actor in a Supporting Role» in 1996?
Answer: Ed Harris

1439. What is the name of the character Emma Thompson plays in the movie «Men in Black 3»?
Answer: Agent O

1440. When did Diane Venora marry Andrzej Bartkowiak?
Answer: 1980

1441. Where did Paul Simon get his high school diploma from?
Answer: Forest Hills High School, in New York

1442. Whom did Becky Ann Baker marry in the year 1990?
Answer: Dylan Baker

1443. In which year did Jessica Hecht marry Adam Bernstein?
Answer: 1995

1444. Whom did Elyssa Davalos marry in the year 1982?
Answer: Jeff Dunas

1445. What is the full name of Mick Foley?
Answer: Michael Francis Foley

1446. Who was the composer for the 2009 film «Harry Potter and the Half-Blood Prince»?
Answer: Nicholas Hooper

1447. For which film did Julia Roberts receive the «Golden Globe Award for Best Supporting Actress – Motion Picture» in 1990?
Answer: Steel Magnolias

1448. For his work in the movie «Wild Wild West», who won the «Golden Raspberry Award for Worst Screen Couple/Ensemble» in 1999?
Answer: Kevin Kline

1449. When did Mary Stuart Masterson marry Damon Santostefano?
Answer: 2000

1450. For which film did Halle Berry receive the «BET Award for Best Actor & Actress» in 2008?
Answer: Things We Lost in the Fire

1451. Whom did Piper Perabo marry in the year 2014?
Answer: Stephen Kay

1452. For which film did Martin Scorsese receive the «Cannes Best Director Award» in 1986?
Answer: After Hours

1453. For her work in the movie «Gothika», who won the «BET Award for Best Actor & Actress» in 2004?
Answer: Halle Berry

1454. Which film won the Golden Globe Award for Best Screenplay in the year 1965?
Answer: Doctor Zhivago

1455. When did Angelina Jolie marry Brad Pitt?
Answer: 2014

1456. What's the birth name of Asa Akira?
Answer: Asa Tagikami

1457. Whom did Maura Tierney marry in the year 1993?
Answer: Billy Morrissette

1458. Who directed the 1995 film «Two Bits»?
Answer: James Foley

1459. Which film won the Academy Award for Best Documentary Feature in the year 1991?
Answer: In the Shadow of the Stars

1460. In which year did Dixie Carter marry Hal Holbrook?

Answer: 1984

1461. Who directed the 2019 film «Captive State»?
Answer: Rupert Wyatt

1462. What's the birth name of Megan Fox?
Answer: Megan Denise Fox

1463. Who was the composer for the 2018 film «Black Panther»?
Answer: Ludwig Göransson

1464. When did Tia Carrere marry Elie Samaha?
Answer: 1992

1465. Who was the composer for the 2018 film «Holmes & Watson»?
Answer: Christophe Beck

1466. Who was the composer for the 2014 film «Teenage Mutant Ninja Turtles»?
Answer: Brian Tyler

1467. Where was Beulah Bondi born?
Answer: Valparaiso

1468. What is the name of the character Geoffrey Rush plays in the movie «Gods of Egypt»?
Answer: Ra

1469. Whom did Deborah Richter marry in the year 1985?
Answer: Charles Haid

1470. Whom did Elizabeth Berridge marry in the year 2001?
Answer: Kevin Corrigan

1471. Which film won the Academy Award for Best Documentary Feature in the year 1960?
Answer: The Horse with the Flying Tail

1472. For which film did Holly Hunter receive the «New York Film Critics Circle Award for Best Actress» in 1993?
Answer: The Piano

1473. What is the full name of Lily Collins?
Answer: Lily Jane Collins

1474. Whom did Krista Allen marry in the year 2010?
Answer: Mams Taylor

1475. In which year did Téa Leoni marry Neil Tardio Jr.?
Answer: 1991

1476. What's the birth name of Halston Sage?
Answer: Halston Jean Schrage

1477. Who directed the 1986 film «The Texas Chainsaw Massacre 2»?
Answer: Tobe Hooper

1478. For which film did Adam Sandler receive the «Golden Raspberry Award for Worst Actor» in 1999?
Answer: Jack and Jill

1479. Who directed the 1987 film «Can't Buy Me Love»?
Answer: Steve Rash

1480. Which film won the Academy Award for Best Film Editing in the year 2018?
Answer: Dunkirk

1481. For which film did Katharine Hepburn receive the «Academy Award for Best Actress» in 1933?
Answer: Morning Glory

1482. Where did Corey Hawkins get his Bachelor of Fine Arts degree from?
Answer: Juilliard School, in Manhattan

1483. Whom did Leelee Sobieski marry in the year 2010?
Answer: Adam Kimmel

1484. Which film won the Academy Award for Best

Writing, Adapted Screenplay in the year 2015?
Answer: The Imitation Game

1485. Who directed the 2003 film «Bad Boys II»?
Answer: Michael Bay

1486. Where was Kelly Stables born?
Answer: St. Louis

1487. What is the full name of Thomas Dekker?
Answer: Thomas Alexander Dekker

1488. Whom did Gillian Anderson marry in the year 1994?
Answer: Clyde Klotz

1489. For which film did Holly Hunter receive the «Los Angeles Film Critics Association Award for Best Actress» in 1993?
Answer: The Piano

1490. Who directed the 1989 film «The Karate Kid, Part III»?
Answer: John G. Avildsen

1491. For his work in the movie «Cadillac Records», who won the «Black Reel Award for Best Ensemble» in 2008?
Answer: Jeffrey Wright

1492. What's the birth name of George Clooney?
Answer: George Timothy Clooney

1493. For which film did Alan Arkin receive the «Screen Actors Guild Award for Outstanding Performance by a Cast in a Motion Picture» in 2013?
Answer: Argo

1494. Whom did Mary McDonnell marry in the year 1984?
Answer: Randle Mell

1495. Whom did Berry Berenson marry in the year 1973?
Answer: Anthony Perkins

1496. Whom did Kathleen Quinlan marry in the year 1994?
Answer: Bruce Abbott

1497. Where did Micaela Dee get her bachelor's degree from?
Answer: Eastern Nazarene College, in Massachusetts

1498. What is the full name of Billy Unger?
Answer: William Brent Unger

1499. Who directed the 2018 film «Entebbe»?
Answer: José Padilha

1500. Who directed the 2019 film «Alita: Battle Angel»?
Answer: Robert Rodriguez

1501. What is the full name of Liev Schreiber?
Answer: Isaac Liev Schreiber

1502. When did Leslie Mann marry Judd Apatow?
Answer: 1997

1503. What is the full name of Jon Bernthal?
Answer: Jonathan Edward Bernthal

1504. Whom did Marilu Henner marry in the year 1980?
Answer: Frederic Forrest

1505. What is the full name of Jeri Ryan?
Answer: Jeri Lynn Zimmermann Ryan

1506. Whom did Bridgette Wilson marry in the year 2000?
Answer: Pete Sampras

1507. For which film did Jennifer Hudson receive the «NAACP Image Award for Outstanding Supporting Actress in a Motion Picture» in 2007?
Answer: Dreamgirls

1508. What's the birth name of Clark Gregg?
Answer: Robert Clark Gregg

1509. Which film won the Academy Award for Best Picture in the year 1930?
Answer: The Broadway Melody

1510. For her work in the movie «The Piano», who won the «BAFTA Award for Best Actress in a Leading Role» in 1994?
Answer: Holly Hunter

1511. Whom did Talisa Soto marry in the year 1997?
Answer: Costas Mandylor

1512. In which year did Britney Spears marry Kevin Federline?
Answer: 2004

1513. What's the birth name of Colton Haynes?
Answer: Colton Lee Haynes

1514. Who directed the 2015 film «The Devil's Candy»?
Answer: Sean Byrne

1515. Who was the composer for the 2003 film «American Wedding»?
Answer: Christophe Beck

1516. What's the birth name of David Silverman?
Answer: David Marshall Silverman

1517. What's the birth name of India Summer?
Answer: Jody Jean Olson

1518. Whom did Riley Keough marry in the year 2015?
Answer: Ben Smith-Petersen

1519. Who directed the 2013 film «The Frozen Ground»?
Answer: Scott Walker

1520. What is the name of the character Marisa Tomei plays in the movie «Captain America: Civil War»?

Answer: May Parker

1521. For which film did Jessica Alba receive the «Golden Raspberry Award for Worst Supporting Actress» in 2011?
Answer: Valentine's Day

1522. What's the birth name of Robin Wright?
Answer: Robin Gayle Wright

1523. When did Alexandra Breckenridge marry Casey Hooper?
Answer: 2015

1524. What is the name of the character Tommy Lee Jones plays in the movie «Men in Black II»?
Answer: Agent K

1525. Who directed the 1994 film «A Low Down Dirty Shame»?
Answer: Keenen Ivory Wayans

1526. In which year did Melinda Clarke marry Ernie Mirich?
Answer: 1997

1527. In which year did Tisha Campbell-Martin marry Duane Martin?
Answer: 1996

1528. What's the birth name of Jason Gedrick?
Answer: Jason Michael Gedroic

1529. Who was the composer for the 2017 film «Guardians of the Galaxy Vol. 2»?
Answer: Tyler Bates

1530. What is the full name of Willow Smith?
Answer: Willow Camille Reign Smith

1531. What is the name of the character Gwyneth Paltrow plays in the movie «Captain America: Civil War»?
Answer: Pepper Potts

1532. When did Laura San Giacomo marry Cameron Dye?
Answer: 1990

1533. What is the name of the character Gene Hackman plays in the movie «Wyatt Earp»?
Answer: Nicholas Porter Earp

1534. What is the full name of Candice King?
Answer: Candice Rene Accola

1535. For his work in the movie «Mrs. Doubtfire», who won the «MTV Movie Award for Best Comedic Performance» in 1994?
Answer: Robin Williams

1536. Who was the composer for the 1999 film «Never Been Kissed»?
Answer: David Newman

1537. For which film did Adam Sandler receive the «Golden Raspberry Award for Worst Actor» in 2011?
Answer: Jack and Jill

1538. What's the birth name of Sean Astin?
Answer: Sean Patrick Duke

1539. Whom did Jennifer Schwalbach Smith marry in the year 1999?
Answer: Kevin Smith

1540. Whom did Susan Saint James marry in the year 1981?
Answer: Dick Ebersol

1541. For which film did Jamie Lee Curtis receive the «Golden Globe Award for Best Actress – Motion Picture Musical or Comedy» in 1994?
Answer: True Lies

1542. For his work in the movie «Anastasia», who won the «National Board of Review Award for Best Actor» in 1956?

Answer: Yul Brynner

1543. Who was the composer for the 1998 film «Star Trek: Insurrection»?
Answer: Jerry Goldsmith

1544. For which film did Fredric March receive the «Academy Award for Best Actor» in 1931?
Answer: Dr. Jekyll and Mr. Hyde

1545. What is the name of the character Robert De Niro plays in the movie «The Godfather Part II»?
Answer: Vito Corleone

1546. For her work in the movie «Nell», who won the «Screen Actors Guild Award for Outstanding Performance by a Female Actor in a Leading Role» in 1995?
Answer: Jodie Foster

1547. Who directed the 2014 film «The Amazing Spider-Man 2»?
Answer: Marc Webb

1548. Who directed the 2017 film «Three Billboards Outside Ebbing, Missouri»?
Answer: Martin McDonagh

1549. For his work in the movie «Bright Star», who won the «National Society of Film Critics Award for Best Supporting Actor» in 2009?
Answer: Paul Schneider

1550. For her work in the movie «Trading Places», who won the «BAFTA Award for Best Actress in a Supporting Role» in 1984?
Answer: Jamie Lee Curtis

1551. In which year did Juliette Lewis marry Steve Berra?
Answer: 1999

1552. Whom did Heather Langenkamp marry in the year 1989?

Answer: David LeRoy Anderson

1553. Who acted as Padmé Amidala in the movie «Star Wars: Episode III – Revenge of the Sith»?
Answer: Natalie Portman

1554. Whom did Linda Lovelace marry in the year 1971?
Answer: Chuck Traynor

1555. When did Angelina Jolie marry Jonny Lee Miller?
Answer: 1996

1556. Who directed the 2003 film «Duplex»?
Answer: Danny DeVito

1557. Who acted as Léon Rom in the movie «The Legend of Tarzan»?
Answer: Christoph Waltz

1558. For her work in the movie «Walk the Line», who won the «Golden Globe Award» in 2006?
Answer: Reese Witherspoon

1559. Where was Wendell Pierce born?
Answer: New Orleans

1560. Who was the composer for the 1994 film «Stargate»?
Answer: David Arnold

1561. Which film won the Golden Globe Award for Best Motion Picture – Drama in the year 1978?
Answer: Midnight Express

1562. Whom did Geena Davis marry in the year 1993?
Answer: Renny Harlin

1563. Who directed the 2003 film «Bruce Almighty»?
Answer: Tom Shadyac

1564. Who directed the 2001 film «Piñero»?
Answer: Leon Ichaso

1565. Who directed the 2016 film «Independence Day: Resurgence»?
Answer: Roland Emmerich

1566. Whom did Tricia Leigh Fisher marry in the year 2007?
Answer: Byron Thames

1567. Who directed the 1993 film «Hot Shots! Part Deux»?
Answer: Jim Abrahams

1568. Who acted as Adrian Cronauer in the movie «Good Morning, Vietnam»?
Answer: Robin Williams

1569. For her work in the movie «The Break-Up», who won the «Teen Choice Award for Choice Movie – Comedy» in 2006?
Answer: Jennifer Aniston

1570. When did Melanie Griffith marry Antonio Banderas?
Answer: 1996

1571. Whom did Jean Peters marry in the year 1971?
Answer: Stan Hough

1572. When did Heidi Klum marry Ric Pipino?
Answer: 1997

1573. Who directed the 1994 film «Beverly Hills Cop III»?
Answer: John Landis

1574. Who acted as Alfred Pennyworth in the movie «Batman Begins»?
Answer: Michael Caine

1575. For her work in the movie «Capote», who won the «Toronto Film Critics Association Award for Best Supporting Actress» in 2005?
Answer: Catherine Keener

1576. For her work in the movie «Pleasantville», who won the «Broadcast Film Critics Association Award for Best Supporting Actress» in 1998?
Answer: Joan Allen

1577. Whom did Pia Zadora marry in the year 1977?
Answer: Meshulam Riklis

1578. Who was the composer for the 2016 film «The Legend of Tarzan»?
Answer: Rupert Gregson-Williams
1579. What's the birth name of Sarah Drew?
Answer: Sarah White Drew

1580. For her work in the movie «Precious», who won the «Independent Spirit Award for Best Female Lead» in 2010?
Answer: Gabourey Sidibe

1581. For which film did David Lynch receive the «Palme d'Or» award in 1990?
Answer: Wild at Heart

1582. When did Heidi Klum marry Seal?
Answer: 2005

1583. In which year did Amy Adams marry Darren Le Gallo?
Answer: 2015

1584. When did Lela Rochon marry Antoine Fuqua?
Answer: 1999

1585. Who were the composers of the 2018 film «The Happytime Murders»?
Answer: Christopher Lennertz and Rupert Gregson-Williams

1586. In which year did Jamie Lee Curtis marry Christopher Guest?
Answer: 1984

1587. Who acted as Mazer Rackham in the movie «Ender's Game»?
Answer: Ben Kingsley

1588. Which film won the Academy Award for Best Picture in the year 1976?
Answer: One Flew Over the Cuckoo's Nest

1589. In which year did Joanne Dru marry C.V. Wood?
Answer: 1972

1590. Whom did Betsy Russell marry in the year 1989?
Answer: Vincent Van Patten

1591. Which film won the Academy Award for Best Original Score in the year 1965?
Answer: Doctor Zhivago

1592. For his work in the movie «Manchester by the Sea», who won the «Golden Globe Award for Best Actor – Motion Picture Drama» in 2017?
Answer: Casey Affleck

1593. Which film won the Academy Award for Best Documentary Feature in the year 1977?
Answer: Who Are the DeBolts? And Where Did They Get Nineteen Kids?

1594. Whom did Ali MacGraw marry in the year 1973?
Answer: Steve McQueen

1595. What is the full name of Lucy Liu?
Answer: Lucy Alexis Liu

1596. Who was the composer for the 2018 film «Future World»?
Answer: TOYDRUM

1597. What is the full name of Faune A. Chambers?
Answer: Faune Alecia Chambers

1598. Whom did Elizabeth Perkins marry in the year 1984?
Answer: Terry Kinney

1599. Who acted as Joker in the movie «Batman»?
Answer: Jack Nicholson

1600. Whom did Mamie Gummer marry in the year 2011?
Answer: Benjamin Walker

1601. What is the name of the character Lupita Nyong'o plays in the movie «Black Panther»?
Answer: Nakia

1602. Who acted as Agent Smith in the movie «The Matrix»?
Answer: Hugo Weaving

1603. For his work in the movie «The Deer Hunter», who won the «Academy Award for Best Supporting Actor» in 1978?
Answer: Christopher Walken

1604. Who was the composer for the 2009 film «Surrogates»?
Answer: Richard Marvin

1605. For which film did Allison Janney receive the «Academy Award for Best Supporting Actress» in 2018?
Answer: I, Tonya

1606. Who was the composer for the 1990 film «Dances with Wolves»?
Answer: John Barry

1607. Whom did Zoe Saldana marry in the year 2013?
Answer: Marco Perego

1608. What is the full name of Leelee Sobieski?
Answer: Liliane Rudabet Gloria Elsveta Sobieski

1609. What's the birth name of Adam Shankman?
Answer: Adam Michael Shankman

1610. Which film won the Academy Award for Best Picture in the year 1995?
Answer: Forrest Gump

1611. Who was the composer for the 2018 film «Welcome to Marwen»?
Answer: Alan Silvestri

1612. What's the birth name of Hillary Wolf?
Answer: Hillary Jocelyn Wolf

1613. For which film did Tom Noonan receive the «U.S. Grand Jury Prize: Dramatic» award in 1994?
Answer: What Happened Was

1614. For her work in the movie «Rachel Getting Married», who won the «Satellite Award for Best Supporting Actress – Motion Picture» in 2008?
Answer: Rosemarie DeWitt

1615. Whom did Brooke Burke Charvet marry in the year 2001?
Answer: Garth Fisher

1616. What is the name of the character Jared Leto plays in the movie «Alexander»?
Answer: Hephaestion

1617. Who were the composers of the 2017 film «Jumanji: Welcome to the Jungle»?
Answer: Henry Jackman and James Newton Howard

1618. Who directed the 2016 film «Eva Hesse»?
Answer: Marcie Begleiter

1619. Who was the composer for the 2018 film «Blockers»?
Answer: Mateo Messina

1620. When did Janeane Garofalo marry Robert Cohen?
Answer: 1992

1621. In which year did Gwen Stefani marry Gavin Rossdale?
Answer: 2002

1622. For which film did Regina King receive the «BET Award for Best Actor & Actress» in 2005?
Answer: A Cinderella Story

1623. Which film won the Academy Award for Best Picture in the year 2017?
Answer: Moonlight

1624. In which year did Audra McDonald marry Will Swenson?
Answer: 2012

1625. Who acted as Boggs in the movie «The Hunger Games: Mockingjay – Part 2»?
Answer: Mahershala Ali

1626. What is the full name of Amy Poehler?
Answer: Amy Meredith Poehler

1627. Who was the composer for the 2013 film «Pain & Gain»?
Answer: Steve Jablonsky

1628. In which year did Rebecca De Mornay marry Patrick O'Neal?
Answer: 1995

1629. Who acted as Betty Ross in the movie «Hulk»?
Answer: Jennifer Connelly

1630. Which film won the Academy Award for Best Picture in the year 2004?
Answer: The Lord of the Rings: The Return of the King

1631. What is the full name of Gina Carano?
Answer: Gina Joy Carano

1632. Who directed the 1993 film «Loaded Weapon 1»?
Answer: Gene Quintano

1633. Whom did Constance Zimmer marry in the year 1999?
Answer: Steve Johnson

1634. Where was Steve Harris born?
Answer: Chicago

1635. In which year did Katharine Houghton marry Ken Jenkins?
Answer: 1970

1636. Which film won the Academy Award for Best Picture in the year 1944?
Answer: Casablanca

1637. When did Donna Murphy marry Shawn Elliott?
Answer: 1990

1638. Whom did LaTanya Richardson marry in the year 1980?
Answer: Samuel L. Jackson

1639. Whom did Angela Bassett marry in the year 1997?
Answer: Courtney B. Vance

1640. Who acted as Debbie Ocean in the movie «Ocean's 8»?
Answer: Sandra Bullock

1641. Whom did Karen Allen marry in the year 1988?
Answer: Kale Browne

1642. Which film won the Academy Award for Best Production Design in the year 1990?

Answer: Batman

1643. Who was the composer for the 2015 film «The Wedding Ringer»?
Answer: Christopher Lennertz

1644. For his work in the movie «Terminator 2: Judgment Day», who won the «MTV Movie Award for Best Male Performance» in 1992?
Answer: Arnold Schwarzenegger

1645. Who acted as Little John in the movie «Robin Hood»?
Answer: Jamie Foxx

1646. Who directed the 2004 film «The Life Aquatic with Steve Zissou»?
Answer: Wes Anderson

1647. What is the full name of Jessica Simpson?
Answer: Jessica Ann Simpson

1648. When did Sofia Coppola marry Thomas Mars?
Answer: 2011

1649. In which year did Deborah Pratt marry Donald Bellisario?
Answer: 1984

1650. For her work in the movie «Boys Don't Cry», who won the «Independent Spirit Award for Best Supporting Female» in 2000?
Answer: Chloë Sevigny

1651. For which film did Adam Sandler receive the «Golden Raspberry Award for Worst Actor» in 1999?
Answer: Big Daddy

1652. For her work in the movie «Broadcast News», who won the «Los Angeles Film Critics Association Award for Best Actress» in 1987?

Answer: Holly Hunter

1653. What is the full name of Keri Russell?
Answer: Keri Lynn Russell

1654. Where did Katherine Dunham get her Doctor of Philosophy degree from?
Answer: University of Chicago

1655. In which year did Mare Winningham marry A Martinez?
Answer: 1981

1656. What's the birth name of Drew Barrymore?
Answer: Drew Blythe Barrymore

1657. For his work in the movie «The Philadelphia Story», who won the «Academy Award for Best Actor» in 1940?
Answer: James Stewart

1658. For her work in the movie «L.A. Confidential», who won the «Golden Globe Award for Best Supporting Actress – Motion Picture» in 1997?
Answer: Kim Basinger

1659. Whom did Jeri Ryan marry in the year 1991?
Answer: Jack Ryan

1660. Which film won the Academy Award for Best Documentary Feature in the year 1981?
Answer: Genocide

1661. Who directed the 2018 film «Ben Is Back»?
Answer: Peter Hedges

1662. What's the birth name of Lindsay Lohan?
Answer: Lindsay Dee Lohan

1663. Who directed the 1987 film «Masters of the Universe»?
Answer: Gary Goddard

1664. Which film won the Academy Award for Best Picture in the year 1971?
Answer: Patton

1665. Whom did Donna Hanover marry in the year 1984?
Answer: Rudy Giuliani

1666. Who directed the 1990 film «Arachnophobia»?
Answer: Frank Marshall

1667. Which film won the Academy Award for Best Picture in the year 1938?
Answer: The Life of Emile Zola

1668. What's the birth name of Gabriel Mann?
Answer: Gabriel Wilhoit Amis Mick

1669. When did Mandy Moore marry Taylor Goldsmith?
Answer: 2018
1670. When did Abigail Spencer marry Andrew Pruett?
Answer: 2004

1671. Which film won the Academy Award for Best Writing, Adapted Screenplay in the year 1991?
Answer: The Silence of the Lambs

1672. For his work in the movie «Michael Collins», who won the «Golden Lion» award in 1996?
Answer: Liam Neeson

1673. Which film won the Academy Award for Best Picture in the year 1998?
Answer: Titanic

1674. For her work in the movie «The Twilight Saga: Eclipse», who won the «MTV Movie Award for Best Female Performance» in 2011?
Answer: Kristen Stewart

1675. When did Jill Schoelen marry Anthony Marinelli?

Answer: 1993

1676. For which film did Tom Hanks receive the «Golden Globe Award for Best Actor – Motion Picture Drama» in 1995?
Answer: Forrest Gump

1677. What's the birth name of Elijah Wood?
Answer: Elijah Jordan Wood

1678. Where was Susan Sarandon born?
Answer: New York City

1679. When did Annie Potts marry Greg Antonacci?
Answer: 1978

1680. Whom did Bridget Fonda marry in the year 2003?
Answer: Danny Elfman

1681. For which film did Gillian Anderson receive the «BIFA Award for Best Performance by an Actress in a British Independent Film» in 2000?
Answer: The House of Mirth

1682. Whom did Mary Elizabeth Winstead marry in the year 2010?
Answer: Riley Stearns

1683. What is the full name of William Levy?
Answer: William Levy Gutiérrez

1684. In which year did Lauren Conrad marry William John Tell?
Answer: 2014

1685. Who was the composer for the 1992 film «Alien 3»?
Answer: Elliot Goldenthal

1686. What's the birth name of Ashanti?
Answer: Ashanti Shequoiya Douglas

1687. Who acted as Gwen Stacy in the movie «The Amazing Spider-Man 2»?
Answer: Emma Stone

1688. For her work in the movie «The Diary of Anne Frank», who won the «Academy Award for Best Supporting Actress» in 1959?
Answer: Shelley Winters

1689. For which film did Marisa Tomei receive the «Phoenix Film Critics Society Award for Best Supporting Actress» in 2008?
Answer: The Wrestler

1690. In which year did Meg Ryan marry Dennis Quaid?
Answer: 1991

1691. What's the birth name of Bella Thorne?
Answer: Annabella Avery Thorne

1692. Which film won the Academy Award for Best Documentary Feature in the year 2018?
Answer: Icarus

1693. Where did Ron Perlman get his Bachelor of Fine Arts degree from?
Answer: Lehman College, in The Bronx

1694. Whom did Lorraine Bracco marry in the year 1994?
Answer: Edward James Olmos

1695. For which film did Diane Keaton receive the «David di Donatello for Best Foreign Actress» award in 1982?
Answer: Reds

1696. What is the full name of Tinashe?
Answer: Tinashe Jorgensen Kachingwe

1697. Who acted as Mary D'Annunzio in the movie «25th Hour»?
Answer: Anna Paquin

1698. Whom did Sheri Moon Zombie marry in the year 2002?
Answer: Rob Zombie

1699. What's the birth name of Tia Texada?
Answer: Tia Tucker

1700. Who was the composer for the 1994 film «Clerks»?
Answer: Greg Graffin

1701. For his work in the movie «The Wolf of Wall Street», who won the «Golden Globe Award for Best Actor – Motion Picture Musical or Comedy» in 2014?
Answer: Leonardo DiCaprio

1702. Who directed the 1990 film «The Grifters»?
Answer: Stephen Frears

1703. Who was the composer for the 2006 film «Poseidon»?
Answer: Klaus Badelt

1704. In which year did Rachael Leigh Cook marry Daniel Gillies?
Answer: 2004

1705. Who acted as Lex Luthor in the movie «Superman IV: The Quest for Peace»?
Answer: Gene Hackman

1706. For her work in the movie «Girl, Interrupted», who won the «Golden Globe Award for Best Supporting Actress – Motion Picture» in 2000?
Answer: Angelina Jolie

1707. Which film won the Academy Award for Best Sound Editing in the year 2007?
Answer: The Bourne Ultimatum

1708. When did Cynda Williams marry Billy Bob Thornton?

Answer: 1990

1709. Whom did Emily Wickersham marry in the year 2010?
Answer: Blake Hanley

1710. Whom did Alison Brie marry in the year 2017?
Answer: Dave Franco

1711. Who acted as Jor-El in the movie «Man of Steel»?
Answer: Russell Crowe

1712. Who was the composer for the 2018 film «The Hate U Give»?
Answer: Dustin O'Halloran

1713. Who acted as Maid Marian in the movie «Robin Hood»?
Answer: Cate Blanchett

1714. What's the birth name of Daniel Tosh?
Answer: Daniel Dwight Tosh

1715. Whom did Lindsay Crouse marry in the year 1977?
Answer: David Mamet

1716. Who were the directors of the 2002 film «The Transporter»?
Answer: Corey Yuen and Louis Leterrier

1717. Who directed the 2017 film «Spider-Man: Homecoming»?
Answer: Jon Watts

1718. What is the name of the character Nicolas Cage plays in the movie «The Frozen Ground»?
Answer: Jack Halcombe

1719. For his work in the movie «Pocketful of Miracles», who won the «Golden Globe Award for Best Actor – Motion Picture Musical or Comedy» in 1961?
Answer: Glenn Ford

1720. Whom did Shelley Fabares marry in the year 1984?
Answer: Mike Farrell

1721. Whom did Portia de Rossi marry in the year 1996?
Answer: Mel Metcalfe

1722. For which film did James Dunn receive the «Academy Award for Best Supporting Actor» in 1945?
Answer: A Tree Grows in Brooklyn

1723. Who directed the 2018 film «Mile 22»?
Answer: Peter Berg

1724. Who was the composer for the 2008 film «Marley & Me»?
Answer: Theodore Shapiro

1725. Whom did Jennifer Siebel marry in the year 2008?
Answer: Gavin Newsom

1726. Who directed the 1991 film «What About Bob?»?
Answer: Frank Oz

1727. Who directed the 2018 film «Mission: Impossible – Fallout»?
Answer: Christopher McQuarrie

1728. For which film did Ernest Borgnine receive the «Golden Globe Award for Best Actor – Motion Picture Drama» in 1955?
Answer: Marty

1729. What's the birth name of Miley Cyrus?
Answer: Destiny Hope Cyrus

1730. Who was the composer for the 1989 film «Batman»?
Answer: Danny Elfman

1731. For which film did Al Pacino receive the «Golden Globe Award for Best Actor – Motion Picture Drama» in 1974?

Answer: Serpico

1732. Whom did Maureen Anderman marry in the year 1982?
Answer: Frank Converse

1733. For which film did Steven Spielberg receive the «Boston Society of Film Critics Award for Best Director» in 1983?
Answer: E.T. the Extra-Terrestrial

1734. What is the full name of Frankie Thorn?
Answer: Frankie Lou Thorn

1735. In which year did Amy Madigan marry Ed Harris?
Answer: 1983

1736. Who was the composer for the 2009 film «Orphan»?
Answer: John Ottman

1737. Who was the composer for the 2017 film «It»?
Answer: Benjamin Wallfisch

1738. For which film did Elia Kazan receive the «Golden Globe Award for Best Motion Picture – Drama» in 1955?
Answer: East of Eden

1739. Who was the composer for the 2012 film «Skyfall»?
Answer: Thomas Newman
1740. For which film did Nicolas Cage receive the «National Board of Review Award for Best Actor» in 1995?
Answer: Leaving Las Vegas

1741. What is the full name of Joanna Newsom?
Answer: Joanna Caroline Newsom

1742. What's the birth name of Diane Kruger?
Answer: Diane Heidkrüger

1743. For her work in the movie «Dreamgirls», who won the «Satellite Award for Best Supporting Actress – Motion

Picture» in 2006?
Answer: Jennifer Hudson

1744. Who acted as Thetis in the movie «Troy»?
Answer: Julie Christie

1745. Which film won the Golden Globe Award for Best Motion Picture – Drama in the year 1955?
Answer: East of Eden

1746. Who directed the 2016 film «The Phantom Hour»?
Answer: Brian Patrick Butler

1747. What is the name of the character Philip Seymour Hoffman plays in the movie «The Hunger Games: Mockingjay – Part 1»?
Answer: Plutarch Heavensbee

1748. What is the name of the character Octavia Spencer plays in the movie «Hidden Figures»?
Answer: Dorothy Vaughan

1749. Whom did Karyn Parsons marry in the year 2003?
Answer: Alexandre Rockwell

1750. For which film did Adrien Brody receive the «Academy Award for Best Actor» in 2002?
Answer: The Pianist

1751. For which film did Louis Gossett receive the «NAACP Image Award for Outstanding Actor in a Motion Picture» in 1982?
Answer: An Officer and a Gentleman

1752. For which film did River Phoenix receive the «Independent Spirit Award for Best Male Lead» in 1992?
Answer: My Own Private Idaho

1753. What is the full name of Oleg Taktarov?
Answer: Oleg Nikolaevich Taktarov

1754. Whom did Robin Bartlett marry in the year 1976?
Answer: Alan Rosenberg

1755. For which film did Julia Roberts receive the «Golden Globe Award for Best Actress – Motion Picture Musical or Comedy» in 1991?
Answer: Pretty Woman

1756. Whom did Brooke Burns marry in the year 1999?
Answer: Julian McMahon

1757. Whom did Sarah Wright marry in the year 2012?
Answer: Eric Christian Olsen

1758. For his work in the movie «12 Monkeys», who won the «Golden Globe Award for Best Supporting Actor – Motion Picture» in 1995?
Answer: Brad Pitt

1759. Which film won the Golden Globe Award for Best Motion Picture – Drama in the year 1982?
Answer: E.T. the Extra-Terrestrial

1760. What is the name of the character Al Pacino plays in the movie «The Godfather»?
Answer: Michael Corleone

1761. Who directed the 2014 film «The Hobbit: The Battle of the Five Armies»?
Answer: Peter Jackson

1762. Who directed the 2014 film «300: Rise of an Empire»?
Answer: Noam Murro

1763. Who directed the 2017 film «The Circle»?
Answer: James Ponsoldt

1764. Who directed the 2018 film «Down a Dark Hall»?
Answer: Rodrigo Cortés

1765. Which film won the Academy Award for Best Picture in the year 1987?
Answer: Platoon

1766. Whom did Christa Miller marry in the year 1999?
Answer: Bill Lawrence

1767. Whom did Molly Price marry in the year 2001?
Answer: Derek Kelly

1768. Who was the composer for the 2002 film «Die Another Day»?
Answer: David Arnold

1769. Which film won the Golden Globe Award for Best Motion Picture – Drama in the year 1958?
Answer: The Defiant Ones

1770. When did Leslie Zemeckis marry Robert Zemeckis?
Answer: 2001

1771. Who directed the 1992 film «A Stranger Among Us»?
Answer: Sidney Lumet

1772. For which film did William Hurt receive the «London Film Critics Circle Award for Actor of the Year» in 1986?
Answer: Kiss of the Spider Woman

1773. Whom did Leighton Meester marry in the year 2014?
Answer: Adam Brody

1774. When did Briana Banks marry Bobby Vitale?
Answer: 2003

1775. When did Tiffani Thiessen marry Brady Smith?
Answer: 2005

1776. Who directed the 2016 film «London Has Fallen»?
Answer: Babak Najafi

1777. In which year did Soon-Yi Previn marry Woody

Allen?
Answer: 1997

1778. When did Wendy Moniz marry Frank Grillo?
Answer: 2000

1779. For his work in the movie «Inglourious Basterds», who won the «Phoenix Film Critics Society Award for Best Cast» in 2009?
Answer: Brad Pitt

1780. Who directed the 2015 film «Survivor»?
Answer: James McTeigue

1781. For which film did Allison Janney receive the «Screen Actors Guild Award for Outstanding Performance by a Cast in a Motion Picture» in 2012?
Answer: The Help

1782. Where did Robert David Hall get his academic degree from?
Answer: University of California, Los Angeles

1783. Whom did Barbra Streisand marry in the year 1998?
Answer: James Brolin

1784. Which film won the Academy Award for Best Original Song in the year 2005?
Answer: The Motorcycle Diaries

1785. Whom did Amanda Peet marry in the year 2006?
Answer: David Benioff

1786. What is the name of the character Alec Guinness plays in the movie «Star Wars Episode IV: A New Hope»?
Answer: Obi-Wan Kenobi

1787. Whom did Dagmara Dominczyk marry in the year 2005?
Answer: Patrick Wilson

1788. Whom did Diahnne Abbott marry in the year 1976?
Answer: Robert De Niro

1789. Who was the composer for the 2017 film «The Shack»?
Answer: Aaron Zigman

1790. Whom did Melanie Griffith marry in the year 1980?
Answer: Steven Bauer

1791. Who was the composer for the 2002 film «The Land Before Time IX: Journey to Big Water»?
Answer: Michael Tavera

1792. Which film won the Academy Award for Best Picture in the year 1972?
Answer: The French Connection

1793. When did Lisa LoCicero marry Michael Patrick Jann?
Answer: 2007

1794. Whom did Ayda Field marry in the year 2010?
Answer: Robbie Williams

1795. Who directed the 1990 film «Tremors»?
Answer: Ron Underwood

1796. Who were the directors of the 1993 film «Tombstone»?
Answer: Kevin Jarre and George P. Cosmatos

1797. For his work in the movie «Superman Returns», who won the «Saturn Award for Best Director» in 2007?
Answer: Bryan Singer

1798. Whom did Jane Alexander marry in the year 1975?
Answer: Edwin Sherin

1799. Who directed the 2017 film «I Am Michael»?
Answer: Justin Kelly

1800. Whom did Brogan Lane marry in the year 1988?
Answer: Dudley Moore

1801. For which film did Alan Arkin receive the «BAFTA Award for Best Actor in a Supporting Role» in 2007?
Answer: Little Miss Sunshine

1802. For which film did Alan Arkin receive the «Screen Actors Guild Award for Outstanding Performance by a Cast in a Motion Picture» in 2007?
Answer: Little Miss Sunshine

1803. For his work in the movie «Traffic», who won the «Screen Actors Guild Award for Outstanding Performance by a Cast in a Motion Picture» in 2001?
Answer: D. W. Moffett

1804. What is the name of the character Holly Hunter plays in the movie «Batman v Superman: Dawn of Justice»?
Answer: June Finch

1805. Who was the composer for the 2003 film «The Land Before Time X: The Great Longneck Migration»?
Answer: Michael Tavera

1806. Which film won the Golden Globe Award for Best Motion Picture – Drama in the year 1996?
Answer: The English Patient

1807. What's the birth name of Woody Harrelson?
Answer: Woodrow Tracy Harrelson

1808. When did Debbe Dunning marry Steve Timmons?
Answer: 1997

1809. Whom did Whitney Houston marry in the year 1992?
Answer: Bobby Brown

1810. Whom did Kathleen Kinmont marry in the year 1989?

Answer: Lorenzo Lamas

1811. For his work in the movie «The Barefoot Contessa», who won the «Academy Award for Best Supporting Actor» in 1954?
Answer: Edmond O'Brien

1812. Who directed the 1989 film «Star Trek V: The Final Frontier»?
Answer: William Shatner

1813. For which film did Brad Pitt receive the «Saturn Award for Best Supporting Actor» in 1996?
Answer: 12 Monkeys

1814. Which film won the Academy Award for Best Documentary Feature in the year 1965?
Answer: The Eleanor Roosevelt Story

1815. Which film won the Academy Award for Best Picture in the year 1937?
Answer: The Great Ziegfeld

1816. What is the full name of Michael Peña?
Answer: Michael Anthony Peña

1817. For his work in the movie «State and Main», who won the «National Board of Review Award for Best Cast» in 2000?
Answer: Clark Gregg

1818. What's the birth name of Joseph Gordon-Levitt?
Answer: Joseph Leonard Gordon-Levitt

1819. Which film won the Academy Award for Best Picture in the year 1935?
Answer: It Happened One Night

1820. What is the full name of Ashlie Brillault?
Answer: Ashlie Nicole Brillault

1821. What's the birth name of Hayley Atwell?
Answer: Hayley Elizabeth Atwell

1822. What is the full name of Kellan Lutz?
Answer: Kellan Christopher Lutz

1823. For which film did Gene Hackman receive the «Golden Globe Award for Best Actor – Motion Picture Musical or Comedy» in 2001?
Answer: The Royal Tenenbaums

1824. Who directed the 1989 film «Dead Poets Society»?
Answer: Peter Weir

1825. What is the full name of Patrick Wilson?
Answer: Patrick Joseph Wilson

1826. For which film did Ron Howard receive the «Directors Guild of America Award for Outstanding Directing – Feature Film» in 1995?
Answer: Apollo 13

1827. For which film did Sidney Poitier receive the «Golden Globe Award for Best Actor – Motion Picture Drama» in 1963?
Answer: Lilies of the Field

1828. For which film did Mary Steenburgen receive the «Golden Globe Award for Best Supporting Actress – Motion Picture» in 1980?
Answer: Melvin and Howard

1829. For which film did Natalie Portman receive the «Independent Spirit Award for Best Female Lead» in 2011?
Answer: Black Swan

1830. Where did Joe Manganiello get his Bachelor of Fine Arts degree from?
Answer: Carnegie Mellon University, in Pittsburgh

1831. Where did Seamus Dever get his Master of Fine Arts degree from?
Answer: Carnegie Mellon University, in Pittsburgh

1832. Who acted as Carl Grissom in the movie «Batman»?
Answer: Jack Palance

1833. Whom did Leelee Sobieski marry in the year 2008?
Answer: Matthew Davis

1834. What's the birth name of Robert Stanton?
Answer: Robert Lloyd Stanton

1835. For his work in the movie «Mrs. Doubtfire», who won the «Golden Globe Award for Best Actor – Motion Picture Musical or Comedy» in 1993?
Answer: Robin Williams

1836. What is the name of the character Jennifer Lawrence plays in the movie «The Hunger Games: Mockingjay – Part 2»?
Answer: Katniss Everdeen

1837. In which year did Salma Hayek marry François-Henri Pinault?
Answer: 2009

1838. Whom did Laura Leighton marry in the year 1998?
Answer: Doug Savant

1839. Where was Danielle Panabaker born?
Answer: Augusta

1840. For which film did Jennifer Hudson receive the «Golden Globe Award for Best Supporting Actress – Motion Picture» in 2006?
Answer: Dreamgirls

1841. Which film won the Academy Award for Best Picture in the year 1943?
Answer: Mrs. Miniver

1842. Who directed the 1995 film «GoldenEye»?

Answer: Martin Campbell

1843. Which film won the Academy Award for Best Picture in the year 1991?
Answer: Dances with Wolves

1844. What's the birth name of Paris Hilton?
Answer: Paris Whitney Hilton

1845. For which film did Elisabeth Shue receive the «Los Angeles Film Critics Association Award for Best Actress» in 1995?
Answer: Leaving Las Vegas

1846. In which year did Lauren Holly marry Danny Quinn?
Answer: 1991

1847. For his work in the movie «The Producers», who won the «Academy Award for Best Writing, Original Screenplay» in 1968?
Answer: Mel Brooks

1848. In which year did Heather Burns marry Ajay Naidu?
Answer: 2012

1849. Who was the composer for the 2013 film «Texas Chainsaw 3D»?
Answer: John Frizzell

1850. When did Diane Lane marry Josh Brolin?
Answer: 2004

1851. In which year did Kim Delaney marry Joseph Cortese?
Answer: 1989

1852. For which film did Joan Chen receive the «AACTA Award for Best Actress in a Leading Role» in 2007?
Answer: The Home Song Stories

1853. What's the birth name of Bob Sapp?
Answer: Robert Malcolm Sapp

1854. Whom did Tia Mowry marry in the year 2008?
Answer: Cory Hardrict

1855. What is the full name of Micaela Dee?
Answer: Micaela Dee Donovan

1856. Who acted as Major Bill Cage in the movie «Edge of Tomorrow»?
Answer: Tom Cruise

1857. Who acted as Leo Getz in the movie «Lethal Weapon 4»?
Answer: Joe Pesci

1858. Who directed the 2014 film «Ask Me Anything»?
Answer: Allison Burnett

1859. Who was the composer for the 2015 film «Mad Max: Fury Road»?
Answer: Junkie XL

1860. For which film did Jeremy Renner receive the «Washington D.C. Area Film Critics Association Award for Best Ensemble» in 2010?
Answer: The Town

1861. What is the full name of Schuyler Fisk?
Answer: Schuyler Elizabeth Fisk

1862. Who was the composer for the 1993 film «Six Degrees of Separation»?
Answer: Jerry Goldsmith

1863. What is the full name of Logan Lerman?
Answer: Logan Wade Lerman

1864. For his work in the movie «The Pianist», who won the «César Award for Best Actor» in 2003?
Answer: Adrien Brody

1865. Whom did Lori Loughlin marry in the year 1989?
Answer: Michael R. Burns

1866. When did Tracy Pollan marry Michael J. Fox?
Answer: 1988

1867. Who directed the 1987 film «Throw Momma from the Train»?
Answer: Danny DeVito

1868. Whom did Alex Borstein marry in the year 1999?
Answer: Jackson Douglas

1869. Who was the composer for the 2018 film «Creed II»?
Answer: Ludwig Göransson

1870. For her work in the movie «The Good Girl», who won the «Independent Spirit Award for Best Female Lead» in 2003?
Answer: Jennifer Aniston

1871. Who was the composer for the 2007 film «Aliens vs. Predator: Requiem»?
Answer: Brian Tyler

1872. For which film did Jean Simmons receive the «Golden Globe Award for Best Actress – Motion Picture Musical or Comedy» in 1955?
Answer: Guys and Dolls

1873. Where did Anders Holm get his bachelor's degree from?
Answer: University of Wisconsin–Madison

1874. What's the birth name of Eddie Cibrian?
Answer: Edward Bryant Cibrian

1875. Which film won the Academy Award for Best Original Score in the year 1987?
Answer: Round Midnight

1876. For her work in the movie «Contact», who won the «Saturn Award for Best Actress» in 1997?

Answer: Jodie Foster

1877. Which film won the Academy Award for Best Documentary Feature in the year 1947?
Answer: Design for Death

1878. Whom did Jennifer Esposito marry in the year 2006?
Answer: Bradley Cooper

1879. Who was the composer for the 2018 film «Colette»?
Answer: Thomas Adès

1880. Whom did Rutanya Alda marry in the year 1977?
Answer: Richard Bright

1881. Who acted as Galadriel in the movie «The Hobbit: The Battle of the Five Armies»?
Answer: Cate Blanchett

1882. For her work in the movie «A Stranger Among Us», who won the «Golden Raspberry Award for Worst Actress» in 1992?
Answer: Melanie Griffith

1883. Whom did Elizabeth McGovern marry in the year 1992?
Answer: Simon Curtis

1884. Who was the composer for the 2005 film «Hotel Rwanda»?
Answer: Andrea Guerra

1885. Who directed the 2018 film «Breaking In»?
Answer: James McTeigue

1886. Who acted as Meredith Vickers in the movie «Prometheus»?
Answer: Charlize Theron

1887. For her work in the movie «Kramer vs. Kramer»,

who won the «Academy Award for Best Supporting Actress» in 1980?
Answer: Meryl Streep

1888. In which year did Michelle Phillips marry Dennis Hopper?
Answer: 1970

1889. For which film did Sarah Michelle Gellar receive the «Teen Choice Award for Best Villain» in 1999?
Answer: Cruel Intentions

1890. Whom did Jean Seberg marry in the year 1972?
Answer: Dennis Berry

1891. Which film won the Academy Award for Best Picture in the year 1974?
Answer: The Sting

1892. Who directed the 2017 film «Happy Death Day»?
Answer: Christopher B. Landon

1893. Who directed the 1994 film «The House of the Spirits»?
Answer: Bille August

1894. In which year did Gail O'Grady marry John Stamatakis?
Answer: 2004
1895. Which film won the Academy Award for Best Sound Editing in the year 1994?
Answer: Speed

1896. Whom did Zsa Zsa Gabor marry in the year 1976?
Answer: Michael O'Hara

1897. What is the name of the character Natalie Portman plays in the movie «Thor»?
Answer: Jane Foster

1898. Who directed the 1996 film «Evita»?

Answer: Alan Parker

1899. What is the name of the character Rose Byrne plays in the movie «Troy»?
Answer: Briseis

1900. Who was the composer for the 2018 film «Pacific Rim Uprising»?
Answer: John Paesano

1901. Who was the composer for the 2018 film «Bohemian Rhapsody»?
Answer: Brian May

1902. For which film did Catherine Keener receive the «Dallas-Fort Worth Film Critics Association Award for Best Supporting Actress» in 2005?
Answer: Capote

1903. In which year did Mary Elizabeth Mastrantonio marry Pat O'Connor?
Answer: 1990

1904. For his work in the movie «Face/Off», who won the «MTV Movie Award for Best On-Screen Duo» in 1998?
Answer: Nicolas Cage

1905. Who were the composers of the 2014 film «Kingsman: The Secret Service»?
Answer: Henry Jackman and Matthew Margeson

1906. For his work in the movie «Love Story», who won the «David di Donatello for Best Foreign Actor» award in 1971?
Answer: Ryan O'Neal

1907. In which year did Pauley Perrette marry Coyote Shivers?
Answer: 2000

1908. Who acted as Tuya in the movie «Exodus: Gods and

Kings»?
Answer: Sigourney Weaver

1909. What is the full name of Gary Daniels?
Answer: Gary Edward Daniels

1910. When did Whitney Able marry Scoot McNairy?
Answer: 2010

1911. Which film won the Academy Award for Best Production Design in the year 1965?
Answer: Doctor Zhivago

1912. Who was the composer for the 1997 film «Tomorrow Never Dies»?
Answer: David Arnold

1913. Whom did Sable marry in the year 2006?
Answer: Brock Lesnar

1914. In which year did Suzanne Somers marry Alan Hamel?
Answer: 1977

1915. In which year did Kaley Cuoco marry Karl Cook?
Answer: 2018

1916. Who directed the 1990 film «Home Alone»?
Answer: Chris Columbus

1917. In which year did Jodie Foster marry Alexandra Hedison?
Answer: 2014

1918. Whom did Jaclyn Smith marry in the year 1981?
Answer: Anthony B. Richmond

1919. Who directed the 2014 film «Noah»?
Answer: Darren Aronofsky

1920. Whom did Julia Roberts marry in the year 2008?
Answer: Daniel Moder

1921. For which film did Leonardo DiCaprio receive the «Golden Globe Award for Best Actor – Motion Picture Drama» in 2016?
Answer: The Revenant

1922. Whom did Talia Shire marry in the year 1980?
Answer: Jack Schwartzman

1923. Who directed the 2011 film «Ironclad»?
Answer: Jonathan English

1924. Who acted as Jack Torrance in the movie «The Shining»?
Answer: Jack Nicholson

1925. Whom did Mimi Rogers marry in the year 1987?
Answer: Tom Cruise

1926. Whom did Tracy Nelson marry in the year 1987?
Answer: William R. Moses

1927. Where did Jon Hamm get his Bachelor of Arts degree from?
Answer: University of Missouri, in Columbia

1928. Who was the composer for the 1998 film «Lethal Weapon 4»?
Answer: Michael Kamen

1929. Whom did Kathryn Hahn marry in the year 2002?
Answer: Ethan Sandler

1930. Whom did Amber Stevens marry in the year 2014?
Answer: Andrew J. West

1931. Who was the composer for the 2018 film «Deadpool 2»?
Answer: Tyler Bates

1932. In which year did Jessica Drake marry Brad

Armstrong?
Answer: 2006

1933. Who directed the 2018 film «Peppermint»?
Answer: Pierre Morel

1934. What is the name of the character Cate Blanchett plays in the movie «Thor: Ragnarok»?
Answer: Hela

1935. For which film did Charlton Heston receive the «Academy Award for Best Actor» in 1959?
Answer: Ben-Hur

1936. Who was the composer for the 2000 film «Keeping the Faith»?
Answer: Elmer Bernstein

1937. What's the birth name of Jake Johnson?
Answer: Jake Mark Johnson

1938. Who was the composer for the 1996 film «Phenomenon»?
Answer: Thomas Newman

1939. For his work in the movie «The Visitor», who won the «Satellite Award for Best Actor – Motion Picture» in 2008?
Answer: Richard Jenkins

1940. Whom did Frances McDormand marry in the year 1993?
Answer: Joel Coen

1941. Whom did Fergie marry in the year 2009?
Answer: Josh Duhamel

1942. Who directed the 1992 film «Alien 3»?
Answer: David Fincher

1943. What's the birth name of Helen Hunt?

Answer: Helen Elizabeth Hunt

1944. Whom did Catherine Oxenberg marry in the year 1998?
Answer: Robert Evans

1945. What is the name of the character Charlize Theron plays in the movie «Mad Max: Fury Road»?
Answer: Imperator Furiosa

1946. Whom did Linda Thompson marry in the year 1991?
Answer: David Foster

1947. For which film did Marilyn Monroe receive the «Targa d'Oro» award in 1958?
Answer: The Prince and the Showgirl

1948. For his work in the movie «The Fortune Cookie», who won the «Academy Award for Best Supporting Actor» in 1966?
Answer: Walter Matthau

1949. Who was the composer for the 2018 film «If Beale Street Could Talk»?
Answer: Nicholas Britell

1950. Who was the composer for the 1996 film «Curdled»?
Answer: Joseph Julian Gonzalez

1951. For which film did Meryl Streep receive the «Golden Globe Award for Best Actress – Motion Picture Musical or Comedy» in 2009?
Answer: Julie & Julia

1952. What's the birth name of Daphne Zuniga?
Answer: Daphne Eurydice Zuniga

1953. When did Delta Burke marry Gerald McRaney?
Answer: 1989

1954. Who was the composer for the 2019 film «Alita:

Battle Angel»?
Answer: Junkie XL

1955. Which film won the Academy Award for Best Production Design in the year 2018?
Answer: The Shape of Water

1956. For his work in the movie «Goodfellas», who won the «BAFTA Award for Best Direction» in 1991?
Answer: Martin Scorsese

1957. What's the birth name of Whitney Houston?
Answer: Whitney Elizabeth Houston

1958. Whom did Faye Dunaway marry in the year 1983?
Answer: Terry O'Neill

1959. Who directed the 2006 film «Flicka»?
Answer: Michael Mayer

1960. What's the birth name of Ciara Bravo?
Answer: Ciara Quinn Bravo

1961. Who directed the 2019 film «The Beach Bum»?
Answer: Harmony Korine

1962. Who directed the 2004 film «Alexander»?
Answer: Oliver Stone

1963. Who was the composer for the 1989 film «Licence to Kill»?
Answer: Michael Kamen

1964. Where did Gillian Anderson get her Bachelor of Fine Arts degree from?
Answer: DePaul University, in Chicago

1965. For which film did Jennifer Lawrence receive the «Screen Actors Guild Award for Outstanding Performance by a Female Actor in a Leading Role» in 2013?
Answer: Silver Linings Playbook

1966. Who directed the 2016 film «The Land Before Time XIV: Journey of the Heart»?
Answer: Davis Doi

1967. Whom did Arielle Dombasle marry in the year 1993?
Answer: Bernard-Henri Lévy

1968. When did Linda Thompson marry Caitlyn Jenner?
Answer: 1981

1969. What's the birth name of Amanda Seyfried?
Answer: Amanda Michelle Seyfried

1970. When did Jennifer Aniston marry Brad Pitt?
Answer: 2000

1971. For his work in the movie «The Yearling», who won the «Golden Globe Award for Best Actor – Motion Picture Drama» in 1946?
Answer: Gregory Peck

1972. Who was the composer for the 2012 film «Red Tails»?
Answer: Terence Blanchard

1973. For which film did Kristen Stewart receive the «MTV Movie Award for Best Kiss» in 2011?
Answer: The Twilight Saga: Eclipse

1974. In which year did Rosemarie DeWitt marry Chris Messina?
Answer: 1995

1975. What is the full name of Rob Schneider?
Answer: Robert Michael Schneider

1976. For his work in the movie «Good Morning, Vietnam», who won the «Golden Globe Award for Best Actor – Motion Picture Musical or Comedy» in 1987?
Answer: Robin Williams

1977. When did Rosemarie DeWitt marry Ron Livingston?
Answer: 2009

1978. What's the birth name of Jaimie Alexander?
Answer: Jaimie Lauren Tarbush

1979. Who was the composer for the 2018 film «Destroyer»?
Answer: Theodore Shapiro

1980. In which year did Linda Hamilton marry Bruce Abbott?
Answer: 1982

1981. What is the full name of Dita von Teese?
Answer: Heather Renée Sweet

1982. What is the name of the character Christoph Waltz plays in the movie «Spectre»?
Answer: Franz Oberhauser

1983. Which film won the Golden Globe Award for Best Original Score in the year 1982?
Answer: E.T. the Extra-Terrestrial

1984. What is the full name of Kelly Madison?
Answer: Eleanore Marlene Wilmerton

1985. What's the birth name of Justin Long?
Answer: Justin Jacob Long

1986. Who acted as Cameron Poe in the movie «Con Air»?
Answer: Nicolas Cage

1987. Which film won the Academy Award for Best Original Score in the year 1970?
Answer: Love Story

1988. Where did Justin Theroux get his Bachelor of Arts degree from?

Answer: Bennington College

1989. Who acted as Red Miller in the movie «Mandy»?
Answer: Nicolas Cage

1990. Whom did Nikki Reed marry in the year 2011?
Answer: Paul McDonald

1991. For which film did Jack Palance receive the «Academy Award for Best Supporting Actor» in 1991?
Answer: City Slickers

1992. What is the full name of Eli Marienthal?
Answer: Eli David Marienthal

1993. Who was the composer for the 2018 film «Unbroken: Path to Redemption»?
Answer: Brandon Roberts

1995. Who acted as Jack Rafferty in the movie «Sin City»?
Answer: Benicio del Toro

1996. Whom did Finn Carter marry in the year 1985?
Answer: Steven Weber

1997. Who was the composer for the 2018 film «Blindspotting»?
Answer: Michael Yezerski

1998. What is the full name of Norman Reedus?
Answer: Norman Mark Reedus

1999. Who was the composer for the 2001 film «A Knight's Tale»?
Answer: Carter Burwell

2000. For her work in the movie «The Silence of the Lambs», who won the «BAFTA Award for Best Actress in a Leading Role» in 1992?
Answer: Jodie Foster

2001. Who was the composer for the 2018 film «Hotel Artemis»?
Answer: Cliff Martinez

2002. Who acted as June Finch in the movie «Batman v Superman: Dawn of Justice»?
Answer: Holly Hunter

2003. Whom did Vanessa Marcil marry in the year 1989?
Answer: Corey Feldman

2004. Whom did Sasha Alexander marry in the year 2007?
Answer: Edoardo Ponti

2005. Who directed the 1994 film «Radioland Murders»?
Answer: Mel Smith

2006. For which film did David Lynch receive the «César Award for Best Foreign Film» in 1982?
Answer: The Elephant Man

2007. What's the birth name of Kate Upton?
Answer: Katherine Elizabeth Upton

2008. Who was the composer for the 2016 film «Blair Witch»?
Answer: Adam Wingard

2009. Who was the composer for the 2010 film «127 Hours»?
Answer: A. R. Rahman

2010. Whom did Stockard Channing marry in the year 1970?
Answer: Paul Schmidt

2011. Who was the composer for the 2019 film «Isn't It Romantic»?
Answer: Theodore Shapiro

2012. What is the name of the character Forest Whitaker

plays in the movie «Rogue One»?
Answer: Saw Gerrera

2013. For which film did Adam Sandler receive the «Golden Raspberry Award for Worst Actor» in 2012?
Answer: That's My Boy

2014. What's the birth name of Allie Haze?
Answer: Brittany Sturtevant

2015. For her work in the movie «Paper Moon», who won the «Academy Award for Best Supporting Actress» in 1973?
Answer: Tatum O'Neal

2016. Who was the composer for the 2015 film «The Big Short»?
Answer: Nicholas Britell

2017. Whom did Robbi Morgan marry in the year 1987?
Answer: Mark L. Walberg

2018. For his work in the movie «Chasing Amy», who won the «Independent Spirit Award for Best Screenplay» in 1998?
Answer: Kevin Smith

2019. Who was the composer for the 2000 film «Men of Honor»?
Answer: Mark Isham

2020. For his work in the movie «Argo», who won the «Screen Actors Guild Award for Outstanding Performance by a Cast in a Motion Picture» in 2013?
Answer: Christopher Denham

2021. For which film did Jodie Foster receive the «David di Donatello for Best Foreign Actress» award in 1994?
Answer: Nell

2022. When did Cheryl Hines marry Robert F. Kennedy,

Jr.?
Answer: 2014

2023. In which year did Katharine Ross marry Sam Elliott?
Answer: 1984

2024. Whom did Apollonia Kotero marry in the year 1987?
Answer: Kevin Bernhardt

2025. For her work in the movie «The Piano», who won the «London Film Critics Circle Award for Actress of the Year» in 1993?
Answer: Holly Hunter

2026. In which year did Bianca Kajlich marry Michael Catherwood?
Answer: 2012

2027. For which film did Miloš Forman receive the «Academy Award for Best Director» in 1975?
Answer: One Flew Over the Cuckoo's Nest

2028. Whom did Abby Brammell marry in the year 2006?
Answer: Jake La Botz

2029. For which film did Judy Garland receive the «Golden Globe Award for Best Actress – Motion Picture Musical or Comedy» in 1954?
Answer: A Star Is Born

2030. What is the full name of Sarah Shahi?
Answer: Aahoo Jahansouz Shahi

2031. Where did Larry David get his bachelor's degree from?
Answer: University of Maryland, in College Park

2032. For which film did Paul Dano receive the «Screen Actors Guild Award for Outstanding Performance by a Cast in a Motion Picture» in 2007?
Answer: Little Miss Sunshine

2033. Who was the composer for the 2005 film «Mr. & Mrs. Smith»?
Answer: John Powell

2034. For his work in the movie «Chicago», who won the «Broadcast Film Critics Association Award for Best Cast» in 2002?
Answer: Richard Gere

2035. Who was the composer for the 2019 film «What Men Want»?
Answer: Brian Tyler

2036. What is the full name of Harry Connick Jr.?
Answer: Harry Fowler Connick

2037. For which film did Marlon Brando receive the «Golden Globe Award for Best Actor – Motion Picture Drama» in 1972?
Answer: The Godfather

2038. What is the name of the character Heath Ledger plays in the movie «The Dark Knight»?
Answer: Joker (The Dark Knight)

2039. What is the name of the character Sean Connery plays in the movie «Never Say Never Again»?
Answer: James Bond

2040. When did Carrie Preston marry Michael Emerson?
Answer: 1998

2041. Who was the composer for the 2005 film «Melinda and Melinda»?
Answer: Johann Sebastian Bach

2042. Who was the composer for the 2017 film «Logan»?
Answer: Cliff Martinez

2043. Which film won the Golden Globe Award for Best

Motion Picture – Drama in the year 2013?
Answer: 12 Years a Slave

2044. In which year did Kim Kardashian marry Damon Thomas?
Answer: 2000

2045. For his work in the movie «The Revenant», who won the «Academy Award for Best Actor» in 2016?
Answer: Leonardo DiCaprio

2046. What's the birth name of David Lim?
Answer: David Bradley Lim

2047. Whom did Cyndi Lauper marry in the year 1991?
Answer: David Thornton

2048. When did Rebecca Hall marry Morgan Spector?
Answer: 2015

2049. Where was Jeri Ryan born?
Answer: Munich

2050. Which film won the Academy Award for Best Picture in the year 1942?
Answer: How Green Was My Valley

2051. For her work in the movie «Annie Hall», who won the «Academy Award for Best Actress» in 1977?
Answer: Diane Keaton

2052. Which film won the Academy Award for Best Picture in the year 1939?
Answer: You Can't Take It With You

2053. Who directed the 2014 film «Left Behind»?
Answer: Vic Armstrong

2054. What is the full name of Gillian Jacobs?
Answer: Gillian MacLaren Jacobs

2055. What's the birth name of Chris Evans?

Answer: Christopher Robert Evans

2056. Who was the composer for the 2011 film «The Help»?
Answer: Thomas Newman

2057. Whom did Cindy Williams marry in the year 1982?
Answer: Bill Hudson

2058. Whom did Lina Romay marry in the year 2008?
Answer: Jesús Franco

2059. Whom did Ivana Božilović marry in the year 2008?
Answer: Andrew Firestone

2060. For which film did Steve Buscemi receive the «Independent Spirit Award for Best Supporting Male» in 2002?
Answer: Ghost World

2061. What is the full name of Sienna Miller?
Answer: Sienna Rose Miller

2062. What's the birth name of Kim Chambers?
Answer: Kimberly Schafer

2063. For his work in the movie «The Bad Lieutenant: Port of Call New Orleans», who won the «Toronto Film Critics Association Award for Best Actor» in 2009?
Answer: Nicolas Cage

2064. Who directed the 2008 film «Marley & Me»?
Answer: David Frankel

2065. Who directed the 1996 film «Spy Hard»?
Answer: Rick Friedberg

2066. Who directed the 1988 film «Willow»?
Answer: Ron Howard

2067. Which film won the Academy Award for Best Visual

Effects in the year 1986?
Answer: Aliens

2068. What is the full name of Tony Hawk?
Answer: Anthony Frank Hawk

2069. For which film did Britney Spears receive the «Golden Raspberry Award for Worst Actress» in 2003?
Answer: Crossroads

2070. Who directed the 2009 film «Harry Potter and the Half-Blood Prince»?
Answer: David Yates

2071. Who directed the 2015 film «Jurassic World»?
Answer: Colin Trevorrow

2072. Who was the composer for the 2014 film «Ask Me Anything»?
Answer: Jon Ehrlich

2073. Who was the composer for the 1987 film «Outrageous Fortune»?
Answer: Alan Silvestri

2074. For his work in the movie «Cat Ballou», who won the «Academy Award for Best Actor» in 1965?
Answer: Lee Marvin

2075. Who directed the 2001 film «Jurassic Park III»?
Answer: Joe Johnston

2076. What's the birth name of Janet Jackson?
Answer: Janet Damita Jo Jackson

2077. Who directed the 2014 film «Godzilla»?
Answer: Gareth Edwards

2078. For which film did Catherine Keener receive the «Washington D.C. Area Film Critics Association Award for Best Supporting Actress» in 2005?

Answer: Capote

2079. Who directed the 2008 film «Not Bewitched XXX»?
Answer: Will Ryder

2080. Who directed the 2003 film «Uptown Girls»?
Answer: Boaz Yakin

2081. What's the birth name of Minka Kelly?
Answer: Minka Dumont Kelly

2082. Who acted as Agent K in the movie «Men in Black 3»?
Answer: Tommy Lee Jones

2083. Who was the composer for the 1992 film «A Stranger Among Us»?
Answer: Jerry Bock

2084. In which year did Teri Hatcher marry Jon Tenney?
Answer: 1994

2085. What is the name of the character Lionel Barrymore plays in the movie «Home Alone»?
Answer: Mr. Potter

2086. For her work in the movie «The Good Girl», who won the «Teen Choice Award for Choice Movie - Drama» in 2003?
Answer: Jennifer Aniston

2087. What's the birth name of Kim Smith?
Answer: Kimberley Katherine Smith

2088. Where did Ted Danson get his Bachelor of Fine Arts degree from?
Answer: Carnegie Mellon University, in Pittsburgh

2089. When did Leeza Gibbons marry Steve Fenton?
Answer: 2011
2090. What is the full name of Channing Tatum?

Answer: Channing Matthew Tatum

2091. In which year did Erinn Bartlett marry Oliver Hudson?
Answer: 2006

2092. In which year did Iyari Limon marry Efren Ramirez?
Answer: 1998

2093. For her work in the movie «Dangerous», who won the «Academy Award for Best Actress» in 1935?
Answer: Bette Davis

2094. Who was the composer for the 1988 film «Scrooged»?
Answer: Danny Elfman

2095. Who acted as Pepper Potts in the movie «Iron Man»?
Answer: Gwyneth Paltrow

2096. Who directed the 2002 film «Maid in Manhattan»?
Answer: Wayne Wang

2097. In which year did Anna Nicole Smith marry Howard K. Stern?
Answer: 2006

2098. Which film won the Academy Award for Best Sound Editing in the year 2002?
Answer: The Lord of the Rings: The Two Towers

2099. Whom did Fran Drescher marry in the year 1978?
Answer: Peter Marc Jacobson

2100. Which film won the Academy Award for Best Picture in the year 1999?
Answer: Shakespeare in Love

2102. For her work in the movie «The Actress», who won the «National Board of Review Award for Best Actress» in

1953?
Answer: Jean Simmons

2103. Where was Meryl Streep born?
Answer: Summit

2104. Which film won the Academy Award for Best Sound Mixing in the year 1982?
Answer: E.T. the Extra-Terrestrial

2105. Who acted as Red Skull in the movie «Captain America: The First Avenger»?
Answer: Hugo Weaving

2106. Which film won the Academy Award for Best Picture in the year 2018?
Answer: The Shape of Water

2107. Who directed the 2018 film «How to Talk to Girls at Parties»?
Answer: John Cameron Mitchell

2108. Who directed the 2018 film «Unbroken: Path to Redemption»?
Answer: Harold Cronk

2109. For her work in the movie «The Catered Affair», who won the «National Board of Review Award for Best Supporting Actress» in 1956?
Answer: Debbie Reynolds

2110. For which film did Ron Howard receive the «Academy Award for Best Picture» in 2001?
Answer: A Beautiful Mind

2111. Whom did Charlene Tilton marry in the year 1982?
Answer: Johnny Lee

2112. Who directed the 2018 film «Bad Times at the El Royale»?
Answer: Drew Goddard

2113. For which film did Dan Futterman receive the «Boston Society of Film Critics Award for Best Screenplay» in 2005?
Answer: Capote

2114. Whom did Beth Toussaint marry in the year 1996?
Answer: Jack Coleman

2115. When did Lisa Niemi marry Patrick Swayze?
Answer: 1975

2116. For which film did Edward Norton receive the «Boston Society of Film Critics Award for Best Supporting Actor» in 1996?
Answer: Primal Fear

2117. For which film did Joan Chen receive the «Golden Horse Award for Best Leading Actress» in 2007?
Answer: The Home Song Stories

2118. Whom did Amelia Rose Blaire marry in the year 2018?
Answer: Bryan Dechart

2119. Whom did Gilda Radner marry in the year 1980?
Answer: G. E. Smith

2120. In which year did Talia Balsam marry John Slattery?
Answer: 1998

2121. What's the birth name of Chad Coleman?
Answer: Chad William Coleman

2122. For his work in the movie «All the President's Men», who won the «Academy Award for Best Supporting Actor» in 1976?
Answer: Jason Robards

2123. In which year did Stephanie Romanov marry Nick Wechsler?

Answer: 2001

2124. Who were the directors of the 1988 film «A Fish Called Wanda»?
Answer: John Cleese and Charles Crichton

2125. What is the name of the character Melissa Leo plays in the movie «Snowden»?
Answer: Laura Poitras

2126. Who directed the 2009 film «Terminator Salvation»?
Answer: McG

2127. Whom did Julia Ann marry in the year 2003?
Answer: Michael Raven

2128. Which film won the Academy Award for Best Documentary Feature in the year 1950?
Answer: The Titan: Story of Michelangelo

2129. Who directed the 2017 film «Wonder Woman»?
Answer: Patty Jenkins

2130. Who was the composer for the 1991 film «The Five Heartbeats»?
Answer: Stanley Clarke

2131. Who was the composer for the 1997 film «Air Force One»?
Answer: Jerry Goldsmith

2132. Who was the composer for the 2014 film «Left Behind»?
Answer: Jack Lenz
2133. What's the birth name of Eric Underwood?
Answer: Eric Michael Underwood

2134. In which year did Jami Gertz marry Antony Ressler?
Answer: 1989

2135. Who directed the 2011 film «The Ides of March»?

Answer: George Clooney

2136. In which year did Brittany Murphy marry Simon Monjack?
Answer: 2007

2137. Who directed the 1997 film «Alien: Resurrection»?
Answer: Jean-Pierre Jeunet

2138. For her work in the movie «Mrs. Miniver», who won the «Academy Award for Best Supporting Actress» in 1943?
Answer: Teresa Wright

2139. Whom did Gail O'Grady marry in the year 1995?
Answer: Steve Fenton

2140. Whom did Kelly Coffield Park marry in the year 1991?
Answer: Steve Park

2141. Who was the composer for the 2009 film «X-Men Origins: Wolverine»?
Answer: Harry Gregson-Williams

2142. When did Marika Domińczyk marry Scott Foley?
Answer: 2007

2143. Who acted as Newt Scamander in the movie «Fantastic Beasts and Where to Find Them»?
Answer: Eddie Redmayne

2144. When did LisaRaye McCoy-Misick marry Tony Martin?
Answer: 1992

2145. Who was the composer for the 1990 film «Lord of the Flies»?
Answer: Philippe Sarde

2146. Who was the composer for the 2018 film

«Assassination Nation»?
Answer: Ian Hultquist

2147. Who acted as Alfred Pennyworth in the movie «The Dark Knight Rises»?
Answer: Michael Caine

2148. Who was the composer for the 2017 film «Baywatch»?
Answer: Christopher Lennertz

2149. In which year did Julia Migenes marry Peter Medak?
Answer: 1988

2150. Where did Woody Harrelson get his Bachelor of Arts degree from?
Answer: Hanover College

2151. For his work in the movie «The Silence of the Lambs», who won the «New York Film Critics Circle Award for Best Actor» in 1991?
Answer: Anthony Hopkins

2152. Who were the composers of the 1997 film «Con Air»?
Answer: Mark Mancina and Trevor Rabin

2153. Where did Ron Jeremy get his master's degree from?
Answer: Queens College

2154. Which film won the Academy Award for Best Sound Editing in the year 1986?
Answer: Aliens

2155. Which film won the Golden Globe Award for Best Original Score in the year 1996?
Answer: The English Patient

2156. Which film won the Academy Award for Best Picture in the year 1990?

Answer: Driving Miss Daisy

2157. Whom did Christine Lakin marry in the year 2004?
Answer: Andy Fickman

2158. Who was the composer for the 2016 film «The Birth of a Nation»?
Answer: Henry Jackman

2159. For which film did Sydney Pollack receive the «Academy Award for Best Director» in 1986?
Answer: Out of Africa

2160. For which film did Jason Lee receive the «Independent Spirit Award for Best Supporting Male» in 1998?
Answer: Chasing Amy

2161. Who was the composer for the 1992 film «Sister Act»?
Answer: Marc Shaiman

2162. In which year did Clementine Ford marry Cyrus Wilcox?
Answer: 2013

2163. Who was the composer for the 2011 film «Super 8»?
Answer: Michael Giacchino

2164. In which year did Jennifer Aniston marry Justin Theroux?
Answer: 2015

2165. Who acted as Justin Hammer in the movie «Iron Man 2»?
Answer: Sam Rockwell

2166. In which year did Debra Feuer marry Mickey Rourke?
Answer: 1981

2167. Whom did Phylicia Rashād marry in the year 1978?
Answer: Victor Willis

2168. What is the full name of Tiffany Thornton?
Answer: Tiffany Dawn Thornton

2169. For which film did Nicolas Cage receive the «National Society of Film Critics Award for Best Actor» in 1995?
Answer: Leaving Las Vegas

2170. Which film won the Golden Globe Award for Best Motion Picture – Drama in the year 1965?
Answer: Doctor Zhivago

2171. Whom did Halle Berry marry in the year 1993?
Answer: David Justice

2172. What is the full name of Raylene?
Answer: Stacey Briana Bernstein

2173. Who were the composers of the 2017 film «The Greatest Showman»?
Answer: John Debney and Pasek and Paul

2174. Which film won the Academy Award for Best Story in the year 1939?
Answer: Mr. Smith Goes to Washington

2175. Whom did Tatum O'Neal marry in the year 1986?
Answer: John McEnroe

2176. Whom did Christina Applegate marry in the year 2013?
Answer: Martyn LeNoble

2177. What is the full name of Jay Chandrasekhar?
Answer: Jayanth Jambulingam Chandrasekhar

2178. Who were the directors of the 2015 film «Jupiter Ascending»?
Answer: Lilly Wachowski and Lana Wachowski

2179. Whom did Carré Otis marry in the year 1992?
Answer: Mickey Rourke

2180. What is the full name of John Legend?
Answer: John Roger Stephens

2181. For her work in the movie «The Hottie and the Nottie», who won the «Golden Raspberry Award for Worst Screen Couple/Ensemble» in 2008?
Answer: Christine Lakin

2182. In which year did Linda Lavin marry Kip Niven?
Answer: 1982

2183. When did Mena Suvari marry Simone Sestito?
Answer: 2010

2184. When did Wendy Benson marry Michael Landes?
Answer: 2000

2185. What is the name of the character Nicolas Cage plays in the movie «Season of the Witch»?
Answer: Behmen von Bleibruck

2186. In which year did Jeramie Rain marry Richard Dreyfuss?
Answer: 1983

2187. What is the full name of Patrick Schwarzenegger?
Answer: Patrick Arnold Shriver Schwarzenegger

2188. For his work in the movie «Inglourious Basterds», who won the «Screen Actors Guild Award for Outstanding Performance by a Cast in a Motion Picture» in 2009?
Answer: Brad Pitt

2189. Who directed the 2019 film «Velvet Buzzsaw»?
Answer: Dan Gilroy

2190. Who was the composer for the 2010 film «The Book of Eli»?

Answer: Atticus Ross

2191. When did Ann Turkel marry Richard Harris?
Answer: 1974

2192. Who was the composer for the 2008 film «Indiana Jones and the Kingdom of the Crystal Skull»?
Answer: John Williams

2193. Who was the composer for the 2003 film «Duplex»?
Answer: David Newman

2194. What's the birth name of Kristin Chenoweth?
Answer: Kristi Dawn Chenoweth

2195. For which film did Nipsey Russell receive the «NAACP Image Award for Outstanding Supporting Actor in a Motion Picture» in 1979?
Answer: The Wiz

2196. For her work in the movie «Dreamgirls», who won the «Screen Actors Guild Award for Outstanding Performance by a Female Actor in a Supporting Role» in 2007?
Answer: Jennifer Hudson

2197. Who was the composer for the 2019 film «Dumbo»?
Answer: Danny Elfman

2198. What's the birth name of Ice Cube?
Answer: O'Shea Jackson Sr

2199. Who directed the 2015 film «It Follows»?
Answer: David Robert Mitchell

2200. Who directed the 2018 film «Holmes & Watson»?
Answer: Etan Cohen

2201. Who directed the 1995 film «The Tie That Binds»?
Answer: Wesley Strick

2202. For her work in the movie «American Hustle», who won the «Golden Globe Award for Best Supporting Actress – Motion Picture» in 2013?
Answer: Jennifer Lawrence

2203. Who directed the 2014 film «I, Frankenstein»?
Answer: Stuart Beattie

2204. What's the birth name of Sandra Bullock?
Answer: Sandra Annette Bullock

2205. When did Jana Kramer marry Mike Caussin?
Answer: 2015

2206. Which film won the Academy Award for Best Documentary Feature in the year 1945?
Answer: The True Glory

2207. For his work in the movie «The Brothers McMullen», who won the «Independent Spirit Award for Best First Feature» in 1996?
Answer: Edward Burns

2208. Whom did Kim Basinger marry in the year 1993?
Answer: Alec Baldwin

2209. When did Ashlee Simpson marry Evan Ross?
Answer: 2014

2210. What's the birth name of Marc Anthony?
Answer: Marco Antonio Muñiz

2211. Who was the composer for the 1994 film «Legends of the Fall»?
Answer: James Horner

2212. Who were the composers of the 2013 film «Oblivion»?
Answer: M83 and Joseph Trapanese

2213. For his work in the movie «Magnolia», who won the

«Golden Globe Award for Best Supporting Actor – Motion Picture» in 2000?
Answer: Tom Cruise

2214. What's the birth name of Salma Hayek?
Answer: Salma Valgarma Hayek Jiménez

2215. Whom did Jessica Simpson marry in the year 2002?
Answer: Nick Lachey

2216. For his work in the movie «Fast & Furious 6», who won the «MTV Movie Award for Best On-Screen Duo» in 2014?
Answer: Vin Diesel

2217. For his work in the movie «Happy Gilmore», who won the «MTV Movie Award for Best Fight» in 1996?
Answer: Adam Sandler

2218. In which year did Brenda Scott marry Andrew Prine?
Answer: 1973

2219. Which film won the Academy Award for Best Picture in the year 2007?
Answer: The Departed

2220. Who was the composer for the 2011 film «Trespass»?
Answer: David Buckley

2221. For his work in the movie «Amadeus», who won the «Academy Award for Best Director» in 1984?
Answer: Miloš Forman

2222. Which film won the Academy Award for Best Picture in the year 1993?
Answer: Unforgiven

2223. Where did Meryl Streep get her Bachelor of Arts degree from?

Answer: Vassar College, in Poughkeepsie

2224. Where did Ed Harris get his Bachelor of Fine Arts degree from?
Answer: California Institute of the Arts, in Santa Clarita

2225. Who was the composer for the 2017 film «War for the Planet of the Apes»?
Answer: Michael Giacchino

2226. For her work in the movie «I Am Sam», who won the «Broadcast Film Critics Association Award for Best Young Performer» in 2001?
Answer: Dakota Fanning

2227. What's the birth name of Tracy Morgan?
Answer: Tracy Jamal Morgan

2228. Who acted as Noah Kross in the movie «The Humanity Bureau»?
Answer: Nicolas Cage

2229. For which film did Jeremy Renner receive the «National Society of Film Critics Award for Best Actor» in 2009?
Answer: The Hurt Locker

2230. For her work in the movie «State and Main», who won the «Online Film Critics Society Award for Best Cast» in 2000?
Answer: Patti LuPone

2231. Whom did Tami Roman marry in the year 1994?
Answer: Kenny Anderson

2232. For his work in the movie «Apollo 13», who won the «Screen Actors Guild Award for Outstanding Performance by a Cast in a Motion Picture» in 1996?
Answer: Bill Paxton

2233. In which year did Navi Rawat marry Brawley Nolte?
Answer: 2012

2234. Who directed the 2017 film «Keep Watching»?
Answer: Sean Carter

2235. For which film did Katharine Hepburn receive the «Academy Award for Best Actress» in 1981?
Answer: On Golden Pond

2236. For which film did Diane Keaton receive the «Golden Globe Award for Best Actress – Motion Picture Musical or Comedy» in 2003?
Answer: Something's Gotta Give

2237. Who directed the 2018 film «Aquaman»?
Answer: James Wan

2238. What's the birth name of Ludacris?
Answer: Christopher Brian Bridges

2239. For his work in the movie «One Flew Over the Cuckoo's Nest», who won the «David di Donatello for Best Foreign Director» award in 1976?
Answer: Miloš Forman

2240. Who directed the 2018 film «Destroyer»?
Answer: Karyn Kusama

2241. Where did Amy Poehler get her Bachelor of Arts degree from?
Answer: Boston College, in Massachusetts

2242. In which year did Catherine Hicks marry Kevin Yagher?
Answer: 1990

2243. When did Debra Winger marry Timothy Hutton?
Answer: 1986

2245. Who was the composer for the 2011 film «Battle: Los Angeles»?
Answer: Brian Tyler

2246. Who was the composer for the 1989 film «Enemies,

a Love Story»?
Answer: Maurice Jarre

2247. Whom did Kate Upton marry in the year 2017?
Answer: Justin Verlander

2248. For his work in the movie «Apollo 13», who won the «Screen Actors Guild Award for Outstanding Performance by a Cast in a Motion Picture» in 1996?
Answer: Tom Hanks

2249. Which film won the Academy Award for Best Makeup and Hairstyling in the year 1992?
Answer: Terminator 2: Judgment Day

2250. Which film won the Academy Award for Best Cinematography in the year 1996?
Answer: The English Patient

2251. What is the name of the character Lupita Nyong'o plays in the movie «Black Panther»?
Answer: Nakia

2252. Whom did Britney Spears marry in the year 2004?
Answer: Jason Allen Alexander

2253. For which film did Irvin Kershner receive the «Saturn Award for Best Director» in 1981?
Answer: Star Wars Episode V: The Empire Strikes Back

2254. Who was the composer for the 2001 film «Freddy Got Fingered»?
Answer: Michael Simpson

2255. What is the full name of Carlos Girón?
Answer: Carlos Girón Longoria

2256. What's the birth name of Jeff Stryker?
Answer: Charles Casper Peyton

2257. What is the full name of Anna Malle?

Answer: Anna Hotop-Stout

2258. Who acted as Kay Adams-Corleone in the movie «The Godfather Part II»?
Answer: Diane Keaton

2259. Who was the composer for the 2018 film «Mamma Mia! Here We Go Again»?
Answer: Anne Dudley

2260. For which film did Jeremy Renner receive the «Boston Society of Film Critics Award for Best Actor» in 2009?
Answer: The Hurt Locker

2261. Which film won the Academy Award for Best Picture in the year 1970?
Answer: Midnight Cowboy

2262. Whom did Jeanne Tripplehorn marry in the year 2000?
Answer: Leland Orser

2263. Who directed the 2010 film «Gulliver's Travels»?
Answer: Rob Letterman

2264. For her work in the movie «The Wrestler», who won the «Florida Film Critics Circle Award for Best Supporting Actress» in 2008?
Answer: Marisa Tomei

2265. What is the name of the character Hugo Weaving plays in the movie «The Hobbit: The Battle of the Five Armies»?
Answer: Elrond

2266. What is the name of the character Anne Hathaway plays in the movie «The Dark Knight Rises»?
Answer: Catwoman

2267. When did Eileen Davidson marry Vincent Van Patten?

Answer: 2003

2268. What is the full name of Jack Black?
Answer: Thomas Jacob Black

2269. Who directed the 1992 film «Prelude to a Kiss»?
Answer: Norman René

2270. Where was Justin Theroux born?
Answer: Washington, D.C.

2271. For which film did Edward Norton receive the «Boston Society of Film Critics Award for Best Supporting Actor» in 1996?
Answer: Everyone Says I Love You

2272. Who acted as Jim Lovell in the movie «Apollo 13»?
Answer: Tom Hanks

2273. Who directed the 2014 film «The Imitation Game»?
Answer: Morten Tyldum

2274. Whom did Shannen Doherty marry in the year 2011?
Answer: Kurt Iswarienko

2275. What's the birth name of Michelle Rodriguez?
Answer: Mayte Michelle Rodriguez

2276. In which year did Leah Pipes marry A.J. Trauth?
Answer: 2014

2277. Whom did Demi Moore marry in the year 2005?
Answer: Ashton Kutcher

2278. Which film won the Golden Globe Award for Best Screenplay in the year 2003?
Answer: Lost in Translation

2279. Whom did Jenna Elfman marry in the year 1995?
Answer: Bodhi Elfman

2280. In which year did Margaret Colin marry Justin

Deas?
Answer: 1988

2281. What is the name of the character Gene Hackman plays in the movie «Superman II»?
Answer: Lex Luthor

2282. When did Rebecca Pidgeon marry David Mamet?
Answer: 1991

2283. Who directed the 2000 film «Little Nicky»?
Answer: Steven Brill

2284. For her work in the movie «Untamed Heart», who won the «MTV Movie Award for Best Kiss» in 1993?
Answer: Marisa Tomei

2285. For her work in the movie «The Break-Up», who won the «People's Choice Award for Favorite Female Artist» in 2007?
Answer: Jennifer Aniston

2286. For which film did Matthew McConaughey receive the «Academy Award for Best Actor» in 2014?
Answer: Dallas Buyers Club

2287. Whom did Tamar Estine Braxton marry in the year 2008?
Answer: Vincent Herbert

2288. Where was Corey Hawkins born?
Answer: Washington, D.C.

2289. Who was the composer for the 1992 film «Medicine Man»?
Answer: Jerry Goldsmith

2290. Who acted as Electro in the movie «The Amazing Spider-Man 2»?
Answer: Jamie Foxx

2291. For which film did Natalie Portman receive the «Screen Actors Guild Award for Outstanding Performance by a Female Actor in a Leading Role» in 2011?
Answer: Black Swan

2292. Who directed the 2009 film «Transformers: Revenge of the Fallen»?
Answer: Michael Bay

2293. Whom did Lisa Brenner marry in the year 2003?
Answer: Dean Devlin

2294. Who directed the 2015 film «The Hunger Games: Mockingjay – Part 2»?
Answer: Francis Lawrence

2295. Whom did Wendie Malick marry in the year 1982?
Answer: Mitch Glazer

2296. Who directed the 2004 film «The Passion of the Christ»?
Answer: Mel Gibson

2297. What is the full name of Brian J. Smith?
Answer: Brian Jacob Smith

2298. Whom did Miranda July marry in the year 2009?
Answer: Mike Mills

2299. Who directed the 2018 film «Suspiria»?
Answer: Luca Guadagnino

2300. Which film won the Golden Globe Award for Best Screenplay in the year 2013?
Answer: Her

2301. For his work in the movie «Improper Channels», who won the «Genie Award for Best Performance by a Foreign Actor» in 1982?
Answer: Alan Arkin

2302. For her work in the movie «Before Midnight», who

won the «National Society of Film Critics Award for Best Screenplay» in 2013?
Answer: Julie Delpy

2303. What is the name of the character Nicolas Cage plays in the movie «Mom and Dad»?
Answer: Brent Ryan

2304. For which film did Alan Arkin receive the «Golden Globe Award for Best Actor – Motion Picture Musical or Comedy» in 1966?
Answer: The Russians Are Coming, the Russians Are Coming

2305. What is the name of the character Halle Berry plays in the movie «X2»?
Answer: Storm

2307. What is the full name of Kimbo Slice?
Answer: Kevin Ferguson

2308. For his work in the movie «One Flew Over the Cuckoo's Nest», who won the «Academy Award for Best Actor» in 1976?
Answer: Jack Nicholson

2309. Who was the composer for the 2016 film «The Light Between Oceans»?
Answer: Alexandre Desplat

2310. Whom did Rhea Perlman marry in the year 1982?
Answer: Danny DeVito

2311. Who was the composer for the 1994 film «Star Trek: Generations»?
Answer: Dennis McCarthy

2312. For which film did Halle Berry receive the «National Board of Review Award for Best Actress» in 2001?
Answer: Monster's Ball

2313. Who was the composer for the 2018 film «Vice»?

Answer: Nicholas Britell

2314. For which film did Angelina Jolie receive the «Screen Actors Guild Award for Outstanding Performance by a Female Actor in a Supporting Role» in 2000?
Answer: Girl, Interrupted

2315. When did Holly Palance marry Roger Spottiswoode?
Answer: 1983

2316. For his work in the movie «The Ten Commandments», who won the «National Board of Review Award for Best Actor» in 1956?
Answer: Yul Brynner

2317. What is the full name of Christopher Atkins?
Answer: Christopher Atkins Bomann

2318. For his work in the movie «The Fugitive», who won the «Academy Award for Best Supporting Actor» in 1993?
Answer: Tommy Lee Jones

2319. Who directed the 1994 film «Legends of the Fall»?
Answer: Edward Zwick

2320. In which year did Julie Warner marry Jonathan Prince?
Answer: 1995

2321. Where was Gillian Anderson born?
Answer: Chicago

2322. For which film did Brad Pitt receive the «Academy Award for Best Picture» in 2014?
Answer: 12 Years a Slave

2323. In which year did Lori Loughlin marry Mossimo Giannulli?
Answer: 1997

2324. Who was the composer for the 2002 film «Confessions of a Dangerous Mind»?
Answer: Alex Wurman

2325. For his work in the movie «Mystic River», who won the «Golden Globe Award for Best Supporting Actor – Motion Picture» in 2003?
Answer: Tim Robbins

2326. Who directed the 2014 film «Joe»?
Answer: David Gordon Green

2327. Which film won the Academy Award for Best Picture in the year 1966?
Answer: The Sound of Music

2328. What's the birth name of Emily Blunt?
Answer: Emily Olivia Leah Blunt

2329. Who directed the 1997 film «One Eight Seven»?
Answer: Kevin Reynolds

2330. Who directed the 2010 film «127 Hours»?
Answer: Danny Boyle

2331. Which film won the Academy Award for Best Documentary Feature in the year 1971?
Answer: The Hellstrom Chronicle

2332. Who directed the 2016 film «Snowden»?
Answer: Oliver Stone

2333. Where did Eli Wallach get his Bachelor of Arts degree from?
Answer: University of Texas at Austin

2334. For his work in the movie «The French Connection», who won the «Golden Globe Award for Best Actor – Motion Picture Drama» in 1971?
Answer: Gene Hackman
2335. For which film did Britney Spears receive the

«Golden Raspberry Award for Worst Supporting Actress» in 2005?
Answer: Fahrenheit 9/11

2336. What is the full name of Tawny Kitaen?
Answer: Julie E. Kitaen

2337. Which film won the Academy Award for Best Picture in the year 1936?
Answer: Mutiny on the Bounty

2338. Who was the composer for the 2008 film «Choke»?
Answer: Nathan Larson

2339. For which film did Adam Sandler receive the «Golden Raspberry Award for Worst Actor» in 1999?
Answer: That's My Boy

2340. For her work in the movie «Working Girl», who won the «Golden Globe Award for Best Supporting Actress – Motion Picture» in 1988?
Answer: Sigourney Weaver

2341. What's the birth name of Joel McHale?
Answer: Joel Edward McHale

2342. Who directed the 2010 film «The Karate Kid»?
Answer: Harald Zwart

2343. Whom did Kathy Hilton marry in the year 1979?
Answer: Richard Hilton

2344. Where did Stanley Tucci get his Bachelor of Arts degree from?
Answer: State University of New York at Purchase

2345. Who was the composer for the 2018 film «First Man»?
Answer: Justin Hurwitz

2346. For her work in the movie «Wanderlust», who won the «People's Choice Award for Favorite Movie Actress» in 2013?
Answer: Jennifer Aniston

2347. For which film did Joan Allen receive the «National Society of Film Critics Award for Best Supporting Actress» in 1995?
Answer: Nixon

2348. When did Rachael Bella marry Edward Furlong?
Answer: 2006

2349. In which year did Kelly Overton marry Judson Pearce Morgan?
Answer: 2004

2350. In which year did Halle Berry marry Eric Benét?
Answer: 2001

2351. Who directed the 2011 film «Captain America: The First Avenger»?
Answer: Joe Johnston

2352. When did Marisa Ryan marry Jeremy Sisto?
Answer: 1993

2353. Who directed the 2018 film «Mom and Dad»?
Answer: Brian Taylor

2354. Whom did Christie Brinkley marry in the year 1985?
Answer: Billy Joel

2355. What is the full name of Zendaya?
Answer: Zendaya Maree Stoermer Coleman

2356. When did Jenna Dewan marry Channing Tatum?
Answer: 2009

2357. Who acted as Hank Pym in the movie «Ant-Man»?
Answer: Michael Douglas

2358. In which year did Joyce Van Patten marry Dennis Dugan?
Answer: 1973

2359. What's the birth name of Missi Pyle?
Answer: Andrea Kay Pyle

2360. Who was the composer for the 1996 film «Romeo + Juliet»?
Answer: Nellee Hooper

2361. For her work in the movie «A Beautiful Mind», who won the «BAFTA Award for Best Actress in a Supporting Role» in 2002?
Answer: Jennifer Connelly

2362. When did Lisa Blount marry Ray McKinnon?
Answer: 1998

2363. Who directed the 2018 film «Chappaquiddick»?
Answer: John Curran

2365. What is the full name of Saoirse Ronan?
Answer: Saoirse Una Ronan

2366. Who was the composer for the 1990 film «Dick Tracy»?
Answer: Danny Elfman

2367. For which film did Nicolas Cage receive the «Toronto Film Critics Association Award for Best Actor» in 2002?
Answer: Adaptation

2368. For which film did Adrien Brody receive the «National Society of Film Critics Award for Best Actor» in 2002?
Answer: The Pianist

2369. For her work in the movie «Not Easily Broken», who won the «BET Award for Best Actor & Actress» in 2009?

Answer: Taraji P. Henson

2370. Who acted as Two-Face in the movie «Batman Forever»?
Answer: Tommy Lee Jones

2371. Whom did Kelly Le Brock marry in the year 1987?
Answer: Steven Seagal

2372. Who was the composer for the 1991 film «Father of the Bride»?
Answer: Alan Silvestri

2373. Who were the directors of the 2018 film «Game Night»?
Answer: John Francis Daley and Jonathan Goldstein

2374. Who directed the 2005 film «The Great Raid»?
Answer: John Dahl

2375. When did Loni Anderson marry Burt Reynolds?
Answer: 1988

2376. What's the birth name of Michael B. Jordan?
Answer: Michael Bakari Jordan

2377. For which film did Robert Loggia receive the «Saturn Award for Best Supporting Actor» in 1990?
Answer: Big

2378. Who directed the 2018 film «Rampage»?
Answer: Brad Peyton

2379. For which film did Gregory Peck receive the «David di Donatello for Best Foreign Actor» award in 1963?
Answer: To Kill a Mockingbird

2380. In which year did Amy Wright marry Rip Torn?
Answer: 1989

2381. In which year did Stacy Carter marry Nick Cvjetkovich?

Answer: 2010

2382. When did Sarah Clarke marry Xander Berkeley?
Answer: 2002

2383. For which film did Katharine Hepburn receive the «Academy Award for Best Actress» in 1967?
Answer: Guess Who's Coming to Dinner

2384. What is the full name of Ashley Olsen?
Answer: Ashley Fuller Olsen

2385. For which film did Gene Hackman receive the «Academy Award for Best Supporting Actor» in 1992?
Answer: Unforgiven

2386. Who directed the 2011 film «Beastly»?
Answer: Daniel Barnz

2387. Which film won the Golden Globe Award for Best Motion Picture – Drama in the year 1970?
Answer: Love Story

2388. What's the birth name of Aaron Carter?
Answer: Aaron Charles Carter

2389. What is the full name of Chris Bauer?
Answer: Mark Christopher Bauer

2390. What is the name of the character Jennifer Lawrence plays in the movie «The Hunger Games: Mockingjay – Part 1»?
Answer: Katniss Everdeen

2391. What is the full name of J. J. Abrams?
Answer: Jeffrey Jacob Abrams

2392. What is the full name of Jennifer Morrison?
Answer: Jennifer Marie Morrison

2393. For his work in the movie «Everyone Says I Love You», who won the «Los Angeles Film Critics Association

Award for Best Supporting Actor» in 1996?
Answer: Edward Norton

2394. Whom did Amy Hathaway marry in the year 2001?
Answer: Derick Martini

2395. In which year did Tammy Lynn Michaels marry Melissa Etheridge?
Answer: 2003

2396. Who directed the 2017 film «Life»?
Answer: Daniel Espinosa

2397. What's the birth name of Justin Bartha?
Answer: Justin Lee Bartha

2398. In which year did Linda Hamilton marry James Cameron?
Answer: 1997

2399. What is the name of the character Tilda Swinton plays in the movie «Doctor Strange»?
Answer: The Ancient One

2400. For which film did Joel Grey receive the «Golden Globe Award for Best Supporting Actor – Motion Picture» in 1972?
Answer: Cabaret

2401. Who directed the 2007 film «Bratz»?
Answer: Sean McNamara

2402. In which year did Merle Oberon marry Robert Wolders?
Answer: 1975

2403. Whom did Ally Sheedy marry in the year 1992?
Answer: David Lansbury

2404. Whom did Katie Aselton marry in the year 2006?
Answer: Mark Duplass

2405. Where did Joan Allen get her Bachelor of Arts degree from?
Answer: Northern Illinois University

2406. What is the full name of Dane Cook?
Answer: Dane Jeffrey Cook

2407. In which year did Melissa McCarthy marry Ben Falcone?
Answer: 2005

2408. Whom did Catherine O'Hara marry in the year 1992?
Answer: Bo Welch

2409. What's the birth name of Eva Amurri?
Answer: Eva Maria Olivia Amurri

2410. In which year did Jane Seymour marry Geoffrey Planer?
Answer: 1977

2411. For her work in the movie «If Beale Street Could Talk», who won the «Academy Award for Best Supporting Actress» in 2019?
Answer: Regina King

2412. What's the birth name of Maggie Q?
Answer: Margaret Denise Quigley

2413. Where did Beulah Bondi get her master's degree from?
Answer: Valparaiso University

2414. Who was the composer for the 2018 film «The Old Man and the Gun»?
Answer: Daniel Hart

2415. Who directed the 2015 film «The Divergent Series: Insurgent»?
Answer: Robert Schwentke

2416. What's the birth name of Jessica Alba?
Answer: Jessica Marie Alba

2417. Who was the composer for the 2010 film «Middle Men»?
Answer: Brian Tyler

2418. In which year did Lorna Luft marry Jake Hooker?
Answer: 1977

2419. For his work in the movie «North by Northwest», who won the «David di Donatello for Best Foreign Actor» award in 1960?
Answer: Cary Grant

2420. What is the name of the character Nicolas Cage plays in the movie «Looking Glass»?
Answer: Ray

2421. In which year did Persia White marry Saul Williams?
Answer: 2008

2422. Who acted as Domino Vitali in the movie «Never Say Never Again»?
Answer: Kim Basinger

2423. What is the full name of Justin Chon?
Answer: Justin Jitae Chon

2424. When did Jill St. John marry Robert Wagner?
Answer: 1990

2425. Whom did Angelica Bridges marry in the year 2002?
Answer: Sheldon Souray

2426. For her work in the movie «Rachel, Rachel», who won the «Golden Globe Award for Best Actress – Motion Picture Drama» in 1968?
Answer: Joanne Woodward

2427. What is the full name of Milla Jovovich?
Answer: Milica Bogdanovna Jovovich

2428. For which film did Dennis Hopper receive the «MTV Movie Award for Best Villain» in 1995?
Answer: Speed

2429. Who acted as Phil Hammersley in the movie «Enemy of the State»?
Answer: Jason Robards

2430. What is the name of the character Colin Firth plays in the movie «Kingsman: The Golden Circle»?
Answer: Harry Hart

2431. For his work in the movie «Scent of a Woman», who won the «Golden Globe Award for Best Actor – Motion Picture Drama» in 1993?
Answer: Al Pacino

2432. Who acted as Tom Hagen in the movie «The Godfather Part II»?
Answer: Robert Duvall

2433. Whom did Roxanne Hart marry in the year 1984?
Answer: Philip Casnoff

2434. What is the full name of Justin Berfield?
Answer: Justin Tyler Berfield

2435. Who acted as Carol Danvers in the movie «Captain Marvel»?
Answer: Brie Larson

2436. What's the birth name of Mark Ruffalo?
Answer: Mark Alan Ruffalo

2437. For her work in the movie «Casino», who won the «Golden Globe Award for Best Actress – Motion Picture Drama» in 1995?
Answer: Sharon Stone

2438. Who directed the 1995 film «Father of the Bride Part II»?
Answer: Charles Shyer

2439. In which year did Lindsay Wagner marry Michael Brandon?
Answer: 1976

2440. For which film did Taraji P. Henson receive the «BET Award for Best Actor & Actress» in 2006?
Answer: Something New

2441. For which film did Nicolas Cage receive the «Academy Award for Best Actor» in 1996?
Answer: Leaving Las Vegas

2442. For her work in the movie «The Help», who won the «Satellite Award for Best Cast – Motion Picture» in 2011?
Answer: Mary Steenburgen

2443. What is the full name of Kristin Bauer van Straten?
Answer: Kristin Neubauer

2444. For which film did Edward Norton receive the «Golden Globe Award for Best Supporting Actor – Motion Picture» in 1996?
Answer: Primal Fear

2445. Who were the directors of the 2012 film «Red Tails»?
Answer: Anthony Hemingway and George Lucas

2446. Whom did Kay Lenz marry in the year 1977?
Answer: David Cassidy

2447. Who was the composer for the 2007 film «I Think I Love My Wife»?
Answer: Marcus Miller

2448. Where was Mark Harmon born?

Answer: Burbank

2449. Who directed the 2018 film «BlacKkKlansman»?
Answer: Spike Lee

2450. For which film did Sean Penn receive the «Academy Award for Best Actor» in 2008?
Answer: Milk

2451. For her work in the movie «Broadcast News», who won the «New York Film Critics Circle Award for Best Actress» in 1987?
Answer: Holly Hunter

2452. In which year did Marguerite MacIntyre marry Marcos Siega?
Answer: 1990

2453. Which film won the Academy Award for Best Picture in the year 1977?
Answer: Rocky

2454. When did Talia Balsam marry George Clooney?
Answer: 1989

2455. Who directed the 1997 film «Air Force One»?
Answer: Wolfgang Petersen

2456. What's the birth name of Bumper Robinson?
Answer: Larry Clarence Robinson II

2457. What is the name of the character Benicio del Toro plays in the movie «Thor: The Dark World»?
Answer: Collector (comics)

2458. For which film did Diane Keaton receive the «New York Film Critics Circle Award for Best Actress» in 1977?
Answer: Annie Hall

2459. Who was the composer for the 2009 film «Star Trek»?

Answer: Michael Giacchino

2460. What is the full name of Saul Williams?
Answer: Saul Stacey Williams

2461. Who directed the 2002 film «Star Trek: Nemesis»?
Answer: Stuart Baird

2462. Whom did Soleil Moon Frye marry in the year 1998?
Answer: Jason Goldberg

2463. For which film did Halle Berry receive the «BET Award for Best Actor & Actress» in 2004?
Answer: X2

2464. What is the name of the character Anthony Hopkins plays in the movie «Alexander»?
Answer: Ptolemy I Soter

2465. For which film did Joel Grey receive the «National Society of Film Critics Award for Best Supporting Actor» in 1972?
Answer: Cabaret

2466. Whom did Natalie Portman marry in the year 2012?
Answer: Benjamin Millepied

2467. Whom did Chyler Leigh marry in the year 2002?
Answer: Nathan West

2468. What's the birth name of Nikki Tyler?
Answer: Nicole Madison

2469. For his work in the movie «The Social Network», who won the «Golden Globe Award for Best Screenplay» in 2010?
Answer: Aaron Sorkin

2470. Who directed the 1993 film «The Vanishing»?
Answer: George Sluizer

2471. Whom did Anna Camp marry in the year 2010?
Answer: Michael Mosley

2472. What's the birth name of Thomas Kuc?
Answer: Thomas Nicholas Kuc

2473. Which film won the Academy Award for Best Writing, Adapted Screenplay in the year 1973?
Answer: The Exorcist

2474. What is the full name of Bo Burnham?
Answer: Robert Pickering Burnham

2475. Who was the composer for the 1999 film «Dudley Do-Right»?
Answer: Steve Dorff

2476. What is the name of the character Gwyneth Paltrow plays in the movie «Avengers: Infinity War»?
Answer: Pepper Potts

2477. Whom did Kate Capshaw marry in the year 1991?
Answer: Steven Spielberg

2478. What's the birth name of David Conrad?
Answer: David Crawford Conrad

2479. For his work in the movie «The Cove», who won the «Academy Award for Best Documentary Feature» in 2009?
Answer: Fisher Stevens

2480. For his work in the movie «The Hurt Locker», who won the «Chicago Film Critics Association Award for Best Actor» in 2009?
Answer: Jeremy Renner

2481. Who was the composer for the 2017 film «Only the Brave»?
Answer: Joseph Trapanese

2482. For his work in the movie «Police Story 3: Super Cop», who won the «Golden Horse Award for Best Leading Actor» in 1992?
Answer: Jackie Chan

2483. Which film won the Academy Award for Best Documentary Feature in the year 1980?
Answer: From Mao to Mozart: Isaac Stern in China

2484. For which film did Miloš Forman receive the «Golden Bear» award in 1997?
Answer: The People vs. Larry Flynt

2485. Where did Alison Brie get her bachelor's degree from?
Answer: California Institute of the Arts, in Santa Clarita

2486. What is the full name of Chris Pine?
Answer: Christopher Whitelaw Pine

2487. Who directed the 2017 film «Blade Runner 2049»?
Answer: Denis Villeneuve

2488. Whom did Molly Ringwald marry in the year 2007?
Answer: Panio Gianopoulos

2489. What is the full name of Emma Roberts?
Answer: Emma Rose Roberts

2490. For her work in the movie «The Three Faces of Eve», who won the «National Board of Review Award for Best Actress» in 1957?
Answer: Joanne Woodward

2491. What is the full name of Alexis Bledel?
Answer: Kimberly Alexis Bledel

2492. Which film won the Academy Award for Best Picture in the year 1984?
Answer: Terms of Endearment

2493. Who was the composer for the 2004 film «Alexander»?
Answer: Vangelis

2494. What is the full name of Angus T. Jones?
Answer: Angus Turner Jones

2495. For which film did Jennifer Connelly receive the «Golden Globe Award for Best Supporting Actress – Motion Picture» in 2002?
Answer: A Beautiful Mind

2496. Which film won the Academy Award for Best Film Editing in the year 1996?
Answer: The English Patient

2497. Where did Katherine Dunham get her Doctor of Philosophy degree from?
Answer: University of Chicago

2498. What's the birth name of Billy Ray Cyrus?
Answer: William Ray Cyrus

2499. Where did Andrea Anders get her Master of Fine Arts degree from?
Answer: Rutgers University, in New Jersey

2500. What's the birth name of Nicki Minaj?
Answer: Onika Tanya Maraj

2501. Which film won the Academy Award for Best Picture in the year 1956?
Answer: Marty

2502. For which film did Dakota Fanning receive the «MTV Movie Award for Best Scared-As-St Performance» in 2005?**
Answer: Hide and Seek

2503. What is the full name of Ike Barinholtz?
Answer: Isaac Barinholtz

2504. Whom did Julia Campbell marry in the year 1988?
Answer: Bernard White

2505. Who acted as Storm in the movie «X-Men: The Last Stand»?
Answer: Halle Berry

2506. Who acted as Leo Getz in the movie «Lethal Weapon 2»?
Answer: Joe Pesci

2507. What's the birth name of Michael Jai White?
Answer: Michael Richard Jai White

2508. Which film won the Academy Award for Best Picture in the year 1948?
Answer: Gentleman's Agreement

2509. Who directed the 2017 film «Tomboy, a Revenger's Tale»?
Answer: Walter Hill

2510. What is the full name of Nichole Bloom?
Answer: Nichole Sakura O'Connor

2511. Who acted as Ethan Hunt in the movie «Mission: Impossible II»?
Answer: Tom Cruise

2512. Which film won the Academy Award for Best Costume Design in the year 1996?
Answer: The English Patient

2513. Whom did Nikki Ziering marry in the year 1997?
Answer: Ian Ziering

2514. For which film did Sally Field receive the «Academy Award for Best Actress» in 1984?
Answer: Places in the Heart

2515. Who directed the 2016 film «Hidden Figures»?
Answer: Theodore Melfi

2516. When did Dianna Agron marry Winston Marshall?
Answer: 2016

2517. Who directed the 2008 film «Australia»?
Answer: Baz Luhrmann

2518. Which film won the Academy Award for Best Picture in the year 1963?
Answer: Lawrence of Arabia

2519. Who was the composer for the 2019 film «Shaft»?
Answer: Christopher Lennertz

2520. Who was the composer for the 1999 film «Instinct»?
Answer: Danny Elfman

2521. Which film won the Academy Award for Best Picture in the year 1934?
Answer: Cavalcade

2522. Which film won the Academy Award for Best Picture in the year 1986?
Answer: Out of Africa

2523. Who was the composer for the 1993 film «Teenage Mutant Ninja Turtles III»?
Answer: John Du Prez

2524. What is the full name of Julianna Margulies?
Answer: Julianna Luisa Margulies

2525. Who directed the 2017 film «A Cure for Wellness»?
Answer: Gore Verbinski

2526. When did Gwyneth Paltrow marry Chris Martin?
Answer: 2003

2527. Whom did Courtney Love marry in the year 1992?
Answer: Kurt Cobain

2528. Who acted as President of the United States in the movie «Deep Impact»?
Answer: Morgan Freeman

2529. Who was the composer for the 2009 film «The Road»?
Answer: Nick Cave

2530. Whom did Hilary Duff marry in the year 2010?
Answer: Mike Comrie

2531. When did Kristen Schaal marry Rich Blomquist?
Answer: 2012

2532. Who directed the 2018 film «Looking Glass»?
Answer: Tim Hunter

2533. Whom did Gretchen Egolf marry in the year 2013?
Answer: Adam Chodzko

2534. For her work in the movie «Romeo + Juliet», who won the «London Film Critics Circle Award for Actress of the Year» in 1996?
Answer: Claire Danes

2535. Whom did Heather Langenkamp marry in the year 1984?
Answer: Alan Pasqua

2536. Who was the composer for the 2018 film «Boy Erased»?
Answer: Jonny Greenwood

2537. What's the birth name of Rachael Harris?
Answer: Rachael Elaine Harris

2538. For which film did Michael Moore receive the «César Award for Best Foreign Film» in 2003?
Answer: Bowling for Columbine

2539. What's the birth name of Bradley Cooper?

Answer: Bradley Charles Cooper

2540. For which film did Leonardo DiCaprio receive the «Golden Globe Award for Best Actor – Motion Picture Drama» in 2005?
Answer: The Aviator

2541. What's the birth name of Amanda Bynes?
Answer: Amanda Laura Bynes

2542. In which year did Meredith Baxter marry Michael Blodgett?
Answer: 1995

2543. What is the name of the character Tommy Lee Jones plays in the movie «JFK»?
Answer: Clay Shaw

2544. What's the birth name of Beyoncé?
Answer: Beyoncé Giselle Knowles

2545. Whom did Josie Bissett marry in the year 1992?
Answer: Rob Estes

2546. In which year did Kylie Ireland marry Eli Cross?
Answer: 2002

2547. In which year did Ellen DeGeneres marry Portia de Rossi?
Answer: 2008

2548. When did Jada Pinkett Smith marry Will Smith?
Answer: 1997

2549. Whom did Mila Kunis marry in the year 2015?
Answer: Ashton Kutcher

2550. When did Stacey Dash marry Brian Lovell?
Answer: 1999

2551. When did Rita Wilson marry Tom Hanks?
Answer: 1988

2552. Who directed the 2017 film «Dragonheart: Battle for the Heartfire»?
Answer: Patrik Syversen

2553. Whom did Tracey Ullman marry in the year 1983?
Answer: Allan McKeown

2554. Who was the composer for the 1993 film «Loaded Weapon 1»?
Answer: Robert Folk

2555. What is the full name of Poppy Montgomery?
Answer: Poppy Petal Emma Elizabeth Devereaux Donahue

2556. Where was Shaquille O'Neal born?
Answer: Newark

2557. For which film did Lee Marvin receive the «British Academy of Film and Television Arts» award in 1965?
Answer: Cat Ballou

2558. When did Susanna Hoffs marry Jay Roach?
Answer: 1993
2559. For his work in the movie «Blue Velvet», who won the «National Society of Film Critics Award for Best Supporting Actor» in 1986?
Answer: Dennis Hopper

2560. When did Yvette Mimieux marry Stanley Donen?
Answer: 1972

2561. What is the name of the character Richard Dreyfuss plays in the movie «Jaws»?
Answer: Matt Hooper

2562. For which film did Debbi Morgan receive the «Independent Spirit Award for Best Supporting Female» in 1998?
Answer: Eve's Bayou

2563. Whom did Jayma Mays marry in the year 2007?
Answer: Adam Campbell

2564. In which year did Jamie-Lynn Sigler marry A. J. DiScala?
Answer: 2003

2565. Who directed the 1990 film «Predator 2»?
Answer: Stephen Hopkins

2566. For which film did Jane Fonda receive the «Academy Award for Best Actress» in 1971?
Answer: Klute

2567. What is the full name of Keke Palmer?
Answer: Lauren Keyana Palmer

2568. What's the birth name of Aaron Sorkin?
Answer: Aaron Benjamin Sorkin

2569. For his work in the movie «Cabaret», who won the «BAFTA Award for Most Promising Newcomer to Leading Film Roles» in 1973?
Answer: Joel Grey

2570. In which year did Noureen DeWulf marry Ryan Miller?
Answer: 2011

2571. Where did Patton Oswalt get his Bachelor of Arts degree from?
Answer: College of William & Mary, in Williamsburg

2572. Whom did Jill Kelly marry in the year 1993?
Answer: Cal Jammer

2573. Whom did Virginia Madsen marry in the year 1989?
Answer: Danny Huston

2574. What is the full name of Abigail Spencer?
Answer: Abigail Leigh Spencer

2575. Who was the composer for the 2006 film «X-Men: The Last Stand»?
Answer: John Powell

2576. Which film won the Academy Award for Best Picture in the year 1950?
Answer: All the King's Men

2577. What's the birth name of Jonah Hill?
Answer: Jonah Hill Feldstein

2578. What is the full name of Huckleberry Fox?
Answer: George Miller Fox

2579. Who directed the 2002 film «The Land Before Time IX: Journey to Big Water»?
Answer: Charles Grosvenor

2580. When did Farrah Fawcett marry Lee Majors?
Answer: 1973

2581. When did Grace Hightower marry Robert De Niro?
Answer: 1997

2582. For which film did Kristen Stewart receive the «MTV Movie Award for Best Kiss» in 2010?
Answer: The Twilight Saga: New Moon

2583. What is the name of the character Javier Bardem plays in the movie «Skyfall»?
Answer: Raoul Silva

2584. Who was the composer for the 2011 film «The Ides of March»?
Answer: Alexandre Desplat

2585. For her work in the movie «The Piano», who won the «Golden Globe Award for Best Actress – Motion Picture Drama» in 1993?
Answer: Holly Hunter

2586. For which film did Dustin Hoffman receive the «Academy Award for Best Actor» in 1979?
Answer: Kramer vs. Kramer

2587. Whom did Madeleine Stowe marry in the year 1982?
Answer: Brian Benben

2588. Who directed the 2019 film «It: Chapter Two»?
Answer: Andrés Muschietti

2589. For which film did Fredric March receive the «Academy Award for Best Actor» in 1946?
Answer: The Best Years of Our Lives

2590. For which film did Ali Larter receive the «MTV Movie Award for Best Fight» in 2010?
Answer: Obsessed

2591. Where did Kelly Stables get her bachelor's degree from?
Answer: University of Missouri

2592. Where did Betty Gabriel get her Bachelor of Science degree from?
Answer: Iowa State University, in Ames

2593. What is the full name of Katherine Waterston?
Answer: Katherine Boyer Waterston

2594. When did Milla Jovovich marry Paul W. S. Anderson?
Answer: 2009

2595. In which year did Judith Malina marry Hanon Reznikov?
Answer: 1988

2596. Who was the composer for the 1999 film «Blast from the Past»?
Answer: Steve Dorff

2597. Who directed the 2002 film «Spider-Man»?

Answer: Sam Raimi

2598. What is the full name of Jer Adrianne Lelliott?
Answer: Jeremy Lelliott

2599. When did Charlotte Ross marry Michael Goldman?
Answer: 2003

2600. Who directed the 2016 film «Passengers»?
Answer: Morten Tyldum

2601. Whom did Mandy Moore marry in the year 2009?
Answer: Ryan Adams

2602. For which film did Kristen Stewart receive the «MTV Movie Award for Best Female Performance» in 2010?
Answer: The Twilight Saga: New Moon

2603. What is the full name of Jace Norman?
Answer: Jace Lee Norman

2604. Who was the composer for the 2013 film «The Wolverine»?
Answer: Marco Beltrami

2605. Who directed the 2016 film «Moonlight»?
Answer: Barry Jenkins

2606. Whom did Mia Sara marry in the year 2010?
Answer: Brian Henson

2607. Who directed the 1989 film «Turner & Hooch»?
Answer: Roger Spottiswoode

2608. When did Cecilia Hart marry James Earl Jones?
Answer: 1982

2609. Who directed the 2005 film «Blast»?
Answer: Anthony Hickox

2610. Which film won the Academy Award for Best Picture

in the year 2000?

Answer: American Beauty

2611. Whom did Elizabeth Avellán marry in the year 1990?

Answer: Robert Rodriguez

2612. What's the birth name of Catherine Bell?

Answer: Catherine Lisa Bell

2613. In which year did Marcia Gay Harden marry Thaddaeus Scheel?

Answer: 1996

2614. Who was the composer for the 1986 film «Top Gun»?

Answer: Harold Faltermeyer

2615. What is the name of the character Anthony Hopkins plays in the movie «Thor: Ragnarok»?

Answer: Odin

2616. Whom did Maryse Ouellet marry in the year 2014?

Answer: The Miz

2617. Who was the composer for the 1989 film «The War of the Roses»?

Answer: David Newman

2618. What is the full name of Wiz Khalifa?

Answer: Cameron Jibril Thomaz

2619. Who was the composer for the 2018 film «Mortal Engines»?

Answer: Atli Örvarsson

2620. Who directed the 2007 film «The Man from Earth»?

Answer: Richard Schenkman

2621. What is the name of the character Hugo Weaving plays in the movie «Captain America: The First Avenger»?

Answer: Red Skull

2622. Who was the composer for the 2015 film «Room»?

Answer: Stephen Rennicks

2624. In which year did Jane Seymour marry Michael Attenborough?
Answer: 1971

2625. For her work in the movie «The Graduate», who won the «Golden Globe Award for Best Actress – Motion Picture Musical or Comedy» in 1967?
Answer: Anne Bancroft

2626. In which year did Cindy Crawford marry Richard Gere?
Answer: 1991

2627. What's the birth name of Randy Couture?
Answer: Randy Duane Couture

2628. Who acted as Alfred Pennyworth in the movie «Batman v Superman: Dawn of Justice»?
Answer: Jeremy Irons

2629. What is the full name of Nicole Scherzinger?
Answer: Nicole Prascovia Elikolani Valiente

2630. When did Natalie Zea marry Travis Schuldt?
Answer: 2014

2631. What is the full name of William Bibbiani?
Answer: William Brewster Bibbiani

2632. Whom did Jane Seymour marry in the year 1993?
Answer: James Keach

2633. Where was Katherine Dunham born?
Answer: Glen Ellyn

2634. Which film won the Academy Award for Best Documentary Feature in the year 2004?
Answer: Born into Brothels

2635. Who was the composer for the 2005 film

«Flightplan»?
Answer: James Horner

2636. For her work in the movie «The Hunger Games», who won the «Saturn Award for Best Actress» in 2013?
Answer: Jennifer Lawrence

2637. Who was the composer for the 2017 film «Dunkirk»?
Answer: Hans Zimmer

2638. Whom did Kelly Preston marry in the year 1985?
Answer: Kevin Gage

2639. Who directed the 2008 film «Cloverfield»?
Answer: Matt Reeves

2640. Who acted as Odin in the movie «Thor: Ragnarok»?
Answer: Anthony Hopkins

2641. Where was Shaquille O'Neal born?
Answer: Newark

2642. Who was the composer for the 2007 film «Live Free or Die Hard»?
Answer: Marco Beltrami

2643. For which film did Vince Vaughn receive the «MTV Movie Award for Best On-Screen Duo» in 2006?
Answer: Wedding Crashers

2644. What is the full name of Nicole Anderson?
Answer: Nicole Gale Anderson

2645. Who directed the 2006 film «The Guardian»?
Answer: Andrew Davis

2646. What's the birth name of Shane West?
Answer: Shannon Bruce Snaith

2647. Who directed the 2015 film «Spectre»?
Answer: Sam Mendes

2648. What is the name of the character Nicolas Cage plays in the movie «Outcast»?
Answer: Gallain

2649. For which film did Fred Astaire receive the «BAFTA Award for Best Actor in a Supporting Role» in 1976?
Answer: The Towering Inferno

2650. What is the full name of Dr. Dre?
Answer: Andre Romelle Young

2651. What is the full name of Miranda Cosgrove?
Answer: Miranda Taylor Cosgrove

2652. Who was the composer for the 1986 film «Aliens»?
Answer: James Horner

2653. Who directed the 1995 film «Fair Game»?
Answer: Andrew Sipes

2654. For which film did Jennifer Lawrence receive the «Central Ohio Film Critics Association Award for Best Actress» in 2012?
Answer: Silver Linings Playbook

2655. Which film won the Academy Award for Best Costume Design in the year 1965?
Answer: Doctor Zhivago

2656. Whom did Dorothy Malone marry in the year 1971?
Answer: Charles Huston Bell

2657. Which film won the Academy Award for Best Picture in the year 1929?
Answer: Wings

2658. Whom did Loretta Swit marry in the year 1983?
Answer: Dennis Holahan

2659. For which film did Ron Howard receive the «Directors Guild of America Award for Outstanding

Directing – Feature Film» in 2001?
Answer: A Beautiful Mind

2660. Who directed the 2015 film «Avengers: Age of Ultron»?
Answer: Joss Whedon

2661. Who directed the 2005 film «Hotel Rwanda»?
Answer: Terry George

2662. What's the birth name of Ever Carradine?
Answer: Ever Dawn Carradine

2663. Who directed the 1991 film «Twenty-One»?
Answer: Don Boyd

2664. For which film did Mary Pickford receive the «Academy Award for Best Actress» in 1929?
Answer: Coquette

2665. Whom did Gretchen Mol marry in the year 2004?
Answer: Kip Williams

2666. For which film did Jeremy Renner receive the «Online Film Critics Society Award for Best Actor» in 2010?
Answer: The Hurt Locker

2667. Who was the composer for the 1996 film «Tremors 2: Aftershocks»?
Answer: Jay Ferguson

2668. In which year did Patricia Arquette marry Thomas Jane?
Answer: 2006

2669. Whom did Sutton Foster marry in the year 2014?
Answer: Ted Griffin

2670. For his work in the movie «The Last Picture Show», who won the «Academy Award for Best Supporting Actor»

in 1971?
Answer: Ben Johnson

2671. Whom did Elizabeth Daily marry in the year 1995?
Answer: Rick Salomon

2672. Whom did Stacey Nelkin marry in the year 1987?
Answer: Barry Bostwick

2673. What is the full name of Larry the Cable Guy?
Answer: Daniel Lawrence Whitney

2674. For his work in the movie «Leaving Las Vegas», who won the «New York Film Critics Circle Award for Best Actor» in 1995?
Answer: Nicolas Cage

2675. What's the birth name of Terrence Howard?
Answer: Terrence Dashon Howard

2676. Which film won the Academy Award for Best Picture in the year 1931?
Answer: Cimarron

2677. For which film did Brad Pitt receive the «Broadcast Film Critics Association Award for Best Cast» in 2009?
Answer: Inglourious Basterds

2678. What is the name of the character Gwyneth Paltrow plays in the movie «The Avengers»?
Answer: Pepper Potts

2679. Whom did Meagan Good marry in the year 2012?
Answer: DeVon Franklin

2680. What is the name of the character Hugo Weaving plays in the movie «The Matrix Revolutions»?
Answer: Agent Smith

2681. What is the full name of Mariska Hargitay?
Answer: Mariska Magdolna Hargitay

2682. Who acted as Alma Coin in the movie «The Hunger Games: Mockingjay – Part 1»?
Answer: Julianne Moore

2683. Whom did Tori Spelling marry in the year 2004?
Answer: Charlie Shanian

2684. What's the birth name of Jon Glaser?
Answer: Jonathan Daniel Glaser

2685. Who was the composer for the 1998 film «Bulworth»?
Answer: Ennio Morricone

2686. For which film did Stanley Tucci receive the «Primetime Emmy Award for Outstanding Lead Actor in a Miniseries or a Movie» in 1999?
Answer: Winchell

2687. For his work in the movie «Schindler's List», who won the «BAFTA Award for Best Film» in 1993?
Answer: Steven Spielberg

2688. Whom did Christina Moore marry in the year 2008?
Answer: John Ducey

2689. What is the full name of Jason Bateman?
Answer: Jason Kent Bateman

2691. Who was the composer for the 1996 film «Evita»?
Answer: Andrew Lloyd Webber

2692. Who directed the 1990 film «Dances with Wolves»?
Answer: Kevin Costner

2693. Who directed the 2001 film «Joe Dirt»?
Answer: Dennie Gordon

2694. Who was the composer for the 1989 film «Blaze»?
Answer: Bennie Wallace

2695. When did Jewel De'Nyle marry Michael Stefano?
Answer: 2002

2696. Who directed the 2017 film «Kingsman: The Golden Circle»?
Answer: Matthew Vaughn

2697. When did Natasha Gregson Wagner marry Barry Watson?
Answer: 2015

2698. Who directed the 2017 film «Blood Will Have Blood»?
Answer: Jesse Keller

2699. When did Shirley Jones marry Marty Ingels?
Answer: 1977

2700. For his work in the movie «It Happened One Night», who won the «Academy Award for Best Actor» in 1934?
Answer: Clark Gable

2701. For which film did Emma Stone receive the «Golden Globe Award» in 2017?
Answer: La La Land

2702. Who directed the 2009 film «Star Trek»?
Answer: J. J. Abrams

2703. Who directed the 2017 film «mother!»?
Answer: Darren Aronofsky

2704. Whom did Meg Gibson marry in the year 2007?
Answer: Keith Reddin

2705. Who was the composer for the 2015 film «Heart of a Dog»?
Answer: Laurie Anderson

2706. For her work in the movie «Clouds of Sils Maria», who won the «César Award for Best Supporting Actress»

in 2015?
Answer: Kristen Stewart

2707. When did Kerry Washington marry Nnamdi Asomugha?
Answer: 2013

2708. What is the full name of André 3000?
Answer: André Lauren Benjamin

2709. When did Elizabeth Berkley marry Greg Lauren?
Answer: 2003

2710. For which film did Melanie Griffith receive the «Golden Globe Award for Best Actress – Motion Picture Musical or Comedy» in 1988?
Answer: Working Girl

2711. Who directed the 1995 film «Die Hard with a Vengeance»?
Answer: John McTiernan

2712. Where did Billy Crystal get his Bachelor of Fine Arts degree from?
Answer: New York University Tisch School of the Arts, in New York City

2713. Who was the composer for the 2004 film «Hotel Rwanda»?
Answer: Andrea Guerra

2714. Whom did Kaitlin Riley marry in the year 2012?
Answer: Jordi Vilasuso

2715. What is the name of the character Anthony Hopkins plays in the movie «Thor»?
Answer: Odin

2716. What is the name of the character Rami Malek plays in the movie «Bohemian Rhapsody»?
Answer: Freddie Mercury

2717. Whom did Julie Condra marry in the year 1998?
Answer: Mark Dacascos

2718. Whom did Joanna Going marry in the year 2004?
Answer: Dylan Walsh

2719. Who was the composer for the 2008 film «Punisher: War Zone»?
Answer: Christopher Franke

2720. What is the full name of Mischa Barton?
Answer: Mischa Anne Marsden Barton

2721. For which film did Taraji P. Henson receive the «BET Award for Best Actor & Actress» in 2009?
Answer: The Curious Case of Benjamin Button

2722. Who acted as Jean Paul Getty in the movie «All the Money in the World»?
Answer: Christopher Plummer

2723. In which year did Mary-Kate Olsen marry Olivier Sarkozy?
Answer: 2014

2724. In which year did Drew Barrymore marry Tom Green?
Answer: 2001

2725. Whom did Olivia Wilde marry in the year 2003?
Answer: Tao Ruspoli

2726. Who acted as Uncle Ben in the movie «Spider-Man»?
Answer: Cliff Robertson

2727. What is the full name of Selena Gomez?
Answer: Selena Marie Gomez

2728. Who was the composer for the 1987 film «Beverly Hills Cop II»?

Answer: Harold Faltermeyer

2729. Who directed the 1987 film «Three Men and a Baby»?
Answer: Leonard Nimoy

2730. For his work in the movie «The Departed», who won the «Academy Award for Best Director» in 2006?
Answer: Martin Scorsese

2731. Who acted as Jane Foster in the movie «Thor: The Dark World»?
Answer: Natalie Portman

2732. In which year did Julianne Hough marry Brooks Laich?
Answer: 2017

2733. Which film won the Academy Award for Best Picture in the year 2013?
Answer: Argo

2734. Who directed the 2010 film «Middle Men»?
Answer: George Gallo

2735. What is the full name of Anna Malle?
Answer: Anna Hotop-Stout

2736. Who directed the 2019 film «An Acceptable Loss»?
Answer: Joe Chappelle

2737. For which film did Regina King receive the «BET Award for Best Actor & Actress» in 2005?
Answer: Miss Congeniality 2: Armed and Fabulous

2738. Who was the composer for the 1990 film «Kindergarten Cop»?
Answer: Randy Edelman

2739. When did Debra Messing marry Daniel Zelman?
Answer: 2000

2740. What's the birth name of Max Carver?
Answer: Robert Maxwell Martensen

2741. For which film did Thomas Haden Church receive the «National Society of Film Critics Award for Best Supporting Actor» in 2004?
Answer: Sideways

2742. For which film did Al Pacino receive the «Academy Award for Best Actor» in 1993?
Answer: Scent of a Woman

2743. Whom did Megan Mullally marry in the year 2003?
Answer: Nick Offerman

2744. Who was the composer for the 2013 film «Iron Man 3»?
Answer: Brian Tyler

2745. Where was Bill Wallace born?
Answer: Portland

2746. Who was the composer for the 2011 film «The Descendants»?
Answer: Craig Armstrong

2747. For her work in the movie «The Twilight Saga: Breaking Dawn – Part 2», who won the «Golden Raspberry Award for Worst Actress» in 2012?
Answer: Kristen Stewart

2748. Who was the composer for the 2017 film «Tomboy, a Revenger's Tale»?
Answer: Ry Cooder

2749. Whom did Kimberly Williams-Paisley marry in the year 2003?
Answer: Brad Paisley

2750. Who directed the 1997 film «Batman & Robin»?

Answer: Joel Schumacher

2751. Who was the composer for the 2004 film «The Village»?
Answer: James Newton Howard

2752. What's the birth name of Ben Platt?
Answer: Benjamin Schiff Platt

2753. For his work in the movie «Double Team», who won the «Golden Raspberry Award for Worst Supporting Actor» in 1997?
Answer: Dennis Rodman

2754. For her work in the movie «The Great Ziegfeld», who won the «Academy Award for Best Actress» in 1936?
Answer: Luise Rainer

2755. When did Penny Marshall marry Rob Reiner?
Answer: 1971

2756. What's the birth name of Martin Lawrence?
Answer: Martin Fitzgerald Lawrence

2757. Who were the directors of the 2015 film «Vacation»?
Answer: Jonathan Goldstein and John Francis Daley

2758. Whom did Sandra Bullock marry in the year 2005?
Answer: Jesse James

2759. What is the full name of Elisabeth Moss?
Answer: Elisabeth Singleton Moss

2760. Who was the composer for the 1999 film «The Matrix»?
Answer: Don Davis

2761. For which film did Anton Yelchin receive the «Young Artist Award for Best Leading Young Actor in a Feature Film» in 2002?
Answer: Hearts in Atlantis

2762. Whom did Elizabeth Franz marry in the year 1984?
Answer: Edward Binns

2763. Which film won the Golden Globe Award for Best Motion Picture – Drama in the year 1986?
Answer: Platoon

2764. Who was the composer for the 1990 film «Three Men and a Little Lady»?
Answer: James Newton Howard

2765. In which year did Laura Dern marry Ben Harper?
Answer: 2005

2766. Which film won the Academy Award for Best Film Editing in the year 1940?
Answer: Gone with the Wind

2767. When did Johanna Braddy marry Freddie Stroma?
Answer: 2016

2768. Whom did Alexa Vega marry in the year 2008?
Answer: Sean Covel

2769. When did Ashlee Simpson marry Pete Wentz?
Answer: 2008

2770. Where did Dwayne Johnson get his Bachelor of General Studies degree from?
Answer: University of Miami, in Coral Gables

2771. Who directed the 2014 film «Love, Rosie»?
Answer: Christian Ditter

2772. Who directed the 2018 film «Ocean's 8»?
Answer: Gary Ross

2773. What is the name of the character Benicio del Toro plays in the movie «Avengers: Infinity War»?
Answer: Collector (comics)

2774. What's the birth name of Kim Kardashian?
Answer: Kimberly Noel Kardashian

2775. For which film did Jonathan Demme receive the «Academy Award for Best Director» in 1991?
Answer: The Silence of the Lambs

2776. Whom did Amber Valletta marry in the year 2003?
Answer: Chip McCaw

2777. Which film won the Academy Award for Best Picture in the year 2016?
Answer: Spotlight

2778. Where was "Weird Al" Yankovic born?
Answer: Downey

2779. When did Lorna Raver marry Yuri Rasovsky?
Answer: 1987

2780. For which film did Nicolas Cage receive the «Los Angeles Film Critics Association Award for Best Actor» in 1995?
Answer: Leaving Las Vegas

2781. For his work in the movie «Wonder Boys», who won the «Satellite Award for Best Actor in a Musical or Comedy» in 2001?
Answer: Michael Douglas
2782. Where was Woody Harrelson born?
Answer: Midland

2783. For his work in the movie «The More the Merrier», who won the «Academy Award for Best Supporting Actor» in 1943?
Answer: Charles Coburn

2784. When did Jill Eikenberry marry Michael Tucker?
Answer: 1973

2785. Whom did Jane Fonda marry in the year 1973?

Answer: Tom Hayden

2786. Who directed the 2017 film «Alien: Covenant»?
Answer: Ridley Scott

2787. For her work in the movie «Five Easy Pieces», who won the «National Society of Film Critics Award for Best Supporting Actress» in 1970?
Answer: Lois Smith

2788. What's the birth name of Michelle Williams?
Answer: Michelle Ingrid Williams

2789. Whom did Robin Mattson marry in the year 2006?
Answer: Werner Roth

2790. When did Shelley Hack marry Harry Winer?
Answer: 1990

2791. For which film did Heather Graham receive the «MTV Movie Award for Best Breakthrough Performance» in 1998?
Answer: Boogie Nights

2792. Where was Robert David Hall born?
Answer: East Orange

2793. For which film did Kim Kardashian receive the «Golden Raspberry Award for Worst Supporting Actress» in 2013?
Answer: Temptation: Confessions of a Marriage Counselor

2794. What's the birth name of Mackenzie Foy?
Answer: Mackenzie Christine Foy

2795. When did Madolyn Smith Osborne marry Mark Osborne?
Answer: 1988

2796. Who directed the 1988 film «Big»?
Answer: Penny Marshall

2797. Whom did Suzanne Pleshette marry in the year 2001?
Answer: Tom Poston

2798. What's the birth name of Norah Jones?
Answer: Geethali Norah Jones Shankar

2799. Who was the composer for the 1992 film «The Bodyguard»?
Answer: Alan Silvestri

2800. What's the birth name of Tatyana Ali?
Answer: Tatyana Marisol Ali

2801. When did Kristin Cavallari marry Jay Cutler?
Answer: 2013

2802. In which year did Geena Davis marry Jeff Goldblum?
Answer: 1987

2803. For his work in the movie «Primal Fear», who won the «Los Angeles Film Critics Association Award for Best Supporting Actor» in 1996?
Answer: Edward Norton

2804. Who was the composer for the 1996 film «Independence Day»?
Answer: David Arnold

2805. For her work in the movie «The Deep Blue Sea», who won the «New York Film Critics Circle Award for Best Actress» in 2012?
Answer: Rachel Weisz

2806. Where did Wood Harris get his Bachelor of Arts degree from?
Answer: Northern Illinois University

2807. Who directed the 2018 film «The Front Runner»?
Answer: Jason Reitman

2808. What is the full name of Emma Stone?
Answer: Emily Jean Stone

2809. For his work in the movie «Minority Report», who won the «Saturn Award for Best Director» in 2003?
Answer: Steven Spielberg

2810. When did Kate Hudson marry Chris Robinson?
Answer: 2000

2811. What is the full name of Lily-Rose Depp?
Answer: Lily-Rose Melody Depp

2812. What's the birth name of Miracle Davis?
Answer: Miracle Nicole Davis

2813. Whom did Amy Brenneman marry in the year 1995?
Answer: Brad Silberling

2814. Who directed the 1997 film «A Simple Wish»?
Answer: Michael Ritchie

2815. What's the birth name of Jake Gyllenhaal?
Answer: Jacob Benjamin Gyllenhaal

2816. What is the full name of Lynn LeMay?
Answer: Laurie Lynn Emery

2817. For which film did Jessica Lange receive the «Academy Award for Best Supporting Actress» in 1982?
Answer: Tootsie

2818. Who was the composer for the 1990 film «Rocky V»?
Answer: Bill Conti

2819. What's the birth name of Anthony Mackie?
Answer: Anthony Dwane Mackie

2820. For which film did Jennifer Lawrence receive the «Premio Marcello Mastroianni» award in 2008?

Answer: The Burning Plain

2821. For which film did Martin Scorsese receive the «Palme d'Or» award in 1976?
Answer: Taxi Driver

2822. When did Kaley Cuoco marry Ryan Sweeting?
Answer: 2013

2823. What's the birth name of Ryan Hansen?
Answer: Ryan Albert Hansen

2824. Whom did Solange Knowles marry in the year 2014?
Answer: Alan Ferguson

2825. Who acted as Jor-El in the movie «Superman»?
Answer: Marlon Brando

2826. What's the birth name of Lady Bunny?
Answer: Jon Ingle

2827. When did Connie Sellecca marry John Tesh?
Answer: 1992

2828. In which year did Andrea Martin marry Bob Dolman?
Answer: 1980

2829. Who directed the 2014 film «Exodus: Gods and Kings»?
Answer: Ridley Scott

2830. Who was the composer for the 2018 film «Tully»?
Answer: Thomas Newman

2831. Which film won the Academy Award for Best Documentary Feature in the year 1974?
Answer: Hearts and Minds

2832. What's the birth name of Tyler, the Creator?
Answer: Tyler Gregory Okonma

2833. Whom did Jane Seymour marry in the year 1981?
Answer: David Flynn

2834. For his work in the movie «The Fisher King», who won the «Golden Globe Award for Best Actor – Motion Picture Musical or Comedy» in 1991?
Answer: Robin Williams

2835. Who directed the 2008 film «The Incredible Hulk»?
Answer: Louis Leterrier

2836. What's the birth name of Halle Berry?
Answer: Maria Halle Berry

2837. What is the name of the character Nicolas Cage plays in the movie «Inconceivable»?
Answer: Brian

2838. For which film did Holly Hunter receive the «Academy Award for Best Actress» in 1993?
Answer: The Piano

2839. For her work in the movie «Some Like It Hot», who won the «Golden Globe Award for Best Actress – Motion Picture Musical or Comedy» in 1959?
Answer: Marilyn Monroe

2840. Which film won the Academy Award for Best Picture in the year 1994?
Answer: Schindler's List

2841. Whom did Amber Tamblyn marry in the year 2012?
Answer: David Cross

2842. For which film did Gregory Peck receive the «Golden Globe Award for Best Actor – Motion Picture Drama» in 1962?
Answer: To Kill a Mockingbird

2843. What's the birth name of Owen Wilson?
Answer: Owen Cunningham Wilson

2844. Who directed the 2017 film «It»?
Answer: Andrés Muschietti

2845. For which film did Holly Hunter receive the «National Society of Film Critics Award for Best Actress» in 1993?
Answer: The Piano

2846. Who was the composer for the 2007 film «Spider-Man 3»?
Answer: Christopher Young

2847. For her work in the movie «The Piano», who won the «National Board of Review Award for Best Actress» in 1993?
Answer: Holly Hunter

2848. For his work in the movie «The Big Country», who won the «Golden Globe Award for Best Supporting Actor – Motion Picture» in 1958?
Answer: Burl Ives

2849. What is the name of the character Joe Pesci plays in the movie «JFK»?
Answer: David Ferrie

2850. Who was the composer for the 2012 film «The Cabin in the Woods»?
Answer: David Julyan

2851. Which film won the Academy Award for Best Documentary Feature in the year 1972?
Answer: Marjoe

2852. Who was the composer for the 2014 film «The Giver»?
Answer: Marco Beltrami

2853. Which film won the Golden Globe Award for Best Motion Picture – Drama in the year 2018?
Answer: Three Billboards Outside Ebbing, Missouri

2854. Whom did Jennifer Garner marry in the year 2000?
Answer: Scott Foley

2855. Whom did Lauren Holly marry in the year 2001?
Answer: Francis Greco

2856. Where did Woody Harrelson get his Bachelor of Arts degree from?
Answer: Hanover College, in Indiana

2857. Who directed the 1990 film «Paint It Black»?
Answer: Tim Hunter

2858. What is the full name of Sasha Grey?
Answer: Marina Ann Hantzis

2859. Who was the composer for the 2015 film «Jurassic World»?
Answer: Michael Giacchino

2860. For her work in the movie «Erin Brockovich», who won the «BAFTA Award for Best Actress in a Leading Role» in 2001?
Answer: Julia Roberts

2861. Where did Susan Sarandon get her Bachelor of Arts degree from?
Answer: The Catholic University of America, in Washington, D.C.

2862. Where did Rozonda Thomas get her high school degree from?
Answer: Benjamin Elijah Mays High School, in Georgia

2863. Whom did Meredith Salenger marry in the year 2017?
Answer: Patton Oswalt

2864. Whom did Kim Kardashian marry in the year 2014?
Answer: Kanye West

2865. For her work in the movie «The Sun Also Rises»,

who won the «Asian Film Award for Best Supporting Actress» in 2007?
Answer: Joan Chen

2866. Where did Brian Bosworth get his Bachelor of Science degree from?
Answer: University of Oklahoma, in Norman

2867. For his work in the movie «The Silence of the Lambs», who won the «Chicago Film Critics Association Award for Best Actor» in 1991?
Answer: Anthony Hopkins

2868. In which year did Cassandra Jean marry Stephen Amell?
Answer: 2012

2869. Which film won the Academy Award for Best Sound Editing in the year 2009?
Answer: The Dark Knight

2870. Whom did Alexis Bledel marry in the year 2014?
Answer: Vincent Kartheiser

2871. Who was the composer for the 2002 film «Men in Black II»?
Answer: Danny Elfman

2872. Which film won the Academy Award for Best Documentary Feature in the year 1983?
Answer: He Makes Me Feel Like Dancin'

2873. In which year did Julianne Moore marry Bart Freundlich?
Answer: 2003

2874. For which film did Michael Moore receive the «Academy Award for Best Documentary Feature» in 2002?
Answer: Bowling for Columbine

2875. Who directed the 2006 film «Hollywoodland»?
Answer: Allen Coulter

2876. Who were the directors of the 1987 film «Deadly Illusion»?
Answer: William Tannen and Larry Cohen

2877. Who directed the 1991 film «Terminator 2: Judgment Day»?
Answer: James Cameron

2878. In which year did Mary Steenburgen marry Ted Danson?
Answer: 1995

2879. For which film did Jack Nicholson receive the «Academy Award for Best Supporting Actor» in 1984?
Answer: Terms of Endearment

2880. Which film won the Academy Award for Best Documentary Feature in the year 2019?
Answer: Free Solo

2881. What is the name of the character William Hurt plays in the movie «The Incredible Hulk»?
Answer: Thaddeus Ross

2882. Who was the composer for the 1993 film «Schindler's List»?
Answer: John Williams

2883. Which film won the Academy Award for Best Picture in the year 1973?
Answer: The Godfather

2884. What is the full name of Alexis Arquette?
Answer: Robert Arquette

2885. For which film did Jeffrey Wright receive the «Black Reel Award for Best Supporting Actor» in 2008?
Answer: Cadillac Records

2886. In which year did Sunny Mabrey marry Ethan Embry?
Answer: 2005

2887. For her work in the movie «King Kong», who won the «Golden Globe Award for New Star of the Year – Actress» in 1976?
Answer: Jessica Lange

2888. What is the full name of Tracey Gold?
Answer: Tracey Claire Fisher

2889. For which film did Jane Fonda receive the «Academy Award for Best Actress» in 1978?
Answer: Coming Home

2890. Whom did Gina Torres marry in the year 2002?
Answer: Laurence Fishburne

2891. Who was the composer for the 2008 film «The Day the Earth Stood Still»?
Answer: Tyler Bates

2892. Which film won the Academy Award for Best Picture in the year 1947?
Answer: The Best Years of Our Lives

2893. What's the birth name of Liam Aiken?
Answer: Liam Pádraic Aiken

2894. Which film won the Academy Award for Best Film Editing in the year 1992?
Answer: Unforgiven

2895. Who was the composer for the 1992 film «Patriot Games»?
Answer: James Horner

2896. What is the name of the character Forest Whitaker plays in the movie «Phenomenon»?
Answer: Nate Pope

2897. What is the full name of Arija Bareikis?
Answer: Arija Allison Bareikis

2898. Where was Jon Hamm born?
Answer: St. Louis

2899. In which year did Kiele Sanchez marry Zach Gilford?
Answer: 2012

2900. In which year did Meredith Baxter marry David Birney?
Answer: 1974

2901. What is the name of the character Halle Berry plays in the movie «Die Another Day»?
Answer: Jinx Johnson

2902. Who was the composer for the 2006 film «Scary Movie 4»?
Answer: James L. Venable

2903. What's the birth name of Bill Goldberg?
Answer: William Scott Goldberg

2904. Where did Alan Ritchson get his associate degree from?
Answer: Northwest Florida State College

2905. What is the full name of Christopher Castile?
Answer: Christopher Jon Castile

2906. Whom did Zoë Wanamaker marry in the year 1994?
Answer: Gawn Grainger

2907. Who was the composer for the 1990 film «Home Alone»?
Answer: John Williams

2908. Whom did Eileen Davidson marry in the year 1997?
Answer: Jon Lindstrom

2909. For her work in the movie «Black Swan», who won the «Academy Award for Best Actress» in 2011?
Answer: Natalie Portman

2910. Where did Vince Vaughn get his high school diploma from?
Answer: Lake Forest High School, in Illinois

2911. What is the full name of Dean Norris?
Answer: Dean Joseph Norris

2912. What is the name of the character Viola Davis plays in the movie «Ender's Game»?
Answer: Major Anderson

2913. Who was the composer for the 2013 film «Lone Survivor»?
Answer: Steve Jablonsky

2914. Who was the composer for the 2016 film «Southside with You»?
Answer: Stephen James Taylor

2915. What's the birth name of Simon Helberg?
Answer: Simon Maxwell Helberg

2916. What is the full name of Mike Myers?
Answer: Michael John Myers

2917. For which film did Jean Simmons receive the «Targa d'Oro» award in 1956?
Answer: Footsteps in the Fog

2918. What is the full name of Parker Posey?
Answer: Parker Christian Posey

2919. Who directed the 2002 film «Far from Heaven»?
Answer: Todd Haynes

2920. What is the name of the character Gwyneth Paltrow plays in the movie «Iron Man 2»?

Answer: Pepper Potts

2921. Who was the composer for the 1989 film «The Fabulous Baker Boys»?
Answer: Dave Grusin

2922. For his work in the movie «Philadelphia», who won the «Academy Award for Best Actor» in 1994?
Answer: Tom Hanks

2923. Whom did Maddie Corman marry in the year 1998?
Answer: Jace Alexander

2924. When did Nancy Travis marry Robert N. Fried?
Answer: 1994

2925. Where did "Weird Al" Yankovic get his Bachelor of Architecture degree from?
Answer: California Polytechnic State University

2926. Whom did Gena Lee Nolin marry in the year 2004?
Answer: Cale Hulse

2927. For which film did Rami Malek receive the «Academy Award for Best Actor» in 2019?
Answer: Bohemian Rhapsody

2928. What is the full name of Todd Giebenhain?
Answer: Todd Ronald Giebenhain

2929. What's the birth name of Selena?
Answer: Selena Quintanilla

2930. What is the full name of Brad Pitt?
Answer: William Bradley Pitt

2931. Whom did Ashley Judd marry in the year 2001?
Answer: Dario Franchitti

2932. For which film did Sam Rockwell receive the «Academy Award for Best Supporting Actor» in 2018?

Answer: Three Billboards Outside Ebbing, Missouri

2933. For his work in the movie «The Player», who won the «Golden Globe Award for Best Actor – Motion Picture Musical or Comedy» in 1992?
Answer: Tim Robbins

2934. What is the name of the character Jennifer Connelly plays in the movie «Spider-Man: Homecoming»?
Answer: Karen

2935. When did Selma Blair marry Ahmet Zappa?
Answer: 2004

2936. Whom did Kim Little marry in the year 1994?
Answer: David Michael Latt

2937. Whom did Melody Thomas Scott marry in the year 1985?
Answer: Edward J. Scott

2938. When did Annette Bening marry Warren Beatty?
Answer: 1992

2939. Which film won the Academy Award for Best Original Score in the year 2018?
Answer: The Shape of Water

2940. Which film won the Academy Award for Best Picture in the year 1980?
Answer: Kramer vs. Kramer

2941. For his work in the movie «Goodfellas», who won the «BAFTA Award for Best Film» in 1991?
Answer: Martin Scorsese

2942. What is the full name of Scott Foley?
Answer: Scott Kellerman Foley

2943. Who directed the 2004 film «Spider-Man 2»?
Answer: Sam Raimi

2944. What is the full name of Gillian Anderson?
Answer: Gillian Leigh Anderson

2945. For his work in the movie «Young Frankenstein», who won the «Saturn Award for Best Director» in 1976?
Answer: Mel Brooks

2946. For which film did Steven Spielberg receive the «Saturn Award for Best Director» in 1994?
Answer: Jurassic Park

2947. Who directed the 2000 film «Without Evidence»?
Answer: Gill Dennis

2948. For which film did Anthony Hopkins receive the «Kansas City Film Critics Circle Award for Best Actor» in 1993?
Answer: The Remains of the Day

2949. When did Christine Ebersole marry Peter Bergman?
Answer: 1976

2950. For his work in the movie «A Madea Christmas», who won the «Golden Raspberry Award for Worst Actress» in 2013?
Answer: Tyler Perry

2951. For her work in the movie «To Gillian on Her 37th Birthday», who won the «Young Artist Award» in 1996?
Answer: Claire Danes

2952. What is the name of the character Tom Hanks plays in the movie «Bridge of Spies»?
Answer: James B. Donovan

2953. Whom did Morena Baccarin marry in the year 2011?
Answer: Austin Chick

2954. Whom did Stephanie Seymour marry in the year 1995?
Answer: Peter M. Brant

2955. Who was the composer for the 2016 film «Underworld: Blood Wars»?
Answer: Michael Wandmacher

2956. What is the name of the character Rose Byrne plays in the movie «Star Wars Episode II: Attack of the Clones»?
Answer: Dormé

2957. Whom did Rachael Harris marry in the year 2015?
Answer: Christian Hebel

2958. Whom did Rya Kihlstedt marry in the year 1994?
Answer: Gil Bellows

2959. For which film did Holly Hunter receive the «Cannes Film Festival Award for Best Actress» in 1993?
Answer: The Piano

2960. When did Penelope Ann Miller marry Will Arnett?
Answer: 1994

2961. Who acted as Galadriel in the movie «The Hobbit: The Desolation of Smaug»?
Answer: Cate Blanchett

2962. In which year did Phoebe Cates Kline marry Kevin Kline?
Answer: 1989

2963. Whom did Laura Harring marry in the year 1987?
Answer: Carl-Eduard von Bismarck

2964. In which year did Marcheline Bertrand marry Jon Voight?
Answer: 1971

2965. Who was the composer for the 2017 film «Black Panther»?
Answer: Ludwig Göransson

2966. What's the birth name of Eric McCormack?
Answer: Eric James McCormack

2967. Who was the composer for the 1992 film «Lethal Weapon 3»?
Answer: Michael Kamen

2968. Where did Bill Fagerbakke get his Bachelor of Arts degree from?
Answer: University of Idaho, in Moscow

2969. Who was the composer for the 2013 film «After Earth»?
Answer: James Newton Howard

2970. For which film did Tom Hanks receive the «Golden Globe Award for Best Actor – Motion Picture Drama» in 1994?
Answer: Philadelphia

2971. What's the birth name of Method Man?
Answer: Clifford Smith

2972. Whom did Jessica Harper marry in the year 1989?
Answer: Tom Rothman

2973. Who was the composer for the 2014 film «The Guest»?
Answer: Steve Moore

2974. In which year did Dixie Carter marry George Hearn?
Answer: 1977

2975. Whom did Kirstie Alley marry in the year 1983?
Answer: Parker Stevenson

2976. Who was the composer for the 2018 film «A Quiet Place»?
Answer: Marco Beltrami

2977. For which film did Rachel Weisz receive the «Academy Award for Best Supporting Actress» in 2005?

Answer: The Constant Gardener

2978. When did Margot Kidder marry John Heard?
Answer: 1979

2979. In which year did Ana Brenda Contreras marry Alejandro Amaya?
Answer: 2013

2980. When did Diane Kruger marry Guillaume Canet?
Answer: 2001

2981. What is the name of the character Marlon Brando plays in the movie «The Godfather»?
Answer: Vito Corleone

2982. Who was the composer for the 1995 film «Losing Isaiah»?
Answer: Mark Isham

2983. When did Rileah Vanderbilt marry Adam Green?
Answer: 2010

2984. Whom did Sofía Vergara marry in the year 1991?
Answer: Joe Gonzalez

2985. What's the birth name of Kristanna Loken?
Answer: Kristanna Sommer Løken

2986. Who directed the 1999 film «Summer of Sam»?
Answer: Spike Lee

2987. Where was Denzel Washington born?
Answer: Mount Vernon

2988. Who was the composer for the 2017 film «Monster Trucks»?
Answer: Dave Sardy

2989. What is the name of the character Hugo Weaving plays in the movie «The Matrix Reloaded»?

Answer: Agent Smith

2990. For which film did Robin Williams receive the «Golden Globe Award for Best Motion Picture – Musical or Comedy» in 1993?
Answer: Mrs. Doubtfire

2991. When did Mary Jo Deschanel marry Caleb Deschanel?
Answer: 1972

2992. What is the name of the character Christian Bale plays in the movie «The Dark Knight Rises»?
Answer: Batman

2993. Which film won the Academy Award for Best Documentary Feature in the year 2001?
Answer: Murder on a Sunday Morning

2994. In which year did Rachel Nichols marry Scott Stuber?
Answer: 2008

2995. Who acted as Uncle Ben in the movie «Spider-Man 2»?
Answer: Cliff Robertson

2996. Where was Amy Poehler born?
Answer: Newton

2997. What's the birth name of Jon Bon Jovi?
Answer: John Francis Bongiovi

2998. What's the birth name of Chandra Wilson?
Answer: Chandra Danette Wilson

2999. What's the birth name of Joelle Carter?
Answer: Joelle Marie Carter

3000. Which film won the Academy Award for Best Picture in the year 1940?

Answer: Gone with the Wind

3001. Who directed the 2014 film «John Wick»?
Answer: David Leitch

3002. Where was Piper Perabo born?
Answer: Dallas

3003. For which film did Bette Davis receive the «Academy Award for Best Actress» in 1938?
Answer: Jezebel

3004. Whom did Eve Torres marry in the year 2014?
Answer: Rener Gracie

3005. For her work in the movie «Aliens», who won the «Saturn Award for Best Actress» in 1987?
Answer: Sigourney Weaver

3006. When did Silvana Gallardo marry Billy Drago?
Answer: 1980

3007. For which film did Sidney Poitier receive the «Academy Award for Best Actor» in 1963?
Answer: Lilies of the Field

3008. Whom did Michelle Pfeiffer marry in the year 1981?
Answer: Peter Horton

3009. Who acted as Lester in the movie «Blackway»?
Answer: Anthony Hopkins

3010. What's the birth name of Lizzy Caplan?
Answer: Elizabeth Anne Caplan

3011. Who was the composer for the 2018 film «Wildlife»?
Answer: David Lang

3012. For his work in the movie «Raging Bull», who won the «Golden Globe Award for Best Actor – Motion Picture Drama» in 1980?

Answer: Robert De Niro

3013. What is the name of the character Kevin Spacey plays in the movie «All the Money in the World»?
Answer: John Paul Getty Jr.

3014. What is the full name of Edi Gathegi?
Answer: Edi Mue Gathegi

3015. Who directed the 1999 film «Anna and the King»?
Answer: Andy Tennant

3016. For which film did Allison Janney receive the «Broadcast Film Critics Association Award for Best Cast» in 2007?
Answer: Hairspray

3017. What's the birth name of Brandon Call?
Answer: Brandon Spencer Lee Call

3018. Whom did Kelly Bishop marry in the year 1981?
Answer: Lee Leonard

3019. In which year did Jerry Hall marry Mick Jagger?
Answer: 1990

3020. Who were the directors of the 1995 film «Waterworld»?
Answer: Kevin Reynolds and Kevin Costner

3021. In which year did Leeza Gibbons marry Christopher Quinten?
Answer: 1989

3022. Who was the composer for the 2014 film «The Hunger Games: Mockingjay – Part 1»?
Answer: James Newton Howard

3023. Who was the composer for the 1989 film «National Lampoon's Christmas Vacation»?
Answer: Angelo Badalamenti

3024. Who directed the 2012 film «Men in Black 3»?
Answer: Barry Sonnenfeld

3025. For his work in the movie «Antwone Fisher», who won the «Independent Spirit Award for Best Male Lead» in 2003?
Answer: Derek Luke

3026. What's the birth name of Adam Sandler?
Answer: Adam Richard Sandler

3027. For which film did Taraji P. Henson receive the «BET Award for Best Actor & Actress» in 2006?
Answer: Four Brothers

3028. Where did Wilson Cleveland get his Bachelor of Science degree from?
Answer: Boston University, in Massachusetts

3029. Whom did Troian Bellisario marry in the year 2016?
Answer: Patrick J. Adams

3030. Who was the composer for the 2011 film «Captain America: The First Avenger»?
Answer: Alan Silvestri

3031. What's the birth name of Dwayne Johnson?
Answer: Dwayne Douglas Johnson

3032. In which year did Hilary Swank marry Chad Lowe?
Answer: 1997

3033. Who was the composer for the 2016 film «Don't Breathe»?
Answer: Roque Baños

3034. Who directed the 2009 film «Surrogates»?
Answer: Jonathan Mostow

3035. Whom did Sarah Roemer marry in the year 2015?
Answer: Chad Michael Murray

3036. Where did Jeri Ryan get her Bachelor of Fine Arts degree from?
Answer: Northwestern University, in Illinois

3037. What is the name of the character Anna Paquin plays in the movie «X2»?
Answer: Rogue

3038. Whom did Melora Hardin marry in the year 1997?
Answer: Gildart Jackson

3039. What is the full name of Matt Doyle?
Answer: Matthew Finnen Doyle

3040. Who was the composer for the 1996 film «Scream»?
Answer: Marco Beltrami

3041. Whom did Laurette Spang-McCook marry in the year 1980?
Answer: John McCook

3042. What is the full name of Ginger Lynn?
Answer: Ginger Lynn Allen

3043. What's the birth name of Shannon Woodward?
Answer: Shannon Marie Woodward

3044. Where did Piper Perabo get her bachelor's degree from?
Answer: Ohio University, in Athens

3045. For which film did Walter Huston receive the «Academy Award for Best Supporting Actor» in 1948?
Answer: The Treasure of the Sierra Madre

3046. Whom did Julie Gibson marry in the year 1973?
Answer: Charles Barton
3047. Who directed the 2001 film «Enemy at the Gates»?
Answer: Jean-Jacques Annaud

3048. Who was the composer for the 1996 film «Escape from L.A.»?
Answer: Shirley Walker

3049. What is the full name of Cynthia Watros?
Answer: Cynthia Michele Watros

3050. For his work in the movie «The Truman Show», who won the «Golden Globe Award for Best Supporting Actor – Motion Picture» in 1998?
Answer: Ed Harris

3051. When did Amy Poehler marry Will Arnett?
Answer: 2003

3052. Who was the composer for the 2019 film «The Upside»?
Answer: Rob Simonsen

3053. Who directed the 2019 film «The Aftermath»?
Answer: James Kent

3054. Who was the composer for the 2011 film «Rise of the Planet of the Apes»?
Answer: Patrick Doyle

3055. Who was the composer for the 1997 film «Starship Troopers»?
Answer: Basil Poledouris

3056. Where was Fred Thompson born?
Answer: Sheffield

3057. In which year did Dina Merrill marry Ted Hartley?
Answer: 1989

3058. What's the birth name of Becki Newton?
Answer: Rebecca Sara Newton

3059. Whom did Sherri Saum marry in the year 2007?
Answer: Kamar de los Reyes

3060. Who directed the 2017 film «Only the Brave»?
Answer: Joseph Kosinski

3061. Whom did Sable marry in the year 1994?
Answer: Marc Mero

3062. Whom did Brooklyn Decker marry in the year 2009?
Answer: Andy Roddick

3063. Who directed the 1989 film «Enemies, a Love Story»?
Answer: Paul Mazursky

3064. Who was the composer for the 2018 film «A Private War»?
Answer: H. Scott Salinas

3065. Who directed the 2001 film «Pearl Harbor»?
Answer: Michael Bay

3066. For her work in the movie «The Constant Gardener», who won the «BIFA Award for Best Performance by an Actress in a British Independent Film» in 2005?
Answer: Rachel Weisz

3067. Whom did Susan Walters marry in the year 1986?
Answer: Linden Ashby

3068. Who directed the 1993 film «RoboCop 3»?
Answer: Fred Dekker

3069. Who was the composer for the 2018 film «Eighth Grade»?
Answer: Anna Meredith

3070. Which film won the Academy Award for Best Documentary Feature in the year 1997?
Answer: The Long Way Home

3071. Whom did Laura San Giacomo marry in the year

2000?
Answer: Matt Adler

3072. Who directed the 1987 film «Full Metal Jacket»?
Answer: Stanley Kubrick

3073. Whom did Jennifer Jason Leigh marry in the year 2005?
Answer: Noah Baumbach

3074. For which film did Richard Gere receive the «Screen Actors Guild Award for Outstanding Performance by a Cast in a Motion Picture» in 2003?
Answer: Chicago

3075. What is the name of the character Christian Bale plays in the movie «Terminator Salvation»?
Answer: John Reese Connor

3076. Who was the composer for the 2013 film «Percy Jackson: Sea of Monsters»?
Answer: Andrew Lockington

3077. Who acted as Minerva McGonagall in the movie «Harry Potter and the Half-Blood Prince»?
Answer: Maggie Smith

3078. Who were the composers of the 2016 film «Batman v Superman: Dawn of Justice»?
Answer: Junkie XL and Hans Zimmer

3079. When did Mary Steenburgen marry Malcolm McDowell?
Answer: 1980

3080. Who directed the 1998 film «The Thin Red Line»?
Answer: Terrence Malick

3081. What is the full name of Sticky Fingaz?
Answer: Kirk Jones

3082. Who directed the 2018 film «Colette»?
Answer: Wash Westmoreland

3083. When did Iman marry David Bowie?
Answer: 1992

3084. Whom did Heather Menzies marry in the year 1975?
Answer: Robert Urich

3085. For his work in the movie «Little Miss Sunshine», who won the «Academy Award for Best Supporting Actor» in 2006?
Answer: Alan Arkin

3086. Whom did Marla Sokoloff marry in the year 2009?
Answer: Alec Puro

3087. Which film won the Academy Award for Best Picture in the year 1955?
Answer: On the Waterfront

3088. When did Cassandra Harris marry Pierce Brosnan?
Answer: 1980

3089. For which film did DeWayne Jessie receive the «NAACP Image Award for Outstanding Supporting Actor in a Motion Picture» in 1977?
Answer: The Bingo Long Traveling All-Stars & Motor Kings

3090. When did Paula Patton marry Robin Thicke?
Answer: 2005

3091. In which year did Whoopi Goldberg marry Alvin Martin?
Answer: 1973

3092. Which film won the Academy Award for Best Picture in the year 2006?
Answer: Crash

3093. What is the name of the character Benicio del Toro

plays in the movie «Licence to Kill»?
Answer: Dario

3094. Which film won the Golden Globe Award for Best Original Score in the year 1965?
Answer: Doctor Zhivago

3095. What's the birth name of Beth Littleford?
Answer: Elizabeth Ann Halcyon Littleford

3096. Who acted as Pepper Potts in the movie «Iron Man 3»?
Answer: Gwyneth Paltrow

3097. In which year did Rosa Blasi marry Jim Finn?
Answer: 2004

3098. When did Raquel Welch marry André Weinfeld?
Answer: 1980

3099. For which film did George Kennedy receive the «Academy Award for Best Supporting Actor» in 1967?
Answer: Cool Hand Luke

3100. In which year did Morena Baccarin marry Ben McKenzie?
Answer: 2014

3101. For which film did Sarah Michelle Gellar receive the «MTV Movie Award for Best Performance» in 2000?
Answer: Cruel Intentions

3102. For which film did Sigourney Weaver receive the «Golden Globe Award for Best Actress – Motion Picture Drama» in 1988?
Answer: Gorillas in the Mist

3103. Whom did Linda Purl marry in the year 1993?
Answer: Alexander Cary, Master of Falkland

3104. Who was the composer for the 2018 film «Woman

Walks Ahead»?
Answer: George Fenton

3105. For his work in the movie «The Towering Inferno», who won the «Golden Globe Award for Best Supporting Actor – Motion Picture» in 1974?
Answer: Fred Astaire

3106. Who was the composer for the 2016 film «The Land Before Time XIV: Journey of the Heart»?
Answer: Michael Tavera

3107. For her work in the movie «State and Main», who won the «National Board of Review Award for Best Cast» in 2000?
Answer: Patti LuPone

3108. Whom did Tawny Kitaen marry in the year 1997?
Answer: Chuck Finley

3109. For his work in the movie «The Sunshine Boys», who won the «Academy Award for Best Supporting Actor» in 1975?
Answer: George Burns

3110. Who was the composer for the 1987 film «RoboCop»?
Answer: Basil Poledouris

3111. Whom did Mary Elizabeth Ellis marry in the year 2006?
Answer: Charlie Day

3112. In which year did Carrie Fisher marry Paul Simon?
Answer: 1983

3113. What is the name of the character Cuba Gooding Jr. plays in the movie «Selma»?
Answer: Fred Gray

3114. Whom did Diahann Carroll marry in the year 1987?
Answer: Vic Damone

3115. For her work in the movie «La La Land», who won the «Academy Award for Best Actress» in 2017?
Answer: Emma Stone

3116. For her work in the movie «The Help», who won the «Broadcast Film Critics Association Award for Best Cast» in 2011?
Answer: Allison Janney

3117. For which film did Halle Berry receive the «Screen Actors Guild Award for Outstanding Performance by a Female Actor in a Leading Role» in 2002?
Answer: Monster's Ball

3118. What is the name of the character William Hurt plays in the movie «Captain America: Civil War»?
Answer: Thaddeus Ross

3119. Whom did Rena Sofer marry in the year 2003?
Answer: Sanford Bookstaver

3120. For his work in the movie «Moneyball», who won the «Boston Society of Film Critics Award for Best Actor» in 2011?
Answer: Brad Pitt

3121. Who was the composer for the 1994 film «3 Ninjas Kick Back»?
Answer: Richard Marvin

3122. When did Mary Beth Hurt marry William Hurt?
Answer: 1971

3123. For which film did Vin Diesel receive the «MTV Movie Award for Best On-Screen Duo» in 2002?
Answer: The Fast and the Furious

3124. For her work in the movie «The Silence of the Lambs», who won the «Golden Globe Award» in 1991?
Answer: Jodie Foster

3125. Whom did Liza Weil marry in the year 2006?
Answer: Paul Adelstein

3126. Whom did Elizabeth Taylor marry in the year 1975?
Answer: Richard Burton

3127. For which film did Timothée Chalamet receive the «National Board of Review Award for Breakthrough Performance» in 2017?
Answer: Call Me by Your Name

3128. Who directed the 1989 film «The War of the Roses»?
Answer: Danny DeVito

3129. Who was the composer for the 1988 film «The Naked Gun: From the Files of Police Squad!»?
Answer: Ira Newborn

3130. Who was the composer for the 2015 film «Jupiter Ascending»?
Answer: Michael Giacchino

3131. Where was Julianne Moore born?
Answer: Fort Bragg

3132. Who was the composer for the 2017 film «The Big Sick»?
Answer: Michael Andrews

3133. In which year did Pamela Anderson marry Rick Salomon?
Answer: 2014

3134. Who was the composer for the 2018 film «Ben Is Back»?
Answer: Dickon Hinchliffe

3135. Which film won the Academy Award for Best Original Score in the year 1978?
Answer: Midnight Express

3136. Whom did Reese Witherspoon marry in the year 1999?
Answer: Ryan Phillippe

3137. Who was the composer for the 2001 film «Jurassic Park III»?
Answer: Don Davis

3138. Whom did Sofía Vergara marry in the year 2015?
Answer: Joe Manganiello

3139. For her work in the movie «Walk the Line», who won the «Screen Actors Guild Award» in 2006?
Answer: Reese Witherspoon

3140. Who was the composer for the 2018 film «The Meg»?
Answer: Harry Gregson-Williams

3141. In which year did Shannen Doherty marry Rick Salomon?
Answer: 2002

3142. For her work in the movie «The Help», who won the «Screen Actors Guild Award for Outstanding Performance by a Cast in a Motion Picture» in 2012?
Answer: Mary Steenburgen

3143. Which film won the Academy Award for Best Visual Effects in the year 1979?
Answer: Alien

3144. Whom did Brooke Burns marry in the year 2013?
Answer: Gavin O'Connor

3145. What is the full name of Christa Miller?
Answer: Christa Beatrice Miller

3146. Who directed the 2010 film «Robin Hood»?
Answer: Ridley Scott

3147. Where was Ed Harris born?

Answer: Englewood

3148. What's the birth name of Aaron Paul?
Answer: Aaron Paul Sturtevant

3149. Who was the composer for the 2014 film «Guardians of the Galaxy»?
Answer: Tyler Bates

3150. What is the name of the character Christopher Plummer plays in the movie «Star Trek VI: The Undiscovered Country»?
Answer: Chang

3151. Who were the composers of the 2015 film «The Good Dinosaur»?
Answer: Jeff Danna and Mychael Danna

3152. For her work in the movie «Boys Don't Cry», who won the «National Society of Film Critics Award for Best Supporting Actress» in 1999?
Answer: Chloë Sevigny

3153. For which film did Helen Hayes receive the «Academy Award for Best Actress» in 1931?
Answer: The Sin of Madelon Claudet

3154. What is the full name of Kane?
Answer: Glenn Thomas Jacobs

3155. What is the full name of Forest Whitaker?
Answer: Forest Steven Whitaker

3156. Whom did Ronee Blakley marry in the year 1979?
Answer: Wim Wenders

3157. Whom did Bridget Moynahan marry in the year 2015?
Answer: Andrew Frankel

3158. Whom did Zsa Zsa Gabor marry in the year 1975?

Answer: Jack Ryan

3159. For his work in the movie «Lust for Life», who won the «Golden Globe Award for Best Actor – Motion Picture Drama» in 1956?
Answer: Kirk Douglas

3160. What is the full name of Alden Ehrenreich?
Answer: Alden Caleb Ehrenreich

3161. Who was the composer for the 2003 film «Uptown Girls»?
Answer: Joel McNeely

3162. For her work in the movie «Red Rose White Rose», who won the «Golden Horse Award for Best Leading Actress» in 1994?
Answer: Joan Chen

3163. Who directed the 2019 film «Ford V Ferrari»?
Answer: James Mangold

3164. Who was the composer for the 2014 film «Love, Rosie»?
Answer: Ralf Wengenmayr

3165. Whom did Julie Benz marry in the year 1998?
Answer: John Kassir

3166. Who directed the 2019 film «What Men Want»?
Answer: Adam Shankman

3167. Which film won the Academy Award for Best Production Design in the year 1940?
Answer: Gone with the Wind

3168. For which film did Thomas Haden Church receive the «Independent Spirit Award for Best Supporting Male» in 2005?
Answer: Sideways

3169. In which year did Marsha Mason marry Neil Simon?
Answer: 1973

3170. What is the full name of Tyrese Gibson?
Answer: Tyrese Darnell Gibson

3171. Whom did Rene Russo marry in the year 1992?
Answer: Dan Gilroy

3172. What is the full name of Danica McKellar?
Answer: Danica Mae McKellar

3173. Where did George Lucas get his Bachelor of Fine Arts degree from?
Answer: University of Southern California, in Los Angeles

3174. For his work in the movie «Bad Day at Black Rock», who won the «Cannes Film Festival Award for Best Actor» in 1955?
Answer: Spencer Tracy

3175. What is the full name of Kristen Bell?
Answer: Kristen Anne Bell

3176. Who was the composer for the 2019 film «Missing Link»?
Answer: Carter Burwell

3177. What's the birth name of Ashlee Simpson?
Answer: Ashlee Nicole Simpson

3178. Which film won the Academy Award for Best Documentary Feature in the year 2011?
Answer: Undefeated

3179. What is the name of the character Marisa Tomei plays in the movie «Spider-Man: Homecoming»?
Answer: May Parker

3180. What is the full name of Brooke Shields?
Answer: Brooke Christa Camille Shields

3181. What is the full name of Triple H?
Answer: Paul Michael Levesque

3182. Who directed the 2008 film «City of Ember»?
Answer: Gil Kenan

3183. Whom did Eva Longoria marry in the year 2016?
Answer: José Antonio Bastón

3184. Who was the composer for the 1995 film «Jumanji»?
Answer: James Horner

3185. Who directed the 2007 film «The Land Before Time XII: The Great Day of the Flyers»?
Answer: Charles Grosvenor

3186. Who directed the 2019 film «Missing Link»?
Answer: Chris Butler

3187. What is the full name of Coleby Lombardo?
Answer: Coleby Jason Lombardo

3188. For which film did Billy Crystal receive the «MTV Movie Award for Best Comedic Performance» in 1992?
Answer: City Slickers

3189. What is the full name of Johnny Depp?
Answer: John Christopher Depp

3190. Whom did Patricia Arquette marry in the year 1995?
Answer: Nicolas Cage

3191. In which year did Carmen Electra marry Dennis Rodman?
Answer: 1998

3192. Which film won the Academy Award for Best Visual Effects in the year 1982?
Answer: E.T. the Extra-Terrestrial

3193. What is the full name of Tim Ransom?
Answer: Timothy Ransom Wilson

3194. What's the birth name of Jackie Evancho?
Answer: Jacqueline Marie Evancho

3195. For which film did Brad Pitt receive the «Rembrandt Award» in 2010?
Answer: The Curious Case of Benjamin Button

3196. Whom did LaChanze marry in the year 2005?
Answer: Derek Fordjour

3197. For which film did Jeremy Renner receive the «Screen Actors Guild Award for Outstanding Performance by a Cast in a Motion Picture» in 2014?
Answer: American Hustle

3198. For which film did Dolly Parton receive the «Las Vegas Film Critics Society Award for Best Song» in 2005?
Answer: Transamerica

3199. Who was the composer for the 2001 film «Pearl Harbor»?
Answer: Hans Zimmer

3200. Whom did Gilda Radner marry in the year 1984?
Answer: Gene Wilder

3201. What is the full name of Traci Lords?
Answer: Nora Louise Kuzma

3202. Who directed the 2006 film «Goal!»?
Answer: Danny Cannon

3203. Who was the composer for the 2016 film «Synchronicity»?
Answer: Ben Lovett

3204. Where was Eli Wallach born?
Answer: New York City

3205. Who was the composer for the 2017 film

«Wakefield»?
Answer: Aaron Zigman

3206. Whom did Liv Tyler marry in the year 2003?
Answer: Royston Langdon

3207. Whom did Kathy Baker marry in the year 2003?
Answer: Steven Robman

3208. What is the name of the character Sigourney Weaver plays in the movie «1492 – Conquest of Paradise»?
Answer: Isabella I of Castile

3209. Who were the directors of the 1999 film «American Pie»?
Answer: Chris Weitz and Paul Weitz

3210. In which year did Theresa Russell marry Nicolas Roeg?
Answer: 1982

3211. What's the birth name of Idina Menzel?
Answer: Idina Kim Mentzel

3212. Whom did Odette Annable marry in the year 2010?
Answer: Dave Annable

3213. For which film did Bryan Singer receive the «U.S. Grand Jury Prize: Dramatic» award in 1993?
Answer: Public Access

3214. For her work in the movie «Written on the Wind», who won the «Academy Award for Best Supporting Actress» in 1957?
Answer: Dorothy Malone

3215. For which film did Melanie Griffith receive the «Golden Raspberry Award for Worst Supporting Actress» in 1996?
Answer: Mulholland Falls

3216. What is the full name of Pamela Anderson?
Answer: Pamela Denise Anderson

3217. Who was the composer for the 2017 film «Fist Fight»?
Answer: Dominic Lewis

3218. Who was the composer for the 2014 film «The Internet's Own Boy: The Story of Aaron Swartz»?
Answer: John Dragonetti

3219. When did Didi Conn marry David Shire?
Answer: 1982

3220. Who acted as Hugh Glass in the movie «The Revenant»?
Answer: Leonardo DiCaprio

3221. Which film won the Golden Globe Award for Best Motion Picture – Drama in the year 1953?
Answer: The Robe

3222. Who directed the 2017 film «Diary of a Wimpy Kid: The Long Haul»?
Answer: David Bowers

3223. Who directed the 1997 film «Volcano»?
Answer: Mick Jackson

3224. Who directed the 1998 film «Titanic»?
Answer: James Cameron

3225. Whom did Annie Wersching marry in the year 2009?
Answer: Stephen Full

3226. Who directed the 2018 film «A Private War»?
Answer: Matthew Heineman

3227. Who was the composer for the 2006 film «Goal!»?
Answer: Graeme Revell

3228. Who directed the 1994 film «Drop Zone»?
Answer: John Badham

3229. Whom did Elizabeth Mitchell marry in the year 2000?
Answer: Gary Bakewell

3230. Who was the composer for the 2015 film «The Devil's Candy»?
Answer: Sunn O)))

3231. What is the name of the character Jeremy Irons plays in the movie «Justice League»?
Answer: Alfred Pennyworth

3232. Which film won the Academy Award for Best Documentary Feature in the year 1996?
Answer: When We Were Kings

3233. Who acted as Ellen Ripley in the movie «Alien 3»?
Answer: Sigourney Weaver

3234. What is the name of the character Alicia Vikander plays in the movie «Tomb Raider»?
Answer: Lara Croft

3235. Who was the composer for the 2013 film «12 Years a Slave»?
Answer: Hans Zimmer

3236. Which film won the Academy Award for Best Documentary Feature in the year 2006?
Answer: An Inconvenient Truth

3237. Who was the composer for the 2012 film «The Dark Knight Rises»?
Answer: Hans Zimmer

3238. Which film won the Academy Award for Best Picture in the year 1989?
Answer: Rain Man

3239. When did Ashley Tisdale marry Christopher French?
Answer: 2014

3240. Who was the composer for the 2016 film «10 Cloverfield Lane»?
Answer: Bear McCreary

3241. For his work in the movie «Sideways», who won the «Broadcast Film Critics Association Award for Best Supporting Actor» in 2004?
Answer: Thomas Haden Church

3242. Whom did Tichina Arnold marry in the year 1991?
Answer: Lamon Brewster

3243. What's the birth name of Joanna Angel?
Answer: Joanna Margalir Mostov

3244. What's the birth name of Jamie Foxx?
Answer: Eric Marlon Bishop

3245. Who acted as James Gordon in the movie «Batman Begins»?
Answer: Gary Oldman
3246. What's the birth name of Amber Rayne?
Answer: Meghan Wren

3247. Who was the composer for the 1995 film «Batman Forever»?
Answer: Elliot Goldenthal

3248. Who was the composer for the 2018 film «Breaking In»?
Answer: Johnny Klimek

3249. Which film won the Academy Award for Best Documentary Feature in the year 1978?
Answer: Scared Straight!

3250. Whom did Elizabeth Taylor marry in the year 1976?
Answer: John Warner

3251. For his work in the movie «Syriana», who won the «Academy Award for Best Supporting Actor» in 2005?
Answer: George Clooney

3252. When did Lynn Whitfield marry Brian Gibson?
Answer: 1990

3253. What is the name of the character Nicolas Cage plays in the movie «USS Indianapolis: Men of Courage»?
Answer: Charles B. McVay III

3254. Who were the composers of the 2015 film «Avengers: Age of Ultron»?
Answer: Danny Elfman and Brian Tyler

3255. Which film won the Academy Award for Best Sound Mixing in the year 1994?
Answer: Speed

3256. What is the full name of Vanessa Hudgens?
Answer: Vanessa Anne Hudgens

3257. What is the full name of Dylan Walsh?
Answer: Charles Hunter Walsh

3258. When did Brooke Adams marry Tony Shalhoub?
Answer: 1992

3259. Where did Pandora Peaks get her master's degree from?
Answer: University of Georgia, in Athens

3260. Who directed the 1997 film «Mortal Kombat: Annihilation»?
Answer: John R. Leonetti

3261. Where was Arnold Schwarzenegger born?
Answer: Thal

3262. For his work in the movie «The Island of Dr. Moreau», who won the «Golden Raspberry Award for Worst Supporting Actor» in 1996?
Answer: Marlon Brando

3264. When did Elizabeth Perkins marry Julio Macat?
Answer: 2000

3265. What is the full name of Christine Taylor?
Answer: Christine Joan Taylor

3266. Whom did Sarah Jessica Parker marry in the year 1997?
Answer: Matthew Broderick

3267. Who directed the 2017 film «The Great Wall»?
Answer: Zhang Yimou

3268. Whom did Rebecca Gayheart marry in the year 2004?
Answer: Eric Dane

3269. Who was the composer for the 1988 film «Big»?
Answer: Howard Shore

3270. For which film did Thomas Haden Church receive the «Broadcast Film Critics Association Award for Best Cast» in 2004?
Answer: Sideways

3271. Whom did Mira Sorvino marry in the year 2004?
Answer: Christopher Backus

3272. For her work in the movie «Rhinestone», who won the «Golden Raspberry Award for Worst Original Song» in 1984?
Answer: Dolly Parton

3273. Whom did Claudia Christian marry in the year 1988?
Answer: Gary DeVore

3274. For her work in the movie «Die Another Day», who won the «NAACP Image Award for Outstanding Supporting Actress in a Motion Picture» in 2003?
Answer: Halle Berry

3275. When did Paulina Porizkova marry Ric Ocasek?
Answer: 1989

3276. For his work in the movie «Marty», who won the «National Board of Review Award for Best Actor» in 1955?
Answer: Ernest Borgnine

3277. Who was the composer for the 2012 film «Men in Black 3»?
Answer: Danny Elfman

3278. Whom did Christie Brinkley marry in the year 1996?
Answer: Peter Cook

3279. Who was the composer for the 2016 film «London Has Fallen»?
Answer: Trevor Morris

3280. What is the full name of Thomas Gibson?
Answer: Thomas Ellis Gibson
3281. Who directed the 2013 film «Captain Phillips»?
Answer: Paul Greengrass

3282. Who was the composer for the 1993 film «Tombstone»?
Answer: Bruce Broughton

3283. When did Faye Grant marry Stephen Collins?
Answer: 1985

3284. In which year did Alektra Blue marry Pat Myne?
Answer: 2007

3285. For which film did Grace Kelly receive the «Golden Globe Award for Best Actress – Motion Picture Drama» in

1954?
Answer: The Country Girl

3286. Where was Bob Kirsh born?
Answer: Bristol

3287. Who directed the 2018 film «The Equalizer 2»?
Answer: Antoine Fuqua

3288. What is the full name of Justine Bateman?
Answer: Justine Tanya Bateman

3289. Whom did Melissa Joan Hart marry in the year 2003?
Answer: Mark Wilkerson

3290. Whom did Vanessa Minnillo marry in the year 2011?
Answer: Nick Lachey

3291. Who directed the 1986 film «Howard the Duck»?
Answer: Willard Huyck

3292. Which film won the Academy Award for Best Documentary Feature in the year 2010?
Answer: Inside Job

3293. Who directed the 1993 film «Sister Act 2: Back in the Habit»?
Answer: Bill Duke

3294. What is the full name of Katherine Heigl?
Answer: Katherine Marie Heigl

3295. For his work in the movie «Shadowlands», who won the «Los Angeles Film Critics Association Award for Best Actor» in 1993?
Answer: Anthony Hopkins

3296. For which film did Walter Brennan receive the «Academy Award for Best Supporting Actor» in 1940?
Answer: The Westerner

3297. When did Cameron Diaz marry Benji Madden?
Answer: 2015

3298. Where did Shaquille O'Neal get his Doctor of Education degree from?
Answer: Barry University, in Miami

3299. What is the full name of January Jones?
Answer: January Kristen Jones

3300. For which film did Joanne Woodward receive the «New York Film Critics Circle Award for Best Actress» in 1990?
Answer: Mr. and Mrs. Bridge

3301. Which film won the Academy Award for Best Writing, Original Screenplay in the year 2003?
Answer: Lost in Translation

3302. What is the full name of Wendell Pierce?
Answer: Wendell Edward Piercec

3303. Who directed the 2016 film «The Legend of Tarzan»?
Answer: David Yates

3304. For his work in the movie «The People vs. Larry Flynt», who won the «European Film Academy Achievement in World Cinema Award» in 1997?
Answer: Miloš Forman

3305. In which year did Lela Rochon marry Shabba Doo?
Answer: 1984

3306. What is the full name of Jon Stewart?
Answer: Jonathan Stuart Leibowitz

3307. For which film did Harold Russell receive the «Academy Award for Best Supporting Actor» in 1946?
Answer: The Best Years of Our Lives

3308. For which film did William Hurt receive the «Los Angeles Film Critics Association Award for Best Supporting Actor» in 2005?
Answer: A History of Violence

3309. Who directed the 1991 film «Hot Shots!»?
Answer: Jim Abrahams

3310. Whom did Veronica Alicino marry in the year 1997?
Answer: Tim Hill

3311. Who was the composer for the 2014 film «Godzilla»?
Answer: Alexandre Desplat

3312. When did Laurie Metcalf marry Jeff Perry?
Answer: 1983

3313. Who was the composer for the 2017 film «The Circle»?
Answer: Danny Elfman

3314. Who were the composers of the 2014 film «The Amazing Spider-Man 2»?
Answer: Junkie XL and Hans Zimmer

3315. For which film did Adrien Brody receive the «Boston Society of Film Critics Award for Best Actor» in 2002?
Answer: The Pianist

3316. Whom did Bonnie Raitt marry in the year 1991?
Answer: Michael O'Keefe

3317. When did Mary McCormack marry Michael Morris?
Answer: 2003

3318. Which film won the Academy Award for Best Picture in the year 1954?
Answer: From Here to Eternity

3319. What is the full name of Adam Scott?

Answer: Adam Paul Scott

3320. When did Reese Witherspoon marry Jim Toth?
Answer: 2011

3321. Who was the composer for the 2014 film «Exodus: Gods and Kings»?
Answer: Alberto Iglesias

3322. For which film did Adam Sandler receive the «Golden Raspberry Award for Worst Actor» in 2011?
Answer: Big Daddy

3323. Whom did Eva Longoria marry in the year 2007?
Answer: Tony Parker

3324. Which film won the Golden Globe Award for Best Motion Picture – Drama in the year 2017?
Answer: Moonlight

3325. When did Jean Smart marry Richard Gilliland?
Answer: 1987

3326. Who was the composer for the 1991 film «Terminator 2: Judgment Day»?
Answer: Brad Fiedel

3327. What is the full name of Beatrice Rosen?
Answer: Béatrice Rosenblatt

3328. What is the name of the character Nicolas Cage plays in the movie «The Rock»?
Answer: Stanley Goodspeed

3329. Who directed the 2007 film «300»?
Answer: Zack Snyder

3330. For which film did Frances McDormand receive the «Golden Globe Award for Best Supporting Actress – Motion Picture» in 1993?
Answer: Short Cuts

3331. Whom did Christie Brinkley marry in the year 1973?
Answer: François Allaux

3332. Who directed the 2003 film «Hulk»?
Answer: Ang Lee

3333. Who directed the 1989 film «Lethal Weapon 2»?
Answer: Richard Donner

3334. What is the full name of Amy Ryan?
Answer: Amy Beth Dziewiontkowski

3335. Where did Bob Kirsh get his Master of Fine Arts degree from?
Answer: New York University, in Manhattan

3336. When did Vanessa Williams marry Jim Skrip?
Answer: 2015

3337. For her work in the movie «Taxi Driver», who won the «BAFTA Award for Most Promising Newcomer to Leading Film Roles» in 1977?
Answer: Jodie Foster

3338. What is the name of the character Mark Rylance plays in the movie «Bridge of Spies»?
Answer: Rudolf Abel

3339. When did Stacy Carter marry Jerry Lawler?
Answer: 2000

3340. What is the name of the character Chris Cooper plays in the movie «The Amazing Spider-Man 2»?
Answer: Norman Osborn

3341. Whom did Rena Sofer marry in the year 1995?
Answer: Wally Kurth

3342. For which film did Adam Sandler receive the «Golden Raspberry Award for Worst Actor» in 2011?

Answer: That's My Boy

3343. Where did Carroll O'Connor get his undergraduate degree from?
Answer: University College Dublin

3344. Who was the composer for the 2006 film «The Break-Up»?
Answer: Jon Brion

3345. Who directed the 2018 film «The Meg»?
Answer: Jon Turteltaub

3346. Where did "Weird Al" Yankovic get his Bachelor of Architecture degree from?
Answer: California Polytechnic State University, in San Luis Obispo

3347. Who acted as Gwen Stacy in the movie «The Amazing Spider-Man»?
Answer: Emma Stone

3348. Who was the composer for the 1991 film «The Marrying Man»?
Answer: David Newman

3349. Who directed the 1991 film «The Five Heartbeats»?
Answer: Robert Townsend

3350. What's the birth name of John Krasinski?
Answer: John Burke Krasinski

3351. In which year did Brooke Burke Charvet marry David Charvet?
Answer: 2011

3352. For his work in the movie «Crime Story», who won the «Golden Horse Award for Best Leading Actor» in 1983?
Answer: Jackie Chan

3353. Who directed the 2018 film «Mid90s»?
Answer: Jonah Hill

3354. For her work in the movie «The Good Girl», who won the «Hollywood Film Festival» award in 2002?
Answer: Jennifer Aniston

3355. Whom did Janet Jackson marry in the year 1984?
Answer: James DeBarge

3356. In which year did Karen Young marry Tom Noonan?
Answer: 1992

3357. What is the full name of Michelle Monaghan?
Answer: Michelle Lynn Monaghan

3358. Who acted as Iron Monger in the movie «Iron Man»?
Answer: Jeff Bridges

3359. For which film did Louis Gossett receive the «Golden Globe Award for Best Supporting Actor – Motion Picture» in 1982?
Answer: An Officer and a Gentleman

3360. Whom did Rose McGowan marry in the year 2013?
Answer: Davey Detail

3361. Who was the composer for the 1986 film «Off Beat»?
Answer: James Horner

3362. In which year did Jayne Brook marry John Terlesky?
Answer: 1996

3363. Whom did Jenna Jameson marry in the year 2003?
Answer: Jay Grdina

3364. Where did Jesse Williams get his Bachelor of Arts degree from?
Answer: Temple University, in Philadelphia

3365. For which film did Wallace Beery receive the «Volpi Cup for Best Actor» award in 1934?
Answer: Viva Villa!

3366. What's the birth name of Steven R. McQueen?
Answer: Steven Chadwick McQueen

3367. Who was the composer for the 2002 film «The Good Girl»?
Answer: Tony Maxwell

3368. Who directed the 2017 film «War for the Planet of the Apes»?
Answer: Matt Reeves

3369. For which film did Anthony Hopkins receive the «BAFTA Award for Best Actor in a Leading Role» in 1991?
Answer: The Silence of the Lambs

3370. In which year did Missi Pyle marry Casey Anderson?
Answer: 2008

3371. What is the full name of Zachary Quinto?
Answer: Zachary John Quinto

3372. When did Geraldine Chaplin marry Patricio Castilla?
Answer: 2006

3373. For which film did Carrie Snodgress receive the «Golden Globe Award for Best Actress – Motion Picture Musical or Comedy» in 1970?
Answer: Diary of a Mad Housewife

3374. For which film did Meryl Streep receive the «Golden Globe Award for Best Actress – Motion Picture Musical or Comedy» in 2006?
Answer: The Devil Wears Prada

3375. Who directed the 2000 film «The Next Best Thing»?
Answer: John Schlesinger

3376. When did Katherine Heigl marry Josh Kelley?
Answer: 2007

3377. Who directed the 1986 film «King Kong Lives»?
Answer: John Guillermin

3378. For which film did Halle Berry receive the «BET Award for Best Actor & Actress» in 2008?
Answer: Perfect Stranger

3379. For which film did Anthony Hopkins receive the «Saturn Award for Best Actor» in 1991?
Answer: The Silence of the Lambs

3380. For which film did Jennifer Lawrence receive the «MTV Movie Award for Best Female Performance» in 2012?
Answer: The Hunger Games

3381. Who directed the 1994 film «Ed Wood»?
Answer: Tim Burton

3382. For which film did Robin Williams receive the «Grammy Award for Best Comedy Album» in 1988?
Answer: Good Morning, Vietnam

3383. Which film won the Academy Award for Best Visual Effects in the year 1992?
Answer: Terminator 2: Judgment Day

3384. Who acted as Jacob Elinsky in the movie «25th Hour»?
Answer: Philip Seymour Hoffman

3385. For which film did Dean Jagger receive the «Academy Award for Best Supporting Actor» in 1949?
Answer: Twelve O'Clock High

3386. What's the birth name of Nick Chinlund?
Answer: Zareh Nicholas Chinlund

3387. For his work in the movie «The Silence of the Lambs», who won the «Directors Guild of America Award for Outstanding Directing – Feature Film» in 1991?
Answer: Jonathan Demme

3388. What is the full name of Bow Wow?
Answer: Shad Gregory Moss

3389. Where did Richard Riehle get his Bachelor of Arts degree from?
Answer: University of Notre Dame

3390. Who was the composer for the 2019 film «The Rhythm Section»?
Answer: Jongnic Bontemps

3391. Which film won the Academy Award for Best Documentary Feature in the year 2003?
Answer: The Fog of War

3392. For which film did Ava Gardner receive the «Silver Shell for Best Actress» award in 1964?
Answer: The Night of the Iguana

3393. What is the full name of Eric Close?
Answer: Eric Randolph Close

3394. For his work in the movie «Jerry Maguire», who won the «Golden Globe Award for Best Actor – Motion Picture Musical or Comedy» in 1997?
Answer: Tom Cruise

3395. For her work in the movie «The Human Stain», who won the «Washington D.C. Area Film Critics Association Award for Best Supporting Actress» in 2003?
Answer: Anna Deavere Smith

3396. What's the birth name of Crissy Moran?
Answer: Christina McMillan

3397. What's the birth name of Gauge?
Answer: Elizabeth R. Deans

3398. In which year did Clare Grant marry Seth Green?
Answer: 2010

3399. What is the name of the character Robert De Niro plays in the movie «Taxi Driver»?
Answer: Travis Bickle

3400. When did Rosanna Arquette marry James Newton Howard?
Answer: 1986

3401. Where did Denzel Washington get his Bachelor of Arts degree from?
Answer: Fordham University, in Manhattan

3402. For her work in the movie «Swordfish», who won the «BET Award for Best Actor & Actress» in 2002?
Answer: Halle Berry

3403. What's the birth name of Vera Farmiga?
Answer: Vera Ann Farmiga

3404. What is the name of the character Nicole Kidman plays in the movie «Batman Forever»?
Answer: Dr. Chase Meridian

3405. Which film won the Academy Award for Best Picture in the year 2001?
Answer: Gladiator

3406. Whom did Goldie Hawn marry in the year 1976?
Answer: Bill Hudson

3407. In which year did Ellen Barkin marry Gabriel Byrne?
Answer: 1988

3408. For her work in the movie «Leaving Las Vegas», who won the «National Society of Film Critics Award for

Best Actress» in 1995?
Answer: Elisabeth Shue

3409. What is the full name of Lucy Hale?
Answer: Karen Lucille Hale

3410. What is the full name of R. Kelly?
Answer: Robert Sylvester Kelly

3411. Who were the composers of the 2014 film «Gone Girl»?
Answer: Atticus Ross and Trent Reznor

3412. Who was the composer for the 2013 film «Europa Report»?
Answer: Bear McCreary

3413. When did Cher marry Gregg Allman?
Answer: 1975

3414. For which film did Holly Hunter receive the «AACTA Award for Best Actress in a Leading Role» in 1993?
Answer: The Piano

3415. For which film did Meryl Streep receive the «Satellite Award for Best Actress – Motion Picture Musical or Comedy» in 2006?
Answer: The Devil Wears Prada

3416. In which year did Season Hubley marry Kurt Russell?
Answer: 1979

3417. What's the birth name of Bree Olson?
Answer: Rachel Marie Oberlin

3418. What is the name of the character Al Pacino plays in the movie «The Godfather Part II»?
Answer: Michael Corleone

3419. For which film did Kristen Stewart receive the «MTV

Movie Award for Best Kiss» in 2009?
Answer: Twilight

3420. Who was the composer for the 2017 film «The Belco Experiment»?
Answer: Tyler Bates

3421. Where was Jodie Foster born?
Answer: Los Angeles

3422. Who directed the 2009 film «My Sister's Keeper»?
Answer: Nick Cassavetes

3423. For her work in the movie «Silver Linings Playbook», who won the «Dallas-Fort Worth Film Critics Association Award for Best Actress» in 2012?
Answer: Jennifer Lawrence

3424. Who was the composer for the 2015 film «Survivor»?
Answer: Ilan Eshkeri

3425. Whom did Debrah Farentino marry in the year 1985?
Answer: James Farentino

3426. In which year did Janine Lindemulder marry Jesse James?
Answer: 2002

3427. What is the full name of Seth MacFarlane?
Answer: Seth Woodbury MacFarlane

3428. For which film did Steven Spielberg receive the «New York Film Critics Circle Award for Best Film» in 1998?
Answer: Saving Private Ryan

3429. Whom did Courtney Ford marry in the year 2007?
Answer: Brandon Routh

3430. What is the name of the character Russell Crowe

plays in the movie «Noah»?
Answer: Noah

3431. Who directed the 2000 film «Keeping the Faith»?
Answer: Edward Norton

3432. Where was Pandora Peaks born?
Answer: Atlanta

3433. For his work in the movie «Jack and Jill», who won the «Golden Raspberry Award for Worst Actor» in 2012?
Answer: Adam Sandler

3434. When did Kiersten Warren marry Jonathan Lemkin?
Answer: 1990

3435. Whom did Jennifer Lopez marry in the year 1997?
Answer: Ojani Noa

3436. When did Melanie Griffith marry Don Johnson?
Answer: 1976

3437. For her work in the movie «The Help», who won the «Satellite Award for Best Cast – Motion Picture» in 2011?
Answer: Allison Janney

3438. Whom did Reshma Shetty marry in the year 2011?
Answer: Deep Katdare

3439. Whom did Candace Cameron Bure marry in the year 1996?
Answer: Valeri Bure

3440. For which film did Steven Spielberg receive the «Saturn Award for Best Director» in 1978?
Answer: Close Encounters of the Third Kind

3441. Who was the composer for the 1998 film «Pi»?
Answer: Clint Mansell

3442. What is the full name of India?
Answer: Shamika Brown

3443. For which film did Dustin Hoffman receive the «Academy Award for Best Actor» in 1989?
Answer: Rain Man

3444. For his work in the movie «Catch Me If You Can», who won the «Broadcast Film Critics Association Award for Best Director» in 2002?
Answer: Steven Spielberg

3445. Which film won the Academy Award for Best Picture in the year 1960?
Answer: Ben-Hur

3446. What is the full name of Lana Del Rey?
Answer: Elizabeth Woolridge Grant

3447. Who was the composer for the 2018 film «Johnny English Strikes Again»?
Answer: Howard Goodall

3448. Whom did Kate Jackson marry in the year 1982?
Answer: David Greenwald

3449. When did Demi Moore marry Bruce Willis?
Answer: 1987

3450. What is the full name of Stephen Baldwin?
Answer: Stephen Andrew Baldwin

3451. Who directed the 1991 film «The Addams Family»?
Answer: Barry Sonnenfeld

3452. What is the full name of Michael J. Fox?
Answer: Michael Andrew Fox

3453. For her work in the movie «Paper Moon», who won the «Golden Globe Award for New Star of the Year – Actress» in 1973?
Answer: Tatum O'Neal

3454. Who directed the 2006 film «X-Men: The Last Stand»?
Answer: Brett Ratner

3455. In which year did Melissa Ordway marry Justin Gaston?
Answer: 2012

3456. In which year did Troy Beyer marry Mark Burg?
Answer: 1994

3457. Who was the composer for the 2004 film «13 Going on 30»?
Answer: Theodore Shapiro

3458. For her work in the movie «The Miracle Worker», who won the «National Board of Review Award for Best Actress» in 1962?
Answer: Anne Bancroft

3459. Whom did Susan Blanchard marry in the year 1977?
Answer: Charles Frank

3460. When did Laurie Metcalf marry Matt Roth?
Answer: 1993

3461. Whom did Dita von Teese marry in the year 2005?
Answer: Marilyn Manson

3462. Where did Bryce Dallas Howard get her Bachelor of Fine Arts degree from?
Answer: New York University Tisch School of the Arts, in New York City

3463. For which film did Michael Moore receive the «Palme d'Or» award in 2004?
Answer: Fahrenheit 9/11

3464. What is the full name of Zelda Williams?
Answer: Zelda Rae Williams

3465. Who directed the 1988 film «Ernest Saves

Christmas»?
Answer: John R. Cherry III

3466. Who were the directors of the 2015 film «Still Alice»?
Answer: Richard Glatzer and Wash Westmoreland

3467. Who acted as Ruth Schram in the movie «Keeping the Faith»?
Answer: Anne Bancroft

3468. Whom did Téa Leoni marry in the year 1997?
Answer: David Duchovny

3469. Which film won the Academy Award for Best Sound Editing in the year 2018?
Answer: Dunkirk

3470. For which film did Jeremy Renner receive the «MTV Movie Award for Best Fight» in 2013?
Answer: The Avengers

3471. What's the birth name of Hilary Duff?
Answer: Hilary Erhard Duff

3472. Who acted as Plutarch Heavensbee in the movie «The Hunger Games: Mockingjay – Part 2»?
Answer: Philip Seymour Hoffman

3473. What's the birth name of Christy Canyon?
Answer: Melissa Kaye Bardizbanian

3474. What's the birth name of James Haven?
Answer: James Haven Voight

3475. For her work in the movie «Mother», who won the «Satellite Award for Best Supporting Actress – Motion Picture» in 1997?
Answer: Debbie Reynolds

3476. What's the birth name of Felicity Huffman?

Answer: Felicity Kendall Huffman

3477. Who acted as Talia al Ghul in the movie «The Dark Knight Rises»?
Answer: Marion Cotillard

3478. In which year did Valerie Curtin marry Barry Levinson?
Answer: 1975

3479. Who was the composer for the 1992 film «1492 – Conquest of Paradise»?
Answer: Vangelis

3480. Who directed the 2018 film «Beirut»?
Answer: Brad Anderson

3481. For his work in the movie «Precious», who won the «Independent Spirit Award for Best Director» in 2010?
Answer: Lee Daniels

3482. Who directed the 2008 film «The Dark Knight»?
Answer: Christopher Nolan

3483. Who directed the 2013 film «12 Years a Slave»?
Answer: Steve McQueen

3484. What is the full name of Kim Raver?
Answer: Kimberly Jayne Raver

3485. Whom did Julia Sweeney marry in the year 1989?
Answer: Stephen Hibbert

3486. Whom did Lily Mariye marry in the year 1985?
Answer: Boney James

3487. For which film did Steven Spielberg receive the «National Society of Film Critics Award for Best Director» in 1982?
Answer: E.T. the Extra-Terrestrial

3488. For her work in the movie «The Ballad of Jack and Rose», who won the «Boston Society of Film Critics Award for Best Supporting Actress» in 2005?
Answer: Catherine Keener

3489. When did Angie Everhart marry Ashley Hamilton?
Answer: 1996

3490. Whom did Eva LaRue marry in the year 1996?
Answer: John Callahan

3491. When did Julia Louis-Dreyfus marry Brad Hall?
Answer: 1987

3492. For which film did Melvyn Douglas receive the «Academy Award for Best Supporting Actor» in 1979?
Answer: Being There

3493. Who was the composer for the 2003 film «Hulk»?
Answer: Danny Elfman

3494. Whom did Nancy Allen marry in the year 1979?
Answer: Brian De Palma

3496. Who acted as Batman in the movie «Batman & Robin»?
Answer: George Clooney

3497. Where did Jodie Foster get her bachelor's degree from?
Answer: Yale University, in New Haven

3498. Who directed the 2009 film «Aliens in the Attic»?
Answer: John Schultz

3499. What's the birth name of Ben Daniels?
Answer: David T. Daniels

3500. For which film did Yul Brynner receive the «National Board of Review Award for Best Actor» in 1956?
Answer: The King and I

3501. Who was the composer for the 2018 film «Fantastic Beasts: The Crimes of Grindelwald»?
Answer: James Newton Howard

3502. Whom did Robyn Lively marry in the year 1999?
Answer: Bart Johnson

3503. Who was the composer for the 2018 film «Bumblebee»?
Answer: Dario Marianelli

3504. When did Jennifer Carpenter marry Michael C. Hall?
Answer: 2008

3505. For which film did Dan Futterman receive the «Los Angeles Film Critics Association Award for Best Screenplay» in 2005?
Answer: Capote

3506. Whom did Brooke Shields marry in the year 1997?
Answer: Andre Agassi

3507. Who acted as Anton Chigurh in the movie «No Country for Old Men»?
Answer: Javier Bardem

3508. Who directed the 2018 film «Golden Exits»?
Answer: Alex Ross Perry

3509. For which film did Helen Hayes receive the «Academy Award for Best Supporting Actress» in 1970?
Answer: Airport

3510. What is the full name of Elizabeth Daily?
Answer: Elizabeth Ann Guttman

3511. In which year did Joan Taylor marry Walter Grauman?
Answer: 1976

3512. Which film won the Academy Award for Best Documentary Feature in the year 1987?
Answer: The Ten-Year Lunch

3513. What is the full name of Garret Dillahunt?
Answer: Garret Lee Dillahunt

3514. For which film did Tim Robbins receive the «Cannes Film Festival Award for Best Actor» in 1992?
Answer: The Player

3515. In which year did Iman marry Spencer Haywood?
Answer: 1977

3516. When did Kelly Ripa marry Mark Consuelos?
Answer: 1996

3517. Which film won the Academy Award for Best Documentary Feature in the year 2007?
Answer: Taxi to the Dark Side

3518. Who directed the 2012 film «The Master»?
Answer: Paul Thomas Anderson

3519. Who directed the 2018 film «Overlord»?
Answer: Julius Avery

3520. What's the birth name of Brooklyn Decker?
Answer: Brooklyn Danielle Decker

3521. For which film did Spencer Tracy receive the «Academy Award for Best Actor» in 1938?
Answer: Boys Town

3522. What is the name of the character Meryl Streep plays in the movie «Mamma Mia!»?
Answer: Donna Sheridan-Carmichael

3523. What's the birth name of Melinda Clarke?
Answer: Melinda Patrice Clarke

3524. Who directed the 2002 film «Gangs of New York»?
Answer: Martin Scorsese

3525. For which film did Amy Poehler receive the «MTV Movie Award for Best Jaw Dropping Moment» in 2009?
Answer: Baby Mama

3526. Where did Paul Schneider get his Bachelor of Fine Arts degree from?
Answer: University of North Carolina School of the Arts, in Winston-Salem

3527. For which film did Adrien Brody receive the «Satellite Award for Best Cast – Motion Picture» in 1999?
Answer: The Thin Red Line

3528. Who was the composer for the 2016 film «Arrival»?
Answer: Jóhann Jóhannsson

3529. For his work in the movie «The Remains of the Day», who won the «Los Angeles Film Critics Association Award for Best Actor» in 1993?
Answer: Anthony Hopkins

3530. In which year did Lisa Emery marry Josh Pais?
Answer: 1990

3531. Which film won the Special Achievement Academy Award in the year 1977?
Answer: Star Wars Episode IV: A New Hope

3532. Who was the composer for the 2016 film «Rogue One»?
Answer: Michael Giacchino

3533. For which film did Halle Berry receive the «NAACP Image Award for Outstanding Actress in a Motion Picture» in 2011?
Answer: Frankie and Alice

3534. Who directed the 2002 film «Stuart Little 2»?
Answer: Rob Minkoff

3535. For which film did William Hurt receive the «Academy Award for Best Actor» in 1985?
Answer: Kiss of the Spider Woman

3536. For her work in the movie «Before Sunset», who won the «San Francisco Film Critics Circle Award for Best Actress» in 2004?
Answer: Julie Delpy

3537. Whom did Katherine LaNasa marry in the year 2012?
Answer: Grant Show

3538. For his work in the movie «Ed Wood», who won the «Academy Award for Best Supporting Actor» in 1994?
Answer: Martin Landau

3539. For her work in the movie «Boys Don't Cry», who won the «Academy Award for Best Actress» in 1999?
Answer: Hilary Swank

3540. When did Ginnifer Goodwin marry Josh Dallas?
Answer: 2014

3541. Whom did Lindsay Price marry in the year 2013?
Answer: Curtis Stone

3542. Who directed the 2002 film «The Hot Chick»?
Answer: Tom Brady

3543. In which year did Aaliyah marry Damon Dash?
Answer: 2000

3544. What's the birth name of Adam Driver?
Answer: Adam Douglas Driver

3545. Who acted as John Keating in the movie «Dead Poets Society»?
Answer: Robin Williams

3546. What's the birth name of Jessica Chastain?

Answer: Jessica Michelle Chastain

3547. Whom did Sharon Gless marry in the year 1991?
Answer: Barney Rosenzweig

3548. Which film won the Golden Globe Award for Best Motion Picture – Drama in the year 1973?
Answer: The Exorcist

3549. Where did Stacy Keach get his Bachelor of Arts degree from?
Answer: University of California, Berkeley

3550. For his work in the movie «The Messenger», who won the «Independent Spirit Award for Best Supporting Male» in 2009?
Answer: Woody Harrelson

3551. When did Talisa Soto marry Benjamin Bratt?
Answer: 2002

3552. What is the full name of Kristen Stewart?
Answer: Kristen Jaymes Stewart

3553. In which year did Vera Farmiga marry Sebastian Roché?
Answer: 1997

3554. For her work in the movie «Still Alice», who won the «Academy Award for Best Actress» in 2015?
Answer: Julianne Moore

3555. Whom did Sara Gilbert marry in the year 2014?
Answer: Linda Perry

3556. For which film did Allison Janney receive the «National Board of Review Award for Best Cast» in 2011?
Answer: The Help

3557. In which year did Pamela Gidley marry James Lew?
Answer: 2005

3558. Where did Steve Harris get his Bachelor of Arts degree from?
Answer: Northern Illinois University

3560. Who directed the 1997 film «Home Alone 3»?
Answer: Raja Gosnell

3561. Who acted as Ellen Ripley in the movie «Aliens»?
Answer: Sigourney Weaver

3562. Who was the composer for the 1987 film «Adventures in Babysitting»?
Answer: Michael Kamen

3563. What's the birth name of Chris Hardwick?
Answer: Christopher Ryan Hardwick

3564. Which film won the Academy Award for Best Picture in the year 1962?
Answer: West Side Story

3565. For her work in the movie «The 40-Year-Old Virgin», who won the «Boston Society of Film Critics Award for Best Supporting Actress» in 2005?
Answer: Catherine Keener

3566. Which film won the Academy Award for Best Costume Design in the year 1960?
Answer: Spartacus

3567. Who acted as Carla Dean in the movie «Enemy of the State»?
Answer: Regina King

3568. For which film did Jodie Foster receive the «BAFTA Award for Best Actress in a Supporting Role» in 1977?
Answer: Bugsy Malone

3569. Who was the composer for the 2017 film «Sleepless»?
Answer: Michael Kamm

3570. In which year did Kylie Ireland marry Andy Appleton?
Answer: 2010

3571. For his work in the movie «Winchell», who won the «Golden Globe Award for Best Actor – Miniseries or Television Film» in 1999?
Answer: Stanley Tucci

3572. What's the birth name of Leslie Zemeckis?
Answer: Leslie Harter

3573. When did Mary Kay Bergman marry Dino Andrade?
Answer: 1990

3574. For which film did George Chakiris receive the «Academy Award for Best Supporting Actor» in 1961?
Answer: West Side Story

3575. Which film won the Academy Award for Best Documentary Feature in the year 1993?
Answer: I Am a Promise: The Children of Stanton Elementary School

3576. Who was the composer for the 2009 film «The Proposal»?
Answer: Aaron Zigman

3577. When did Adrienne Barbeau marry Billy Van Zandt?
Answer: 1992

3578. For which film did Mila Kunis receive the «Saturn Award for Best Supporting Actress» in 2011?
Answer: Black Swan

3579. Who were the directors of the 2005 film «Stewie Griffin: The Untold Story»?
Answer: Peter Shin and Pete Michels

3580. Whom did Jessica Biel marry in the year 2012?
Answer: Justin Timberlake

3581. For which film did Rachel Weisz receive the «Golden Globe Award for Best Supporting Actress – Motion Picture» in 2005?
Answer: The Constant Gardener

3582. When did Anna Nicole Smith marry James Howard Marshall II?
Answer: 1994

3583. What's the birth name of Odette Annable?
Answer: Odette Juliette Yustman

3584. For her work in the movie «The Family That Preys», who won the «BET Award for Best Actor & Actress» in 2009?
Answer: Taraji P. Henson

3585. For her work in the movie «Body Double», who won the «National Society of Film Critics Award for Best Supporting Actress» in 1984?
Answer: Melanie Griffith

3586. When did Pam Dawber marry Mark Harmon?
Answer: 1987

3587. For his work in the movie «Saving Private Ryan», who won the «Academy Award for Best Director» in 1998?
Answer: Steven Spielberg

3588. When did Eva Angelina marry Danny Mountain?
Answer: 2007

3589. What's the birth name of Marc Blucas?
Answer: Marcus Paul Blucas

3590. Who acted as Martha Kent in the movie «Superman Returns»?
Answer: Eva Marie Saint

3591. Who directed the 1994 film «The Shawshank

Redemption»?
Answer: Frank Darabont

3592. Which film won the Academy Award for Best Picture in the year 1945?
Answer: Going My Way

3593. Who was the composer for the 1999 film «The World Is Not Enough»?
Answer: David Arnold

3594. For which film did Lauren Bacall receive the «Screen Actors Guild Award for Outstanding Performance by a Female Actor in a Supporting Role» in 1997?
Answer: The Mirror Has Two Faces

3595. For his work in the movie «Do the Right Thing», who won the «NAACP Image Award for Outstanding Supporting Actor in a Motion Picture» in 1989?
Answer: Ossie Davis

3596. What is the name of the character Kim Basinger plays in the movie «Batman»?
Answer: Vicki Vale

3597. For which film did Anne Bancroft receive the «Golden Globe Award for Best Actress – Motion Picture Drama» in 1964?
Answer: The Pumpkin Eater

3598. When did Joanna García marry Nick Swisher?
Answer: 2010

3599. What's the birth name of Seamus Dever?
Answer: Seamus Patrick Dever

3600. Whom did Kristen Bell marry in the year 2013?
Answer: Dax Shepard

3601. Who directed the 2005 film «The Land Before Time XI: Invasion of the Tinysauruses»?

Answer: Charles Grosvenor

3602. For which film did Todd Solondz receive the «U.S. Grand Jury Prize: Dramatic» award in 1996?
Answer: Welcome to the Dollhouse

3603. When did Nicole Ari Parker marry Boris Kodjoe?
Answer: 2005

3604. What is the full name of Sean Combs?
Answer: Sean John Combs

3605. For his work in the movie «Cabaret», who won the «Academy Award for Best Supporting Actor» in 1972?
Answer: Joel Grey

3606. When did Katherine LaNasa marry Dennis Hopper?
Answer: 1989

3607. For her work in the movie «Erin Brockovich», who won the «Academy Award for Best Actress» in 2001?
Answer: Julia Roberts

3608. Whom did Aria Giovanni marry in the year 2002?
Answer: John 5

3609. Whom did Suzy Amis Cameron marry in the year 1985?
Answer: Sam Robards

3610. Which film won the Academy Award for Best Production Design in the year 1960?
Answer: Spartacus

3611. Who directed the 1988 film «Cocktail»?
Answer: Roger Donaldson

3612. Who was the composer for the 1995 film «GoldenEye»?
Answer: Éric Serra

3613. What's the birth name of Rami Malek?
Answer: Rami Said Malek

3614. Where was Al Franken born?
Answer: Manhattan

3615. For his work in the movie «Unforgiven», who won the «Golden Globe Award for Best Supporting Actor – Motion Picture» in 1992?
Answer: Gene Hackman

3616. For which film did Sharon Stone receive the «Golden Raspberry Award for Worst Actress» in 1994?
Answer: Intersection

3617. For his work in the movie «A Beautiful Mind», who won the «Broadcast Film Critics Association Award for Best Director» in 2001?
Answer: Ron Howard

3618. Whom did Asia Carrera marry in the year 2003?
Answer: Don Lemmon

3619. Whom did Moon Zappa marry in the year 2002?
Answer: Paul Doucette

3620. When did Jane Fonda marry Ted Turner?
Answer: 1991

3621. Who was the composer for the 1992 film «The Distinguished Gentleman»?
Answer: Randy Edelman

3622. For his work in the movie «Cocoon», who won the «Academy Award for Best Supporting Actor» in 1985?
Answer: Don Ameche

3623. What is the full name of Michael Brandon?
Answer: Michael Phillips

3624. For her work in the movie «The Wrestler», who won

the «Online Film Critics Society Award for Best Supporting Actress» in 2009?
Answer: Marisa Tomei

3625. For his work in the movie «Finding Forrester», who won the «Young Artist Award for Best Leading Young Actor in a Feature Film» in 2001?
Answer: Rob Brown

3626. In which year did Felicity Huffman marry William H. Macy?
Answer: 1997

3627. Who directed the 1992 film «Universal Soldier»?
Answer: Roland Emmerich

3628. Where was Andrew Stanton born?
Answer: Rockport

3629. Who was the composer for the 1998 film «3 Ninjas: High Noon at Mega Mountain»?
Answer: John Coda

3630. For his work in the movie «Capote», who won the «San Diego Film Critics Society Award for Best Adapted Screenplay» in 2005?
Answer: Dan Futterman

3631. What's the birth name of Chanel Preston?
Answer: Rachel Ann Taylor

3632. Where did Andrea Anders get her Bachelor of Fine Arts degree from?
Answer: University of Wisconsin–Stevens Point

3633. What's the birth name of Courtney Ford?
Answer: Courtney Braden Ford

3634. For which film did Dianne Wiest receive the «Academy Award for Best Supporting Actress» in 1994?
Answer: Bullets Over Broadway

3635. Whom did Melora Walters marry in the year 1996?
Answer: Dylan Walsh

3636. Who directed the 2001 film «American Pie 2»?
Answer: J. B. Rogers

3637. Whom did Trish Van Devere marry in the year 1972?
Answer: George C. Scott

3638. Whom did Cicely Tyson marry in the year 1981?
Answer: Miles Davis

3639. For which film did Louis Gossett receive the «Academy Award for Best Supporting Actor» in 1982?
Answer: An Officer and a Gentleman

3640. What is the full name of Tori Black?
Answer: Michelle Chapman

3641. Who were the composers of the 2008 film «10,000 BC»?
Answer: Thomas Wanker and Harald Kloser

3642. Who directed the 2015 film «No Escape»?
Answer: John Erick Dowdle

3643. Whom did Jane Powell marry in the year 1988?
Answer: Dickie Moore

3644. What is the full name of Stone Cold Steve Austin?
Answer: Steven James Anderson

3645. Who acted as Holly the Angel in the movie «Little Nicky»?
Answer: Reese Witherspoon

3646. Who was the composer for the 1997 film «Titanic»?
Answer: James Horner

3647. What is the name of the character Lupita Nyong'o plays in the movie «Black Panther»?

Answer: Nakia

3648. What is the full name of Bob Clendenin?
Answer: Robert Treman Clendenin

3649. What is the full name of Jodie Foster?
Answer: Alicia Christian Foster

3650. Who was the composer for the 1990 film «The Hunt for Red October»?
Answer: Basil Poledouris

3651. Which film won the Academy Award for Best Sound Mixing in the year 1980?
Answer: Star Wars Episode V: The Empire Strikes Back

3652. Which film won the Academy Award for Best Documentary Feature in the year 2002?
Answer: Bowling for Columbine

3653. Who was the composer for the 2013 film «Scary Movie 5»?
Answer: James L. Venable

3654. For her work in the movie «Cold Mountain», who won the «Academy Award for Best Supporting Actress» in 2004?
Answer: Renée Zellweger

3655. Whom did Sarah Shahi marry in the year 2009?
Answer: Steve Howey

3656. Which film won the Golden Globe Award for Best Screenplay in the year 1968?
Answer: Charly

3657. Whom did Margot Kidder marry in the year 1983?
Answer: Philippe de Broca

3658. What is the name of the character Gary Oldman plays in the movie «The Dark Knight Rises»?

Answer: James Gordon

3659. Whom did Persia White marry in the year 2014?
Answer: Joseph Morgan

3660. For which film did Martin Balsam receive the «Academy Award for Best Supporting Actor» in 1965?
Answer: A Thousand Clowns

3661. Whom did Whoopi Goldberg marry in the year 1994?
Answer: Lyle Trachtenberg

3662. Whom did Robin Wright marry in the year 1996?
Answer: Sean Penn

3663. Who directed the 1986 film «Star Trek IV: The Voyage Home»?
Answer: Leonard Nimoy

3664. Where did Ron Perlman get his master's degree from?
Answer: University of Minnesota, in Falcon Heights

3665. Who was the composer for the 2014 film «RoboCop»?
Answer: Pedro Bromfman

3667. For which film did Meryl Streep receive the «Academy Award for Best Actress» in 2011?
Answer: The Iron Lady

3668. Where was Stacy Keach born?
Answer: Savannah

3669. What is the full name of Jonathan Groff?
Answer: Jonathan Drew Groff

3670. Where did Fred Thompson get his Juris Doctor degree from?
Answer: Vanderbilt University, in Nashville

3671. Whom did Brooke Shields marry in the year 2001?
Answer: Chris Henchy

3672. What is the name of the character Christopher Plummer plays in the movie «Alexander»?
Answer: Aristotle

3673. Whom did Alyson Hannigan marry in the year 2003?
Answer: Alexis Denisof

3674. For which film did Meryl Streep receive the «AACTA Award for Best Actress in a Leading Role» in 1989?
Answer: Evil Angels

3675. Who directed the 2018 film «Puzzle»?
Answer: Marc Turtletaub

3676. When did Liza Minnelli marry David Gest?
Answer: 2002

3677. Whom did Katie Holmes marry in the year 2006?
Answer: Tom Cruise

3678. Which film won the Academy Award for Best Picture in the year 2003?
Answer: Chicago

3679. Which film won the Academy Award for Best Documentary Feature in the year 1962?
Answer: Black Fox: The Rise and Fall of Adolf Hitler

3680. In which year did Heather McComb marry James Van Der Beek?
Answer: 2003

3681. Who directed the 2009 film «2012»?
Answer: Roland Emmerich

3682. Who was the composer for the 2014 film «Joe»?
Answer: Lusine

3683. Whom did Kelly Le Brock marry in the year 1984?

Answer: Victor Drai

3684. For her work in the movie «Fargo», who won the «Academy Award for Best Actress» in 1996?
Answer: Frances McDormand

3685. Whom did Aimee Mullins marry in the year 2016?
Answer: Rupert Friend

3686. What's the birth name of Jacqueline Gill?
Answer: Jacqueline Diana Hill

3687. For which film did Luise Rainer receive the «Academy Award for Best Actress» in 1937?
Answer: The Good Earth

3688. Who was the composer for the 1999 film «The 13th Warrior»?
Answer: Jerry Goldsmith

3689. For her work in the movie «Who's Afraid of Virginia Woolf?», who won the «National Board of Review Award for Best Actress» in 1966?
Answer: Elizabeth Taylor

3690. Who was the composer for the 2012 film «Seeking Justice»?
Answer: J. Peter Robinson

3691. Whom did Jana Kramer marry in the year 2010?
Answer: Johnathon Schaech

3692. Who was the composer for the 2000 film «Mission: Impossible II»?
Answer: Hans Zimmer

3693. Who was the composer for the 2018 film «Ant-Man and the Wasp»?
Answer: Christophe Beck
3694. For her work in the movie «Young Bess», who won the «National Board of Review Award for Best Actress» in

1953?
Answer: Jean Simmons

3695. In which year did Tuesday Weld marry Dudley Moore?
Answer: 1975

3696. Which film won the Academy Award for Best Original Score in the year 2015?
Answer: The Grand Budapest Hotel

3697. Whom did Angie Harmon marry in the year 2001?
Answer: Jason Sehorn

3698. What's the birth name of Jesse Williams?
Answer: Jesse Wesley Williams

3699. For which film did Edward Norton receive the «Los Angeles Film Critics Association Award for Best Supporting Actor» in 1996?
Answer: The People vs. Larry Flynt

3700. What's the birth name of Paz de la Huerta?
Answer: María de la Paz Elizabeth Sofía Adriana de la Huerta y Bruce

3701. For which film did Jessica Lange receive the «Academy Award for Best Actress» in 1994?
Answer: Blue Sky

3702. For which film did Lynn Whitfield receive the «NAACP Image Award for Outstanding Performance in a Youth/Children's Series or Special» in 2000?
Answer: The Planet of Junior Brown

3703. Which film won the Academy Award for Best Visual Effects in the year 1988?
Answer: Innerspace

3704. Who was the composer for the 2014 film «Noah»?
Answer: Clint Mansell

3705. What is the full name of Bradley Pierce?
Answer: Bradley Michael Pierce

3706. Whom did Amy Smart marry in the year 2011?
Answer: Carter Oosterhouse

3707. For which film did Clark Gregg receive the «Saturn Award for Best Supporting Actor» in 2013?
Answer: The Avengers

3708. Who directed the 2017 film «Jumanji: Welcome to the Jungle»?
Answer: Jake Kasdan

3709. In which year did Robin Givens marry Mike Tyson?
Answer: 1988

3710. Which film won the Academy Award for Best Writing, Original Screenplay in the year 1996?
Answer: Fargo

3711. Who directed the 2005 film «Batman Begins»?
Answer: Christopher Nolan

3712. Whom did Alyssa Milano marry in the year 1999?
Answer: Cinjun Tate

3713. For her work in the movie «The Effect of Gamma Rays on Man-in-the-Moon Marigolds», who won the «Cannes Film Festival Award for Best Actress» in 1973?
Answer: Joanne Woodward

3714. Who directed the 1998 film «Armageddon»?
Answer: Michael Bay

3715. What is the name of the character Sean Connery plays in the movie «The Hunt for Red October»?
Answer: Marko Ramius

3716. What is the full name of Casey Affleck?
Answer: Caleb Casey McGuire Affleck-Boldt

3717. For her work in the movie «Broadcast News», who won the «National Board of Review Award for Best Actress» in 1987?
Answer: Holly Hunter

3718. What's the birth name of Olivia Wilde?
Answer: Olivia Jane Cockburn

3719. Whom did Jamie Chung marry in the year 2015?
Answer: Bryan Greenberg

3720. Who acted as Will Gerard in the movie «Seeking Justice»?
Answer: Nicolas Cage

3721. What's the birth name of Kelly Rutherford?
Answer: Kelly Melissa Rutherford

3722. What is the name of the character Gwyneth Paltrow plays in the movie «Spider-Man: Homecoming»?
Answer: Pepper Potts

3723. Whom did Elizabeth Taylor marry in the year 1991?
Answer: Larry Fortensky

3724. What is the full name of Christy Canyon?
Answer: Melissa Bardizbanian

3725. Who was the composer for the 1986 film «At Close Range»?
Answer: Patrick Leonard

3726. What's the birth name of Rebecca Schaeffer?
Answer: Rebecca Lucile Schaeffer

3727. Who directed the 2018 film «Hotel Transylvania 3: Summer Vacation»?
Answer: Genndy Tartakovsky

3728. What is the full name of Jimmy Kimmel?
Answer: James Christian Kimmel

3729. For which film did Lillian Gish receive the «National Board of Review Award for Best Actress» in 1987?
Answer: The Whales of August

3730. Whom did Julianne Nicholson marry in the year 2004?
Answer: Jonathan Cake

3731. Whom did Anita Morris marry in the year 1973?
Answer: Grover Dale

3732. Who were the directors of the 2006 film «Jesus Camp»?
Answer: Rachel Grady and Heidi Ewing

3733. Which film won the Golden Globe Award for Best Motion Picture – Drama in the year 1998?
Answer: Saving Private Ryan

3734. Who was the composer for the 1986 film «Star Trek IV: The Voyage Home»?
Answer: Leonard Rosenman

3735. For which film did Aaron Sorkin receive the «Satellite Award for Best Adapted Screenplay» in 2010?
Answer: The Social Network

3736. For her work in the movie «Boogie Nights», who won the «Florida Film Critics Circle Award for Best Cast» in 1997?
Answer: Heather Graham

3737. In which year did Marija Omaljev-Grbić marry Miraj Grbić?
Answer: 2008

3738. When did Glenn Close marry David Evans Shaw?
Answer: 2006

3739. For his work in the movie «Forrest Gump», who won the «Academy Award for Best Actor» in 1995?

Answer: Tom Hanks

3740. Who directed the 1989 film «The Fly II»?
Answer: Chris Walas

3741. Who directed the 2013 film «Oblivion»?
Answer: Joseph Kosinski

3742. Who directed the 2012 film «The Cabin in the Woods»?
Answer: Drew Goddard

3743. Who acted as Pepper Potts in the movie «The Avengers»?
Answer: Gwyneth Paltrow

3744. What is the name of the character Christian Bale plays in the movie «Ford V Ferrari»?
Answer: Ken Miles

3745. Which film won the Academy Award for Best Film Editing in the year 1977?
Answer: Star Wars Episode IV: A New Hope

3746. In which year did Gwyneth Paltrow marry Brad Falchuk?
Answer: 2018

3747. When did Lucie Arnaz marry Laurence Luckinbill?
Answer: 1980

3748. Who directed the 2018 film «Bumblebee»?
Answer: Travis Knight

3749. What is the full name of Kelly Preston?
Answer: Kelly Kamalelehua Smith

3750. Who directed the 2017 film «My Friend Dahmer»?
Answer: Marc Meyers

3751. For which film did Red Buttons receive the

«Academy Award for Best Supporting Actor» in 1957?
Answer: Sayonara

3752. Where did Andrew Stanton get his Bachelor of Fine Arts degree from?
Answer: California Institute of the Arts, in Santa Clarita

3753. Whom did Salli Richardson marry in the year 2002?
Answer: Dondre Whitfield

3754. For which film did Dan Futterman receive the «Washington D.C. Area Film Critics Association Award for Best Adapted Screenplay» in 2005?
Answer: Capote

3755. In which year did Darcy LaPier marry Mark R. Hughes?
Answer: 1999

3756. Whom did Cecily Adams marry in the year 1989?
Answer: Jim Beaver

3757. Which film won the Academy Award for Best Writing, Adapted Screenplay in the year 1978?
Answer: Midnight Express

3758. Who was the composer for the 1996 film «Girls Town»?
Answer: Guru

3759. Who directed the 2016 film «The Huntsman: Winter's War»?
Answer: Cedric Nicolas-Troyan

3760. What is the name of the character Peter O'Toole plays in the movie «Troy»?
Answer: Priam

3761. In which year did Vanessa Williams marry Rick Fox?
Answer: 1999

3762. Who was the composer for the 1992 film «Consenting Adults»?

Answer: Michael Small

3763. Who directed the 1992 film «Home Alone 2: Lost in New York»?
Answer: Chris Columbus

3764. For which film did Christopher Lambert receive the «César Award for Best Actor» in 1986?
Answer: Subway

3765. What's the birth name of Ashley Benson?
Answer: Ashley Victoria Benson

3766. Who was the composer for the 1993 film «Compassion in Exile: The Life of the 14th Dalai Lama»?
Answer: Philip Glass

3767. Whom did Dina Spybey marry in the year 2000?
Answer: Mark Waters

3768. Whom did Judith Light marry in the year 1985?
Answer: Robert Desiderio

3769. For which film did Ed Begley receive the «Academy Award for Best Supporting Actor» in 1962?
Answer: Sweet Bird of Youth

3770. For her work in the movie «The Business of Strangers», who won the «London Film Critics Circle Award for Actress of the Year» in 2002?
Answer: Stockard Channing

3771. Whom did Michelle Johnson marry in the year 1999?
Answer: Matt Williams

3772. In which year did Rosie Perez marry Seth Zvi Rosenfeld?
Answer: 1991

3773. In which year did Jill Kelly marry Julian?

Answer: 2000

3774. For which film did Reese Witherspoon receive the «Academy Award for Best Actress» in 2005?
Answer: Walk the Line

3775. For her work in the movie «The Robe», who won the «National Board of Review Award for Best Actress» in 1953?
Answer: Jean Simmons

3776. Who was the composer for the 1999 film «The Thirteenth Floor»?
Answer: Harald Kloser

3777. Who was the composer for the 1992 film «Blame It on the Bellboy»?
Answer: Trevor Jones

3778. Whom did Lynda Day George marry in the year 1970?
Answer: Christopher George

3779. What is the full name of Luke Perry?
Answer: Coy Luther Perry III

3780. What's the birth name of Giovanni Ribisi?
Answer: Antonino Giovanni Ribisi

3781. What's the birth name of Nestor Carbonell?
Answer: Nestor Gastizu Carbonell

3782. What's the birth name of Asia Carrera?
Answer: Jessica Andrea Steinhauser

3783. Who acted as Ernst Stavro Blofeld in the movie «Spectre»?
Answer: Christoph Waltz

3784. For his work in the movie «Traffic», who won the «Screen Actors Guild Award for Outstanding Performance

by a Cast in a Motion Picture» in 2001?
Answer: Michael Douglas

3785. Who were the composers of the 2018 film «Annihilation»?
Answer: Geoff Barrow and Ben Salisbury

3786. In which year did Scarlett Johansson marry Ryan Reynolds?
Answer: 2008

3787. When did Nana Visitor marry Alexander Siddig?
Answer: 1997

3788. Where did Brian Tee get his Bachelor of Arts degree from?
Answer: University of California, Berkeley

3789. For her work in the movie «Anthony Adverse», who won the «Academy Award for Best Supporting Actress» in 1937?
Answer: Gale Sondergaard

3790. Whom did Betsy Brantley marry in the year 1989?
Answer: Steven Soderbergh

3791. Whom did Marilu Henner marry in the year 1990?
Answer: Robert Lieberman

3792. For her work in the movie «The Curious Case of Benjamin Button», who won the «NAACP Image Award for Outstanding Supporting Actress in a Motion Picture» in 2009?
Answer: Taraji P. Henson

3793. Who acted as Horace Slughorn in the movie «Harry Potter and the Half-Blood Prince»?
Answer: Jim Broadbent

3794. Where did Kelly Stables get her bachelor's degree from?

Answer: University of Missouri, in Columbia

3795. Who directed the 2016 film «Doctor Strange»?
Answer: Scott Derrickson

3796. What is the full name of Paul Walker?
Answer: Paul William Walker IV

3797. When did Ashley Blue marry Dave Naz?
Answer: 2009

3798. When did Lake Bell marry Scott Campbell?
Answer: 2013

3799. For his work in the movie «Kiss of the Spider Woman», who won the «National Board of Review Award for Best Actor» in 1985?
Answer: William Hurt

3800. What is the full name of Wilson Cleveland?
Answer: Wilson Land Cleveland

3801. Whom did Emmy Rossum marry in the year 2017?
Answer: Sam Esmail

3802. What is the name of the character Nicole Kidman plays in the movie «Queen of the Desert»?
Answer: Gertrude Bell

3803. What is the full name of Lacey Chabert?
Answer: Lacey Nicole Chabert

3805. Who was the composer for the 1998 film «Rushmore»?
Answer: Mark Mothersbaugh

3806. For her work in the movie «The Devil Wears Prada», who won the «London Film Critics Circle Award for Actress of the Year» in 2006?
Answer: Meryl Streep

3807. For which film did Anthony Hopkins receive the

«David di Donatello for Best Foreign Actor» award in 1994?
Answer: The Remains of the Day

3808. What is the name of the character Viola Davis plays in the movie «Widows»?
Answer: Veronica

3809. In which year did Mel Harris marry David Hume Kennerly?
Answer: 1983

3810. Where did Bill Wallace get his bachelor's degree from?
Answer: Ball State University, in Muncie

3811. What's the birth name of Jensen Ackles?
Answer: Jensen Ross Ackles

A Few Bonus Questions

3812. What is the full name of D. B. Sweeney?
Answer: Daniel Bernard Sweeney

3813. For his work in the movie «As You Like It», who won the «Screen Actors Guild Award for Outstanding Performance by a Male Actor in a Miniseries or Television Movie» in 2008?
Answer: Kevin Kline

3814. Which film won the Academy Award for Best Documentary Feature in the year 2015?
Answer: Citizenfour

3815. What is the full name of Annie Parisse?
Answer: Anne Marie Cancelmi

3816. Whom did Barbara Bach marry in the year 1981?
Answer: Ringo Starr

3817. Which film won the Academy Award for Best Picture in the year 1958?
Answer: The Bridge on the River Kwai

3818. Whom did Denise Richards marry in the year 2002?
Answer: Charlie Sheen

3819. Whom did Jenny Mollen marry in the year 2008?
Answer: Jason Biggs

3820. When did Jessica Simpson marry Eric Johnson?
Answer: 2014

3822. Who directed the 1991 film «One Good Cop»?
Answer: Heywood Gould

3823. Whom did Joan Allen marry in the year 1990?
Answer: Peter Friedman

3824. Who was the composer for the 1997 film «One Eight Seven»?
Answer: David Darling

3825. In which year did Nicole Kidman marry Tom Cruise?
Answer: 1990

3826. In which year did Alexandra Hedison marry Jodie Foster?
Answer: 2014

3827. What is the full name of Colin Hanks?
Answer: Colin Lewes Dillingham

3828. What is the name of the character Whoopi Goldberg plays in the movie «Star Trek: Generations»?
Answer: Guinan

3829. Which film won the Academy Award for Best Picture in the year 2008?
Answer: No Country for Old Men

3830. For which film did Paul Muni receive the «Volpi Cup

for Best Actor» award in 1936?
Answer: The Story of Louis Pasteur

3831. Whom did Patricia Richardson marry in the year 1982?
Answer: Ray Baker

3832. Who was the composer for the 1993 film «Sleepless in Seattle»?
Answer: Marc Shaiman

3833. Which film won the Academy Award for Best Sound Mixing in the year 2007?
Answer: The Bourne Ultimatum

3834. In which year did Marcy Lafferty marry William Shatner?
Answer: 1973

3835. Who was the composer for the 1992 film «Straight Talk»?
Answer: Brad Fiedel

3836. For which film did Elizabeth Taylor receive the «Academy Award for Best Actress» in 1966?
Answer: Who's Afraid of Virginia Woolf?

3837. For which film did Jennifer Lawrence receive the «MTV Movie Award for Best Fight» in 2012?
Answer: The Hunger Games

3838. Whom did Rebecca De Mornay marry in the year 1986?
Answer: Bruce Wagner

3839. When did Jenna Jameson marry Brad Armstrong?
Answer: 1996

The End